Quick Results

with SAS/GRAPH® Software

Arthur L. Carpenter and Charles E. Shipp

The correct bibliographic citation for this manual is as follows: Carpenter, Arthur L. and Shipp, Charles E., *Quick Results with SAS/GRAPH® Software*, Cary, NC: SAS Institute Inc., 1995. 249 pp.

Quick Results with SAS/GRAPH® Software

Table of Contents

PREFACE

Quick Results with SAS/GRAPH Software provides an overview to SAS System graphics capabilities, highlights selected base and SAS/STAT graphics procedures, reviews pertinent SAS/GRAPH options, and demonstrates through example the construction and presentation of graphs without the use of the ANNOTATE facility. We assume that the reader has a working knowledge of the SAS System, is able to create and manipulate SAS data sets, and understands to some extent how to use the basic graphics procedures.

It is our hope that this book will be used as a reference guide for specific tasks, as well as an example guide that provides a starting point for those who wish to make similar types of graphs. The focus for most of the book is on the examples. The emphasis, generally, is not on why you might want to create a specific type of graph, but rather, given the desire, how to do it.

We concentrate on the presentation of data without using the ANNOTATE facility in SAS/GRAPH and include discussions of the base product and SAS/STAT graphics, the environment, general presentation considerations, low-resolution plots, and plot construction. The graphics topics contained in this book are very eclectic, and on first glance, some of them may seem to have only a peripheral relationship to the graphical presentation of data. There is, however, a method to our selection of topics. Since SAS/GRAPH was first introduced, we have worked with a large number of users, both novices and experts, who have been in various stages of frustration with the creation of graphs that present the information that they want in the way they want to see it. In this book, we try to address those topics that seem to cause the most confusion and difficulties. We have found that it is not unusual that the little things, the topics that should be easy, take the longest to code, and that a little hint or a trick is what is needed. It is our hope that this book contains that gem of information that gets you over your next graphics hurdle.

The use of graphs to summarize and convey information is an integral part of the SAS System for Information Delivery. The benefits of good graphical presentations are well known. Readers can absorb and assimilate information more quickly and completely when well-constructed graphical presentations are included. The proper use of graphs enhances both the appearance and presentation of information.

x

ACKNOWLEDGMENTS

We would like to thank the following individuals and organizations for their permission to use various examples and data sets.

Joseph Catalano, technical director of AeroComp Inc., Costa Mesa, California, for the use of the California Air Pollution Data (CA88AIR).

Dr. Jan Callahan, president of Callahan Associates, La Jolla, California, for the example data and graphics design used in Section 4.3.3e.

Dr. Hany Elwany for the water quality data (H2OQUAL).

We would also like to thank those who assisted with the review of both technical and grammatical aspects of the manuscript. They contributed a great deal to those things that are right about this book. Special thanks go to Mike Kalt of SAS Institute for his detailed comments and suggestions. In addition to numerous anonymous reviewers at SAS Institute, reviews were done by: Dick Barton, Nelson Pardee, Marilyn Carpenter, Lynnette Shipp, and Rick Smith. Any errors that remain are almost certainly the fault of the authors and our desire to do it our way.

Clinton Carpenter designed and created the sketches of the houses used for the chapter headings.

About the Authors

Both authors have extensive experience with SAS/GRAPH and have consulted in all aspects of SAS for a number of years. Both have taught SAS classes and have presented papers at SAS Users Group International (SUGI) conferences.

Art Carpenter has provided SAS and statistical consulting services with California Occidental Consultants since 1983 and has been using SAS since 1976. He has used SAS/GRAPH extensively since its introduction and has presented several papers at SUGI conferences on various SAS/GRAPH topics. He has written and taught several training courses on SAS/GRAPH, as well as other SAS topics. Mr. Carpenter has served as a steering-committee member and president of the Southern California SAS User's Group, a section chair and conference co-chair at the Western Users of SAS Software regional conference, and in various positions at the SUGI conference. Mr. Carpenter received his M.S. in Mathematics from the Colorado School of Mines.

Charlie Shipp was first introduced to the SAS System in 1981 when he was asked to evaluate the package as a statistical tool for Northrop Corporation. He became the first installer, user, and support person at Northrop. He attended SUGI6 (1981) in San Antonio, Texas, and in 1982 was sent to a SAS Institute training class in Los Angeles. It was taught personally by James Goodnight, John Sall, and Kathy Council. In 1983, he established the Northrop SAS Users Group and also the Southern California SAS Users Group. He has presented four SUGI papers, two on user groups and two on statistical graphics.

Currently, Mr. Shipp works in the Graphics Installation and Support Department of Northrop Corporation and his interest continues in supporting user groups. He has two degrees in physics and is doing pioneer work in simplifying visualization of large amounts of measurement data.

Using This Book

This book was written for readers familiar with the basics of the SAS System. We assume (always dangerous) that you are able to perform simple DATA step operations, understand the mechanics of the DATA step and the PROC step, and know how to use the manuals and user guides for the base and SAS/GRAPH products. You need not have a thorough understanding of SAS/GRAPH. However, some experience will be helpful.

It is one of the hallmarks of the SAS System that SAS runs on a wide variety of operating systems. The syntax of virtually all of the SAS statements is independent of the operating system. Consequently, the example programs contained in the examples and appendices should require very few changes to be used on your operating system. It is likely, however, that you will be required to make some changes and that the resulting graphs will appear somewhat different when created on your system. We decided to address this issue by ignoring it. Examples are simply that, examples, patterns to mimic and learn from. We assume that you will consult the *SAS Companion* associated with your operating system for system-specific details. When the differences are the issue or the point of the example, we will address them.

Differences in the graphs are also likely to occur when different graphics output devices are used. For consistency, we use one device almost exclusively in this book. A variety of graphical aspects change when different devices are used. You should not expect to have your example graphs look just like those reproduced in this book.

Two indices are available: the traditional index of keywords and topics, and a graphical index showing each figure. If you know the appropriate keyword, the first index should be helpful. The second index is designed for those who want to learn how to make a graphic that "looks sort of like this one."

The SAS code used to generate the examples is not always reproduced in its entirety in the text of the book; the complete listing of each example program is contained in Appendix B. The data sets used in the examples are all generated using code contained in Appendix A. All of the SAS code and data sets are available through SAS Online Samples. See the inside back cover for instructions on how to access the online samples. SAS code and data sets are also available on diskette from Arthur L. Carpenter at the following address:

California Occidental Consultants
4239 Serena Avenue
Oceanside, CA 92056-5018

Many of the examples utilize *libref*s that have been defined by a LIBNAME statement that does not appear in the code. Because the structure of the LIBNAME statement varies among operating systems, we have left it to you to provide the appropriate *libref* specification. The base product language guide, *SAS Language: Reference, Version 6, First Edition,* provides additional information on the LIBNAME statement and the companion for your operating system for host-specific information. The program SETUP.SAS, which can be found in both Appendix A and Appendix B, contains the LIBNAME and FILENAME statements used by the examples in this book. The examples were written specifically for Release 6.08 of the SAS System running in the Windows environment.

Most of the examples create a Hewlett-Packard Graphics Language (HP-GL) file using the HP7475A device driver. These HP-GL files were then loaded directly into the text of this book (using the techniques shown in Section 5.2.2). Other equally useful device drivers are available and you will probably want to change this graphics device to whatever is appropriate for you. The graphics option GSFNAME points to a *fileref* that indicates the name of the file where the HP-GL file is written. In most examples, the FILENAME statement is either not included or contains the macro variable &pathhpg. As was the case for the LIBNAME statement, the FILENAME statement is operating system dependent, and is therefore incompletely defined in most examples. See the FILENAME statement in Chapter 9, "SAS Language Statements," in *SAS Language: Reference*, and the companion for your operating system for host-specific information.

At the end of many of the sections there is often information concerning related topics or sources for more detail. "More information" sections indicate other sources, such as SAS manuals and reference guides that discuss similar topics (complete bibliographic information is in the References Section). "See Also" sections refer to other sections within this book that cover related topics.

In this book, SAS procedure names, statement keywords, and options are CAPITALIZED as are user-supplied variable names. Symbolic names, such as *libref*, are in *italics*. SAS code appears in a `non-proportional font` and sections of SAS code are indented.

1 Overview Of Graphics Capabilities in SAS® Software

   **Laying the Foundation**

1.1   Introduction

Several SAS software products contain procedures capable of generating plots. This chapter gives you some basic information about base SAS and SAS/GRAPH graphics capabilities.

While SAS/GRAPH software contains the tools and flexibility to produce high-resolution, presentation quality graphs, the capabilities of the procedures in the base product are not nearly as sophisticated.   Nevertheless, graphs produced with the base product have several advantages, and the graphics procedures from both products deserve consideration.

1.2   Base Product Graphics

With the exception of SAS/GRAPH, SAS/INSIGHT, SAS/LAB, SAS/OR, and SAS/QC software, the plots and charts produced by SAS are designed to be printed on a line or impact printer and, therefore, have low resolution.   This can be an advantage when high-resolution plots are not required, because plots generated through the base product are generally easy and quick to produce, do not require a graphic-capable printer, can be printed faster, and can be stored in smaller, more easily accessed files.

The plots and charts generated from procedures in products such as base SAS typically have from 80 to 132 horizontal plot positions and from 24 to 60 vertical positions. These low-resolution plots are often unable to draw straight or curved lines or round circles, and you have very little control over font and color selection.

You can use these procedures in the base product to generate plots and graphs of data:

CHART   produces histograms and pie, block, and star charts.

PLOT   is used to generate scatter plots of two or more variables.

TIMEPLOT   creates observation-specific plots of sequence data.

UNIVARIATE   produces probability, stem-and-leaf, box, and schematic plots.

CALENDAR   displays data from a SAS data set in the form of a monthly calendar.

Although base product graphs are not intended to serve as report-quality graphs, they do have distinct advantages and are discussed in more detail in Chapter 2, "Plotting without SAS/GRAPH Software."

1.3   SAS/GRAPH Graphics

SAS/GRAPH provides you the flexibility to generate custom-designed, presentation-quality graphs. This flexibility, of course, adds complexity both in programming and in hardware/software requirements. Once mastered, the capabilities of the system are extensive.

The generation of graphs using SAS/GRAPH may increase the time to create the SAS code and will almost certainly increase the production time of individual graphs and charts. There are two major advantages of graphs created by SAS/GRAPH that justify this investment of time. First you can customize graphs created by SAS/GRAPH to convey specific information using almost any format and color scheme allowed by your hardware. Second, your program can be written to allow the attributes of the graph to depend on the data.

Graphs generated with SAS/GRAPH can include all of the necessary elements required for presentation-quality graphs. It is possible to manipulate all aspects of the graph to create graphs that will suit any presentation.

The term presentation quality implies that the developer has control over most, if not all, aspects of the setup of the graph. SAS/GRAPH allows each of the following:

- FONT creation, control, and selection

- TITLE placement and attributes

- LINE, PATTERN, and SYMBOL selection, placement, and attributes

- AXIS and LEGEND design, placement, and attributes

- graphic page layout design and control.

Unlike many other graphics packages, SAS/GRAPH can be run in batch mode with the data defining many of the graphic's attributes. This is a major strength of SAS/GRAPH. Several graphics packages enable the user to create very nice graphs, one at a time. It is not unusual to need a series of graphs where all are similar, but each is based on slightly different data. Creating such a series of graphs is easy in SAS/GRAPH and is impossible in many other packages.

The data can define the titles and axes as well as the plot symbols. The ANNOTATE facility, an integral portion of SAS/GRAPH that is not discussed in this book, is especially useful when the programmer wishes to base the symbols, labels, and titles on parameter values contained in the data.

1.4   Graphics Options for SAS/GRAPH

The graphics environment is set up and controlled by graphics options in much the same way as options are used in the base product. SAS/GRAPH options, GOPTIONS, are described in *SAS/GRAPH Software: Reference, Version 6, First Edition, Volume 1* and *Volume 2* and to some extent in *SAS/GRAPH Software: Usage, Version 6, First Edition*.

Most of the figures in this book were generated using DEVICE=HP7475A. Unless you use the same device, you need to change this option when you execute the programs in Appendix B. Remember, we used Release 6.08 of the

SAS System under the Windows environment to generate and test the examples in this book. Therefore the form of the file name designation may be somewhat different for your system. Also, if the graph is sent directly to the plotter the FILENAME statement and the GSFNAME= and GSFMODE= options may not be needed.

The options presented in the following sections are often either under utilized or used improperly.

MORE INFORMATION:
> *SAS/GRAPH Software: Reference*, pp 291-302 - The GOPTIONS
> statement is covered in Chapter 12.
> *SAS/GRAPH Software: Usage* - Various GOPTIONS are used in examples
> throughout the book.

1.4.1 Checking the GOPTIONS using the GTESTIT procedure

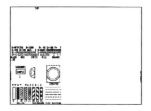

The current settings for the graphics options, especially those that depend on the current graphics device, are often not immediately obvious. You may need to determine the current settings and their effect on the graphs produced on the specified device. Because you need to determine these values for several of the examples in this book, it is fortunate that you can use the GTESTIT procedure to quickly check the current GOPTION settings and their effects.

The following code, which produces Figure 1.4.1a, uses PROC GTESTIT to demonstrate the effects of the current set of graphics options:

```
GOPTIONS DEVICE=hp7475a;

proc gtestit pic=1;
run;
```

The specific results of PROC GTESTIT depend on the graphics device as well as the system options currently in effect. Most of the figures in this book were generated using DEVICE=HP7475A; your PROC GTESTIT results will differ from these, unless you use the same driver.

Figure 1.4.1a is the first of three possible graphs that can be generated using PROC GTESTIT. All of the figures produced for this book are reproduced in black and white even though the original code may have produced a graph containing color. Some of these colors do not show up when they are converted to black and white graphs. Consequently, your graphs may vary from some of the figures shown.

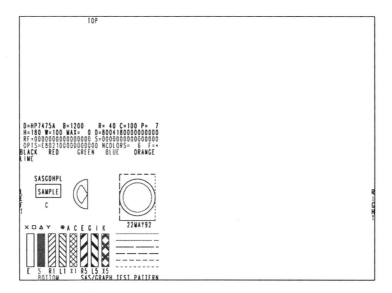

Figure 1.4.1a

Much of the same information that is shown in the graph produced by GTESTIT is also written to the log (Figure 1.4.1b).

```
D=HP7475A  B=1200 R= 40 C=100 P=7
H=180 W=100 MAX=  0 D=8004180000000000
RF=0000000000000000 S=0000000000000000
OPTS=E802100000000000 NCOLORS=  6
Background color = WHITE
Color 1 = BLACK
Color 2 = RED
Color 3 = GREEN
Color 4 = BLUE
Color 5 = ORANGE
Color 6 = LIME
Ratio = 0.71984
Hsize =  9.8424
Vsize =   7.085
F=10
```

Figure 1.4.1b

It is important to understand the relationship between the GTESTIT values shown in Figures 1.4.1a and 1.4.1b, and selected GOPTIONS. These relationships are detailed in *SAS/GRAPH Software: Reference* in the chapter on GTESTIT, and some of these values are also discussed in the following sections in this book.

MORE INFORMATION:
      SAS/GRAPH Software: Reference, Chapter 38 - Discussion and reference for PROC GTESTIT.

1.4.2 Choosing between HSIZE & VSIZE and HPOS & VPOS

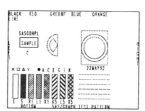

Several factors determine the size of a graph and the size of the letters and numbers on it. Any given device driver has a maximum vertical and horizontal size that is stored as part of that driver's definition (which is controlled through PROC GDEVICE).

Given the hardware constraints, you can also define a plot size. Usually, the plot size is the same as the hardware maximum. However, the size can be changed by using the HSIZE (horizontal size) and VSIZE (vertical size) graphics options.

The units for these options are usually inches but can also be centimeters.

The default size for letters and numbers (h=1) is based on cell size, which is a factor of the number of vertical and horizontal cell positions available for the given HSIZE and VSIZE options. The default varies for different devices but can be changed by using the graphics options HPOS (number of cells horizontally) and VPOS (number of cells vertically).

The default sizes are usually sufficient, but an understanding of how and when to change these options can be useful. Resizing a graph becomes important when

- a smaller physical size is desired

- graphs are truncated when imported into a word processor

- the plot device has insufficient memory to plot the entire graph.

Sizing a graph to fit within specified constraints is common. When HSIZE and VSIZE are reduced and the number of character positions (VPOS and HPOS) stays constant, the individual size of a character cell is reduced (h=1 creates a smaller character). For a constant HSIZE and VSIZE, the cell size can then be increased by decreasing the number of vertical and horizontal positions (VPOS and HPOS). Although it is usually more efficient to increase the size of letters and symbols by using the HTEXT= option or the HEIGHT= option in the TITLE, FOOTNOTE, AXIS, and LABEL statements, there are times when it is necessary to make changes in these options.

The PROC GTESTIT results in the previous section (Figures 1.4.1a and 1.4.1b) show the default values for the HP7475A device. VPOS is the number of rows and is signified by R (in this case 40). The number of columns, HPOS, is designated by C (in this case 100).

You can double the cell size by halving the number of positions (cells) in both directions, as shown in the following GOPTIONS statement:

```
goptions hpos=50 vpos=20;
proc gtestit pic=1;
run;
```

The resulting graph (Figure 1.4.2) contains most of the same information as the previous GTESTIT. However, the letters and figures are larger, and some information is lost.

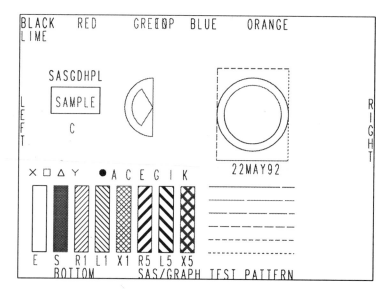

Figure 1.4.2

When changing the cell size by using either HSIZE and VSIZE or HPOS and VPOS, it is usually advisable to change the vertical and horizontal options proportionately. If the change is not proportional, the cell becomes distorted and characters formed by hardware or simulated hardware fonts can be shaped incorrectly.

MORE INFORMATION:

SAS/GRAPH Software: Reference, pp 25-26 - Cell size is discussed further in the section "Defining the Graphics Output Area."

SAS/GRAPH Software: Usage, pp 678-679 - Example and discussion of the use of HPOS= and VPOS=.

SEE ALSO:

Section 1.4.3 - Uses increased HPOS and VPOS values to fit a large block chart.

1.4.3 Using HPOS and VPOS

Increasing the HPOS and VPOS values decreases the cell size and effectively creates more space to create a graph by decreasing the size of each individual character and symbol. When fitting a block chart with a large number of cells or a scatter plot with one or both axes controlled by the ORDER= option with several levels, it is not unusual to receive an error message such as "vertical axis cannot be fit as specified." This occurs when more vertical (or horizontal) character positions are needed than are available.

The following code attempts to create a block chart. The variable MONTH has 12 values, which creates a wide chart.

```
proc gchart data=vol1.ca88air;
title1 h=4 'Block Chart of Average Carbon Monoxide';
footnote j=l h=4 f=simplex 'Figure 1.4.3a';
block month / sumvar=co type=mean
              group=station discrete;
run;
```

The block chart is not created, and the following error message appears in the log.

```
ERROR: A BLOCK chart for MONTH is not possible. At least 43 vertical
       positions and 190 horizontal positions are needed. The device is
       currently defined with 40 vertical positions and 100 horizontal
       positions.
       More positions may be needed if any titles, footnotes, or parts of
       the legend are specified in inches, centimeters, or percent.
```

Figure 1.4.3a

Increasing the HPOS and VPOS values corrects the problem. The following GOPTIONS statement doubles both of these values.

```
goptions vpos=80 hpos=200 htext=2;
```

This produces the following figure:

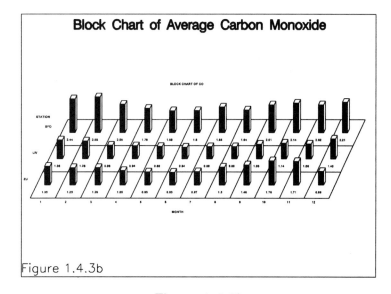

Figure 1.4.3b

Figure 1.4.3b

The HTEXT=2 option increases the default text size to compensate for the decreased cell size. Because HPOS and VPOS were both doubled, so was the HTEXT= option.

1.4.4 Viewing and plotting using the TARGETDEVICE= option

Often, you may find that you develop a graph on one hardware device and display it on another. Unfortunately, the appearance of a graph often changes from device to device, causing carefully positioned legends and labels to fall in the wrong place. Setting GUNIT=PCT on the GOPTIONS statement helps to make the appearance of graphs more consistent among devices.

The problem of the changing appearance of the graph can also be mitigated somewhat by utilizing the TARGETDEVICE= option. This GOPTION allows the developer to view a graph on one device approximately as it will be displayed on a second device (the target device). The graph produced when you use the TARGETDEVICE= option is the best representation of what the graph will look like. A device without color capabilities cannot produce a color plot even if the target device is a color plotter.

The following code runs GTESTIT with TARGETDEVICE=WIN:

```
goptions device=hp7475a targetdevice=win;
proc gtestit pic=1;
run;
```

Compare the following graph (Figure 1.4.4 produced using TARGETDEVICE=WIN) with the GTESTIT graph produced in Section 1.4.1 (Figure 1.4.1a). Both were produced with a DEVICE=HP7475A. However, the target device causes SAS/GRAPH to use the device options associated with that device (in this case, a monitor operating under Release 6.08 of the SAS System for the Windows environment) rather than the device that is actually producing the graph.

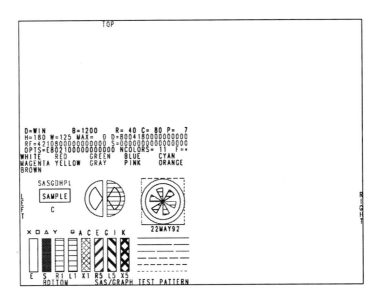

Figure 1.4.4

MORE INFORMATION:

SAS/GRAPH Software: Usage, pp. 603-604 - An example using the TARGETDEVICE= option.

2 Plotting without SAS/GRAPH® Software

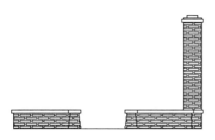

Basic Features

2.1   Introduction

The graphs and charts generated by the base SAS and SAS/STAT products are not intended to be presentation-quality graphs. However, their utility should not be underestimated. These graphs are quickly and easily generated and can convey a great deal of information. This chapter covers four useful procedures you can use to produce plots without using SAS/GRAPH software.

Base product graphs are especially useful for data exploration, quick looks at data displays, and rough-and-ready plots and charts. When you start to spend a lot of time getting a plot or chart to look "just right," the chances are good that a procedure in SAS/GRAPH would be more appropriate.

Base product graphs and charts are designed to be printed (or displayed in the SAS Display Manager System OUTPUT window) rather than plotted. Therefore, the resolution of these types of plots is limited to the number of lines and columns available on the printer or specified by the LINESIZE= and PAGESIZE= options. The fonts are limited to those available on the printer (machine fonts). However, the resulting listing file is easily imported as a text file into word processing documents and can easily be routed to most standard printers. Some laser printers have multiple internal fonts that can be accessed by special commands imbedded in the print stream. Consult your printer owner's manual for designation of these commands.

Plot symbols are limited to the standard character set associated with the printer and cannot be readily connected by lines. Because of the low resolution of these plots, lines may be jagged and circles may not appear to be round.

2.2 Plotting with PROC UNIVARIATE

Many statistical tests assume that the data are normally distributed. When you need to make a determination about the data's normality, plots of the data's distribution can be useful. The UNIVARIATE procedure PLOT option can be used to create both a histogram of the data's distribution and a probability plot with the distribution compared to a normal curve.

The PLOT option makes both requests and there is no control over how the data are presented. The following code generated the plots shown in Figures 2.2a and 2.2b:

```
proc univariate data=vol1.h2oqual plot;
var temp;
title1 'Water Temperature';
footnote1 j=1 'Figure 2.2';
run;
```

Both the histogram and the boxplot show a distribution that is skewed with a few large values and an abundance of smaller ones. Notice that although the JUSTIFY=LEFT option is included without error, it has no effect since this is not a SAS/GRAPH footnote.

```
                        Water Temperature

                        Univariate Procedure

Variable=TEMP          temperature (C)

      Stem Leaf                                             #        Boxplot
        26 11112                                            5           0
        25 3555677889                                      10           |
        24 01                                               2           |
        23 00999999                                         8           |
        22 000179                                           6           |
        21 2334558                                          7           |
        20 7                                                1           |
        19 0022333346666778888999                          23      +-----+
        18 002223555555556666667778888888888899            36      |     |
        17 0001111113333344555567777                       26      *--+--*
        16 02223488999999                                  14      |     |
        15 2222222236678999                                16      |     |
        14 0111122233333455689999999                       25      +-----+
        13 000111112344555566666678888899999               33          |
        12 99                                               2           |
           ----+----+----+----+----+----+----+-

                          Figure 2.2
```

Figure 2.2a

The second plot generated by UNIVARIATE (Figure 2.2b) shows the same distribution. However, here it is compared to a normal distribution. A normally distributed sample would produce a straight line (or as straight as can be plotted with the given resolution).

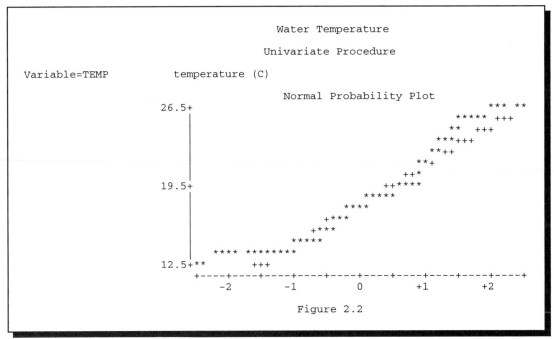

Figure 2.2b

SEE ALSO:
> Section 4.4.1 - This section provides further discussion of normal probability and quantile plots and their generation with SAS/GRAPH.

2.3   Plotting Two or More Variables with PROC PLOT

Since they show the relationship between two or more variables, scatter plots are often used to view the data prior to statistical analysis. In the PLOT procedure, axis control is available in a way analogous to SAS/GRAPH, but without some of the refinements. Other plot options allow multiple plots to be overlaid on a single plot, or plotted individually several to a page.

Figure 2.3 is a simple PROC PLOT of some air quality monitoring data collected in California during 1988. The data are shown in Appendix A. The PLOT statement defines the variables to be included in the scatter plot, in this case O3 and MONTH. The resulting plot shows the relationship between ozone concentrations (O3) and the month of the sample (MONTH).

```
proc plot data=vol1.ca88air;
plot o3 * month;
title1 '1988 Air Quality Data - Ozone';
footnote 'Figure 2.3';
run;
```

Data collected at three separate stations are plotted for each month. When two stations have close to the same monthly value, the letter B is printed to signify two data values at the same place on the plot.

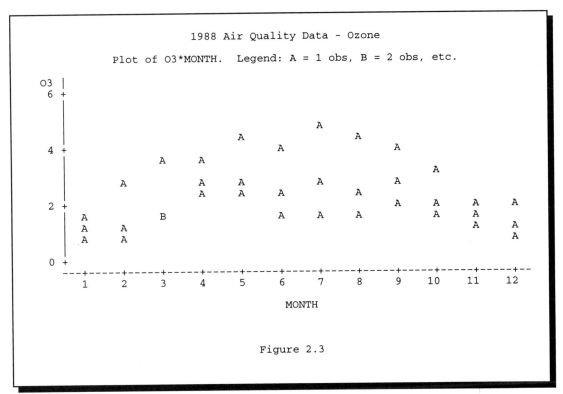

Figure 2.3

SEE ALSO:

Section 2.5 - the REG procedure PLOT statement is also used to explore the relationship between two variables.

2.3.1 Controlling horizontal and vertical axes

Control of the horizontal and vertical axes is handled through the axis options. Remember, if you find that you are spending a great deal of time with axis refinements, SAS/GRAPH may be a more viable option.

The two primary axis options, VAXIS and HAXIS, are used on the PLOT statement to specify the tick marks. The form of the option is similar to that used by an iterative DO statement where the start and end values are specified, and optionally the increment.

The code below produces Figure 2.3.1 in which the vertical axis shown in Figure 2.3 is modified so that it takes on a maximum value of 5 and is incremented by 1. A horizontal line is drawn at 4 parts per hundred million (pphm) of ozone to alert the reader to high ozone conditions.

```
proc plot data=vol1.ca88air;
plot o3 * month / vaxis= 0 to 5 by 1 vexpand vref=4;
title1 '1988 Air Quality Data - Ozone';
footnote1 'Figure 2.3.1';
run;
```

The VEXPAND option minimizes the margins to give the plot maximum resolution, and a horizontal line has been drawn using the VREF option.

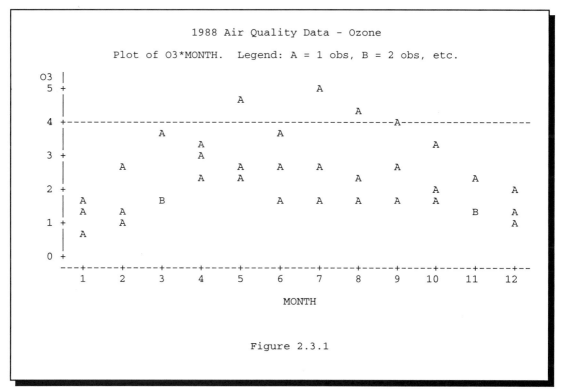

```
                    1988 Air Quality Data - Ozone

           Plot of O3*MONTH.   Legend: A = 1 obs, B = 2 obs, etc.

     O3 |
      5 +                                    A             A
        |                               A
        |                                              A
      4 +-------------------------------------------------A--------------------
        |
        |                 A             A
        |                     A
      3 +           A                   A                         A
        |             A       A  A   A   A        A
        |                 A   A             A         A
      2 +                                A   A   A   A   A             A
        |     A       B                                          A
        |     A   A                     A   A   A   A   A     B   A
      1 +         A                                                  A
        |     A
        |
      0 +
          ---+-----+-----+-----+-----+-----+-----+-----+-----+-----+-----+-----+--
             1     2     3     4     5     6     7     8     9    10    11    12

                                     MONTH


                                 Figure 2.3.1
```

Figure 2.3.1

SAS Procedures Guide, pp 397-432 - Chapter 25 covers PROC PLOT, includes sections on the PLOT statement, and gives examples using the HAXIS and VAXIS options.

2.3.2 Overlaying plots

The typical scatter plot has a vertical (dependent) and a horizontal (independent) variable. However, at times you may wish to plot more than one dependent variable for a given independent variable. This can be done by using the OVERLAY option(s) on the PLOT statement. There are actually a couple of ways to overlay information in PROC PLOT.

Overlaying with the PLOT statement
The plot request typically takes the form of *vertical**horizontal, where *vertical* is the name of the vertical plot variable and *horizontal* is the horizontal plot variable. It is possible to include a third variable on the plot request. A plot request of the form *vertical***horizontal=variable* will produce the same plot as a request without the third variable, except that the plot symbol will be replaced by the first nonblank character contained in *variable*.

The following code is identical to that in Section 2.3, except STATION is being used to define the plot symbols. Since, in this data set, STATION takes on the values of 'AZU', 'LIV', and 'SFO', the three plot symbols will be A,L, and S. In effect, the plots of each of the three stations have been overlaid.

```
proc plot data=vol1.ca88air;
plot o3 * month = station;
footnote1 'Figure 2.3.2a';
title1 '1988 Air Quality Data - Ozone';
run;
```

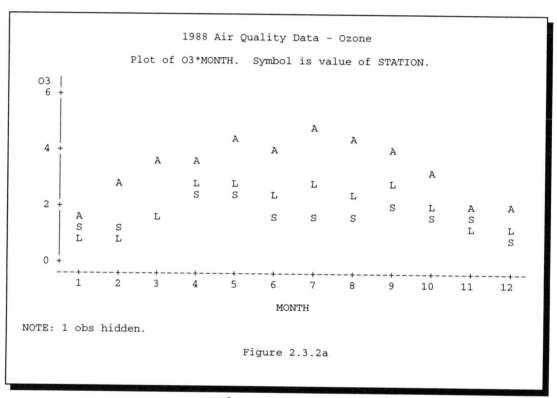

Figure 2.3.2a

One of the disadvantages of using the third variable on the PLOT statement is that when two or more points fall on the same spot, only the first is plotted. PROC PLOT does print a note to alert you to the fact (in this case one point is hidden), but you have to guess where it is (see Figure 2.3). If the user is unaware of the meaning of this warning, incorrect conclusions can be reached.

In Figure 2.3.2a station 'A' is always present, and station 'S' seems to be missing in month 3. You might be misled by the 'missing' information, when in fact 'S' is missing because 'A' comes first alphabetically. Once a symbol has been placed another will not overprint it unless the OVP option has been turned on. Some printers allow multiple strikes at a print position and can effectively utilize overprinting. For these printers OVP should be in effect; otherwise, use the NOOVP option.

Using the OVERLAY option
The OVERLAY option is the second way to place more than one plot within a single set of axes. The OVERLAY option has the additional advantage of allowing more than one vertical variable (although only one axis is used). Remember, multiple plot requests within a single PLOT statement produce separate plots unless the OVERLAY option is used.

The character strings in the plot request in the following code, 'O' (ozone) and 'C' (carbon monoxide), can be used to designate the symbol to be plotted in Figure 2.3.2b:

```
proc plot data=vol1.ca88air;
plot o3 * month = 'O' co * month = 'C' / overlay;
where station='SFO';
footnote1 'Figure 2.3.2b';
title1 '1988 Air Quality Data - SFO';
run;
```

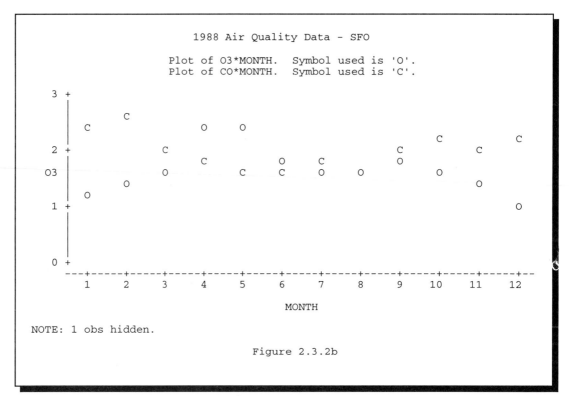

Figure 2.3.2b

As was the case in Figure 2.3.2a, an observation is hidden. Here, however, the dominant symbol (as well as the axis labels) is not selected alphabetically, but instead belongs to the first plot request (O3*MONTH). The vertical axis will be correctly scaled for all variables regardless of which is specified first.

2.3.3 Generating multiple plots per page

The comparison of multiple variables is often accomplished by overlaying two or more variables on one plot. Often this becomes messy and separate plots become necessary. Rather than printing each plot on a separate page, you can generate multiple plots per page.

In order to avoid information loss due to low resolution, it is important to maximize the number of print positions both vertically and horizontally. A printer capable of producing small fonts or equipped with a large carriage is very helpful. The LINESIZE and PAGESIZE options can be used to allow full use of the available space.

The PROC PLOT statement options used to divide the page are HPERCENT and VPERCENT. There is some flexibility as to how the page is subdivided, and it is not necessary for all of the plots to be the same size. HPERCENT is used to designate the portion (percent, not a fraction) to be allotted to each plot horizontally, and VPERCENT is used vertically.

The data used in this example are taken from a study of animals that live in the mud on the ocean bottom. There are several classifications of animals (three are used in this example), and the biomass (weight) of each type is recorded for each sample. The investigator will often want to look at the relationship of biomass among the different pairs of types of animals. Figure 2.3.3 plots all possible two-way pairings of these three classifications in a single presentation.

The following code sets both HPERCENT and VPERCENT equal to 33 to divide the page into nine plot areas. The first three plot requests are used to fill the first three plot spaces on the first row of plots. Notice that the LINESIZE and PAGESIZE values have been increased to allow additional resolution. It may be necessary to try several combinations of these two options in conjunction with your printer and the font choices available on your word processor.

```
options linesize=110 pagesize=50;

proc plot data=vol1.biomass hpercent=33 vpercent=33;
plot bmcrus * bmcrus / vaxis= 0 to 2 by 1 haxis= 0 to 2 by 1;
plot bmcrus * bmmol  / vaxis= 0 to 2 by 1 haxis= 0 to 2 by 1;
plot bmcrus * bmpoly / vaxis= 0 to 2 by 1 haxis= 0 to 2 by 1;
plot bmmol  * bmcrus / vaxis= 0 to 2 by 1 haxis= 0 to 2 by 1;
plot bmmol  * bmmol  / vaxis= 0 to 2 by 1 haxis= 0 to 2 by 1;
plot bmmol  * bmpoly / vaxis= 0 to 2 by 1 haxis= 0 to 2 by 1;
plot bmpoly * bmcrus / vaxis= 0 to 2 by 1 haxis= 0 to 2 by 1;
plot bmpoly * bmmol  / vaxis= 0 to 2 by 1 haxis= 0 to 2 by 1;
plot bmpoly * bmpoly / vaxis= 0 to 2 by 1 haxis= 0 to 2 by 1;

footnote1 'Figure 2.3.3';
title1 'Biomass in GM Wet Weight';
run;
```

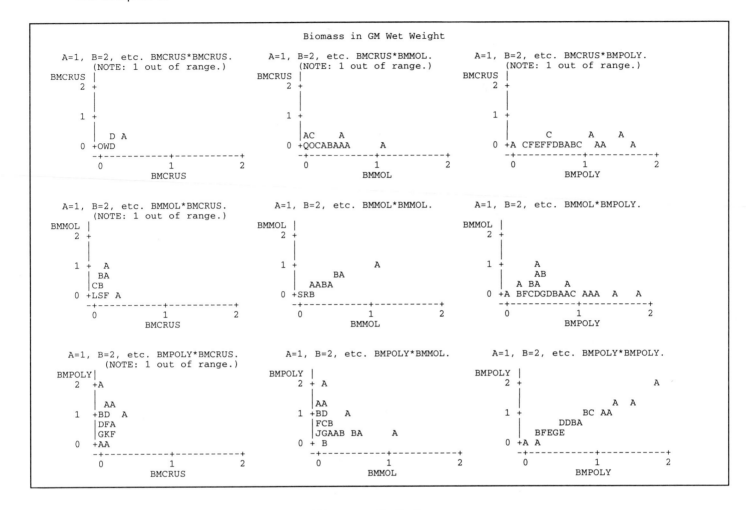

Figure 2.3.3

MORE INFORMATION:

SAS Language: Reference, p. 760 - Defines the LINESIZE system option.
SAS Language: Reference, p. 769 - Defines the PAGESIZE system option.
SAS Procedures Guide, pp. 404-405 - Example of multiple plots per page.

SEE ALSO:

Section 6.3.7 - Multiple plots per page (paired plots) are created using SAS/GRAPH template panels.

2.4 Displaying Data Using PROC TIMEPLOT

Scatter plots show the relationship between two or more variables. However, when you are using PROC PLOT, it is not easy to associate a particular plotted point with the data observation that generated it. PROC TIMEPLOT can be used to highlight individual observations while giving a graphical representation of the data. This procedure prints each observation separately while allowing you to select variables to display graphically at the same time.

PROC TIMEPLOT was designed to display data that have an ordered sequence, usually time series data. Although not strictly designed to do so, this procedure is very useful for plotting other types of data as well and can be especially useful when examining data for outliers.

Using TIMEPLOT on sequence data

The data used in this example (VOL1.DOW) are taken from the SAS Sample Library V6.03 (TIMEPLT1) and the SAS Procedures Guide, Release 6.03 Edition (pp. 386-387). The closing value for 06AUG81 has been altered "by mistake" by 60 points. Inspection of the data does not easily spot the aberrant data point, but it is easily visible in Figure 2.4a.

The PLOT statement is used to note the variable(s) to be plotted on the horizontal axis and optionally overlaid. In the code below a vertical reference line is added at the mean of the low values (REF=MEAN(LOW)) and the high and low values are connected (HILOC).

```
proc timeplot data=vol1.dow;
plot low close high/overlay hiloc ref=mean(low);
id date volume;
format volume 6.1 high low close 6.2;
title1 'PROC TIMEPLOT';
footnote1 'Figure 2.4a';
run;
```

This produces the following table.

```
                              PROC TIMEPLOT

      DATE    volume in     LOW     CLOSE     HIGH      min              max
              thousands                                 883.66        961.47
              of shares                                 *------------------*
    03AUG81   3219.3       940.45   946.25   955.48     |            | LC-H  |
    04AUG81   2938.5       937.40   945.97   951.39     |            | L-CH  |
    05AUG81   4177.8       942.16   953.58   958.81     |            | L--CH |
    06AUG81   3975.7       947.30   892.91   961.47     C-------|-----L--H
    07AUG81   3884.3       938.45   942.54   954.15     |            | LC--H |
    10AUG81   2937.7       935.88   943.68   948.82     |            | L-C-H |
    11AUG81   5262.9       939.50   949.30   955.48     |            | L--CH |
    12AUG81   4005.2       942.26   945.21   955.86     |            | LC--H |
    13AUG81   3680.8       938.55   944.35   952.91     |            | L-C-H |
    14AUG81   3714.1       933.79   936.93   947.77     |          LC-H     |
    17AUG81   3432.7       924.37   926.75   939.40     |      LC--H        |
    18AUG81   4396.7       916.38   924.37   932.74     |     L-C--H        |
    19AUG81   3517.3       918.38   926.46   932.08     |     L|CH          |
    20AUG81   3811.9       923.52   928.37   935.31     |        LC-H       |
    21AUG81   2625.9       917.14   920.57   930.65     |       @|-H        |
    24AUG81   4736.1       896.97   900.11   917.43     |  LC----H          |
    25AUG81   4714.4       887.46   901.83   904.30     L---@   |           |
    26AUG81   3279.6       893.65   899.26   908.39     | LC-H   |          |
    27AUG81   3676.1       883.66   889.08   900.49     LC--H    |          |
    28AUG81   3024.2       884.80   892.22   898.78     L-C-H    |          |
                                                        *------------------*

                              Figure 2.4a
```

Figure 2.4a

The '@' symbol is used when two or more symbols are plotted in the same location. In this example, the order of the letters is also significant and acts as an additional indicator of a data problem.

Using TIMEPLOT on nonsequence data

The following code uses PROC TIMEPLOT on the benthic (bottom of the ocean) biomass data (VOL1.BIOMASS), which has no usable sequencing information. In this table, the user is not at all interested in the pattern of the data other than to search for aberrant values. Symbols may be assigned to variables that are to be plotted; in this case, a 'P' is assigned to the polychaete biomass and a 'C' to the Crustacean biomass value. The two plots are then overlaid.

```
proc timeplot data=vol1.biomass;
plot bmpoly='P' bmcrus='C' /overlay;
where '01aug85'd le date le '31aug85'd;
id date station;
title1 'PROC TIMEPLOT Biomass Data';
footnote1 'Figure 2.4b';
run;
```

In the resulting output shown below (Figure 2.4b), the observation with the different value is obvious (05Aug85 for station D3350-25), and the extent of the difference is also readily apparent.

```
                     PROC TIMEPLOT Biomass Data

         DATE     STATION    POLYCHAETE      CRUSTACEAN      min                  max
                  ID         BIOMASS (GM     BIOMASS (GM     0.01                44.82
                             WET WEIGHT)     WET WEIGHT)     *--------------------*
      05AUG85     DL-25          0.92           0.08         |@                        |
      02AUG85     DL-60          0.40           0.10         |@                        |
      05AUG85     D1100-25       0.18           0.02         |@                        |
      02AUG85     D1100-60       0.39           0.12         |@                        |
      05AUG85     D1900-25       1.23           0.06         |CP                       |
      02AUG85     D1900-60       0.56           0.07         |@                        |
      02AUG85     D3200-60       0.39           0.11         |@                        |
      05AUG85     D3350-25       0.45          44.82         |P                     C  |
      05AUG85     D6700-25       1.13           0.01         |@                        |
      02AUG85     D6700-60       0.43           0.15         |@                        |
      05AUG85     D700-25        0.31           0.02         |@                        |
      02AUG85     D700-60        0.38           0.07         |@                        |
      26AUG85     DL-25          0.57           0.01         |@                        |
      27AUG85     DL-60          0.46           0.05         |@                        |
      26AUG85     D1100-25       0.63           0.02         |@                        |
      27AUG85     D1100-60       0.57           0.04         |@                        |
      26AUG85     D1900-25       0.26           0.03         |@                        |
      27AUG85     D1900-60       0.73           0.07         |@                        |
      27AUG85     D3200-60       0.46           0.07         |@                        |
      26AUG85     D3350-25       0.57           0.02         |@                        |
      26AUG85     D6700-25       0.87           0.01         |@                        |
      27AUG85     D6700-60       0.69           0.07         |@                        |
      26AUG85     D700-25        0.48           0.19         |@                        |
      27AUG85     D700-60        0.25           0.09         |@                        |
                                                             *--------------------*

                               Figure 2.4b
```

Figure 2.4b

It is clear from the plot in Figure 2.4b that one of the crustacean biomass values is different by a factor of 100. Although Figure 2.3.3 warned, "NOTE: 1 out of range," neither the warning nor the extent of the difference was very obvious.

MORE INFORMATION:
Friendly, 1991, p. 70 - TIMEPLOT is used to create a dot chart.
SAS Language and Procedures: *Usage 2*, pp. 383-403 - Chapter 19
contains a number of examples dealing with PROC TIMEPLOT.
SAS Procedures Guide - Chapter 40 provides syntax and examples of the
TIMEPLOT procedure.

2.5   Using PROC REG to Create Scatter Plots

PROC REG, part of SAS/STAT software, is primarily designed for performing regression analysis. Although it is usually thought of as producing tables, it has several built-in plotting and data highlighting capabilities that are underutilized. The PLOT, PAINT, and REWEIGHT statements are recent enhancements and allow the plotting of the data without leaving PROC REG.

The PLOT statement in PROC REG resembles the PLOT statement in PROC PLOT, and it creates a similar scatter plot, but without as many options. The PAINT statement allows you to selectively highlight observations with specific attributes. If selected observations need to receive a weight other than 1, they can be assigned a new weight by the use of the REWEIGHT statement. If observations are identified as outliers, REWEIGHT can be used to assign a weight of 0, causing them to be eliminated from the regression (and therefore the plot).

The data used in the examples in this section deal with physical water measurements taken in a lagoon on the southern California coast. The experimenter has hypothesized that the level of dissolved oxygen in the water can be used to predict its pH through a linear relationship. Figure 2.5 explores this hypothesis by using PROC PLOT to make a scatter plot of these two variables.

The following code produces the plot in Figure 2.5, which can be compared to the others in this section (Figures 2.5.1 and 2.5.2) that are generated using PROC REG:

```
proc plot data=vol1.h2oqual;
by station;
where depth=0 & station='TS6';
plot ph  * do  ;
title1 'Scatter plot prior to PROC REG';
footnote1 'Figure 2.5';
run;
```

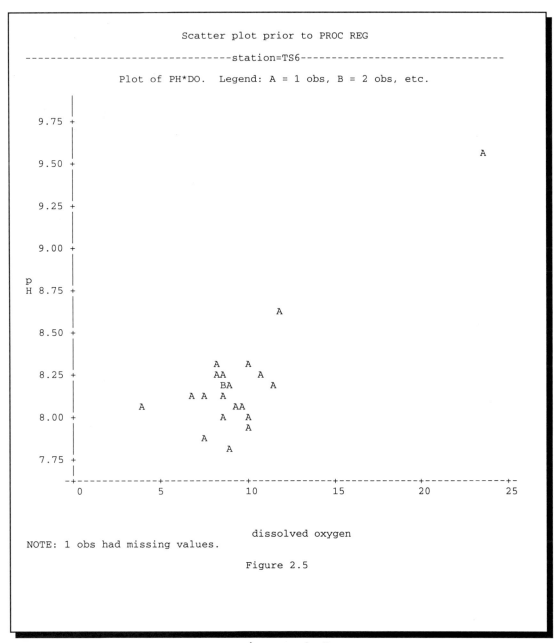

Figure 2.5

A potentially linear relationship can be seen in Figure 2.5 (with possibly one or two high leverage points). Consequently, PROC REG is proposed to further explore the relationship.

PROC REG can be used as a graphical tool to discover more about the data, as well as to calculate regression statistics and parameters. You can use the PLOT statement to create a scatter plot similar to the one shown above. Unlike the PLOT procedure, however, PROC REG has the ability to select and highlight specific observations that influence the regression.

SEE ALSO:
Section 2.3 - Provides additional detail on the use of PROC PLOT.

2.5.1 Using the PLOT statement in PROC REG

The form of the PLOT statement in PROC REG is very similar to the PLOT statement in PROC PLOT. However, the axis and plot control options are not available.

Although not a graphical option, the INFLUENCE option in the MODEL statement can be used to help determine which observations influence the regression equation the most. Points with the most extreme values of the independent variable have the *potential* of having the most influence on the determination of the equation parameters. Influential points are said to have high leverage.

The following code uses PROC REG, the MODEL statement's INFLUENCE option, and the PLOT statement to produce Figures 2.5.1a and 2.5.1b.

```
proc reg data=vol1.h2oqual;
by station;
where depth=0 & station='TS6';
id datetime;
model ph = do / influence;
plot ph * do;
title1 'Regression of pH and dissolved oxygen';
footnote1 'Figure 2.5.1';
run;
```

Only a portion of the output generated by this code is shown below. The Dfbetas produced by the INFLUENCE option (Figure 2.5.1a) indicate a measure of how much an observation influences the equation. The larger the Dfbeta value, the larger the influence of that observation. In this data set, observation 9 has the largest Dfbeta.

```
==========================================
Portions of the listing are not shown
==========================================

Regression of pH and dissolved oxygen

------------------------------ station=TS6 ------------------------------

                                         Hat Diag      Cov
    Obs   DATETIME      Residual  Rstudent       H    Ratio   Dffits

     1    06FEB93:09:43  -0.1090  -0.6333   0.0459   1.1138  -0.1389
     2    10FEB93:12:22  -0.2779  -1.7182   0.0459   0.8700  -0.3771
     3    16FEB93:08:18   0.0653   0.3770   0.0466   1.1451   0.0834
     4    20FEB93:09:50  -0.2347  -1.4206   0.0466   0.9498  -0.3142
     5    02MAR93:14:20  -0.1458  -0.8597   0.0571   1.0888  -0.2116
     6    07MAR93:10:30  -0.1411  -0.8256   0.0456   1.0819  -0.1804
     7    15MAR93:16:43      .        .        .        .        .
     8    27MAR93:14:57   0.1853   1.1131   0.0682   1.0480   0.3011
     9    01APR93:13:40   0.1601   2.2468   0.7970   3.4080   4.4526
    10    03APR93:08:03   0.0295   0.1697   0.0462   1.1582   0.0373
    11    06APR93:11:08  -0.1284  -0.7507   0.0487   1.0987  -0.1699

         ==========================================
         Portions of the listing are not shown
         ==========================================

                        INTERCEP      DO
    Obs   DATETIME       Dfbetas   Dfbetas

     1    06FEB93:09:43  -0.0617    0.0133
     2    10FEB93:12:22  -0.0970   -0.0392
     3    16FEB93:08:18   0.0169    0.0133
     4    20FEB93:09:50  -0.0636   -0.0502
     5    02MAR93:14:20   0.0221   -0.0956
     6    07MAR93:10:30  -0.0563   -0.0085
     7    15MAR93:16:43      .         .
     8    27MAR93:14:57  -0.0749    0.1739
     9    01APR93:13:40  -3.6614    4.3238
    10    03APR93:08:03   0.0175   -0.0046
    11    06APR93:11:08  -0.0997    0.0441

         ==========================================
         Portions of the listing are not shown
         ==========================================

                        Figure 2.5.1
```

Figure 2.5.1a

The PLOT statement produces the following scatter plot (Figure 2.5.1b).

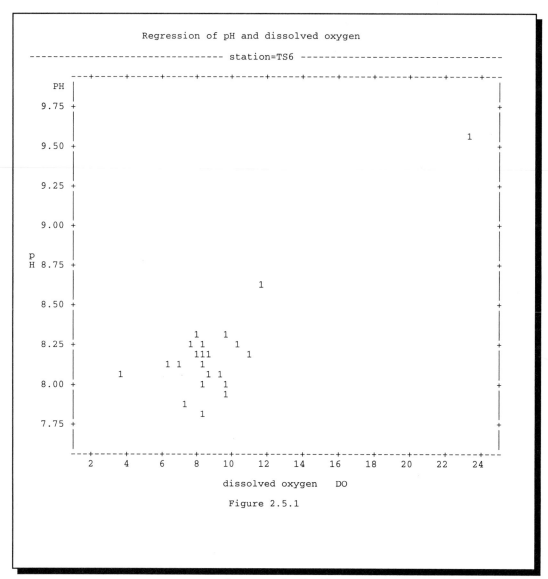

Figure 2.5.1

Figure 2.5.1b

This scatter plot contains the same information as the plot created by PROC PLOT in Figure 2.5. It shows a single point in the upper right corner, which may be the high influence point.

MORE INFORMATION:
>   Freund, 1986, pp. 52-56 - Discusses various influence statistics.
>   ✓ Friendly, 1991, pp. 239-248 - A good discussion and example of influence points. Includes a comparison of influence points with outliers.
>   ✓ Sall, 1990 - Expands the topic of influential points and includes plotting techniques to highlight these points.
>   *SAS/STAT User's Guide*, pp. 1395-1442 - Numerous examples of the PLOT statement as it is used with PROC REG.

2.5.2 Finding and painting influential points

Influential points, i.e., points with the most leverage, will tend to have the extreme values in the column labelled as 'DO Dfbetas' in the previous listing (Figure 2.5.1a). In this data set, observation 9 (DATETIME='01APR93:13:40'dt) has a 'DO Dfbetas' value of over 4. It is therefore of interest to know which point in the scatter plot corresponds to this observation. The PAINT statement can be used to identify this point on the plot with the symbol '@' (you can choose other symbols as well by using the SYMBOL= option).

```
proc reg data=vol1.h2oqual;
by station;
where depth=0 & station='TS6';
id datetime;
model ph = do / influence;
paint datetime = '01apr93:13:40:0'dt;
plot ph * do;
title1 'Regression of pH and dissolved oxygen';
title2 'Paint sample taken 01Apr93 at 13:40';
footnote1 'Figure 2.5.2';
run;
```

The scatter plot generated by the PLOT statement is shown in Figure 2.5.2.

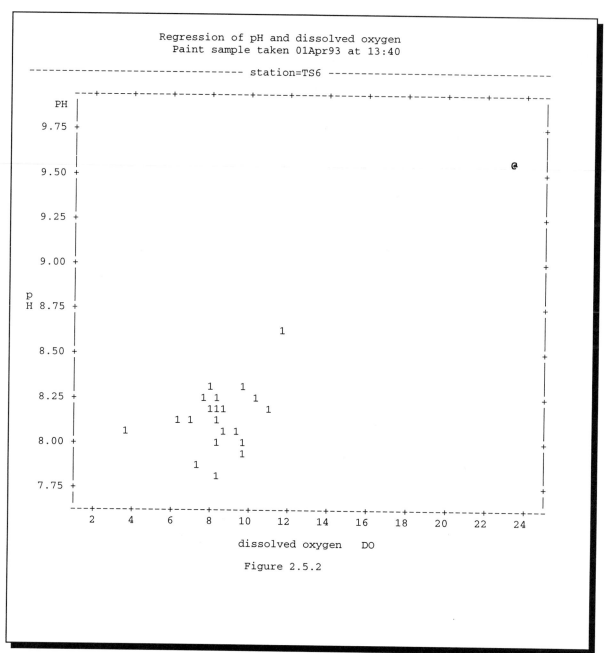

Figure 2.5.2

The painted point, plotted using the @ sign, is in the upper right corner. It is not surprising that this very large value of DO has the most influence on the slope of the line. We would like to remind you that this alone _does not_ make the point an outlier.

MORE INFORMATION:

SAS/STAT User's Guide, pp. 1372-1375 and 1411-1415 - Additional information and examples of the PAINT statement.

3 Titles, Axes, and Legends in SAS/GRAPH® Output

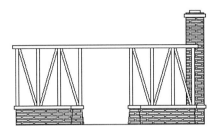

Framing; Adding Structure

3.1 Introduction

Unlike the base product, SAS/GRAPH can be used to create presentation quality graphs. One of the strengths of SAS/GRAPH that you can easily take advantage of is controlling the presentation of lettering and symbols in titles and labels. This chapter highlights the TITLE, AXIS, and LEGEND statements, including a few of those options that users have found to be both useful when presenting information but also somewhat difficult to master.

Not all titles, axes, and legends are created equal. The default values may be adequate, but options and features are available that can turn an ordinary title, axis, or legend into one that becomes an integral part of the graph. For example,

● titles can be enhanced by changing the fonts, color, and text size.

● titles and text can be rotated and moved to various positions on the graph.

● subscripts and superscripts can be easily created.

Further, the AXIS statement can be used to control the appearance of the axes of a chart or plot. Options include the ability to

- control axis scaling

- place special values on the major tick marks

- specify the number and placement of major and minor tick marks.

Legends for plots and charts are customized through the use of the LEGEND statement. The LEGEND statement allows you to

- position the legend anywhere on the graph

- specify the legend's contents

- identify symbols and patterns used in the graph.

3.2   Enhancing Titles

There are a number of details, including TITLE statement options, to know in order to make the title an integral part of the graph. This section covers

- using hardware and software fonts

- changing fonts, color, and text size

- using justification to split text lines

- text rotations and angles

- creating subscripts and superscripts

- using BY and MACRO variables in titles.

Note: This discussion of titles is directed to SAS/GRAPH applications and has little bearing on titles outside SAS/GRAPH. Also, it applies equally to the FOOTNOTE and NOTE statements, which will not be covered separately.

The TITLE statement consists of options and one or more quoted strings. Title options take the form of *OPTIONNAME=optionvalue*. Options are applied to the quoted string that follows and remain in effect for the rest of your SAS session or until changed within the TITLE statement. An option in one title does not affect any other title or footnote, and title options are ignored by procedures other than SAS/GRAPH procedures.

3.2.1 Hardware fonts and when they are used

Each title option has a default value that depends to some extent on the graphics device and to a greater extent on the graphics options (GOPTIONS) in effect. Usually the defaults are adequate and options generally do not need to be changed just to avoid the default. An exception, however, usually needs to be made for font selection.

A default font for titles, labels, and other text can be specified with the GOPTIONS FTEXT= and FTITLE=. These graphics options are especially useful when the default font needs to be changed for a majority of the text on a graph.

When you don't specify fonts in the TITLE statement, SAS/GRAPH makes the following checks to select a default font. For TITLE1 the GOPTION FTITLE= is checked and used if specified. Then (all titles except TITLE1 check here first) FTEXT= is checked and used if specified. When neither FTITLE= nor FTEXT= have been specified, the default font for TITLE1 is SWISS for Releases 6.07 and later, while earlier releases use COMPLEX as the default. The remaining titles (titles 2 through 10) default to a hardware font (or under certain conditions to a simulated hardware font).

Graphs that utilize hardware fonts can often be produced more quickly and require less storage space than graphs with software fonts, but hardware fonts also often have undesirable side effects. If a title or label without any font option specified produces a font that looks similar to simplex, but looks strange, try using the FONT= option to select a specific font. The default hardware font and the logic that determines if a simulated hardware font is to be used are device dependent. Unless you have a specific need to use a hardware font, specify a software font.

The following code demonstrates the differences among the default fonts for one device. The TITLE statements used to create Figure 3.2.1 are

```
proc gslide;
title1
       'Figure 3.2.1  title1 defaults: h=2 f=swiss';
title4 h=2 f=none
       'title4 with h=2 & f=none     (hardware font)';
title5 h=2 f=simplex
       'title5 with h=2 & f=simplex  (Software font)';
run;
```

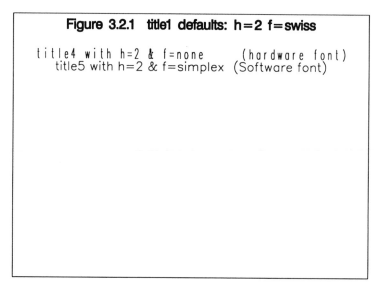

Figure 3.2.1

Titles 1 and 4 do not specify the font. Therefore, SAS/GRAPH will check the FTITLE= and FTEXT= graphics options. Since neither of these options has been specified and Release 6.08 is being used, the default font for TITLE1 is SWISS and the default font for TITLE4 will be either a hardware font or a simulated hardware font. TITLE5 specifies F=SIMPLEX to demonstrate the difference between the font used in TITLE4 and the SIMPLEX font that comes with SAS/GRAPH.

MORE INFORMATION:
> SAS Technical Report P-215 , p.10 - Notes the change to the default font for TITLE1.
> *SAS/GRAPH Software: Reference*, pp.161-164 - This section covers hardware fonts and when they are used.
> *SAS/GRAPH Software: Reference*, pp. 446-462 - Consult the section on TITLE statement options for more details.

3.2.2 Changing fonts, color, and text size

Fonts, along with most of the other title statement options, can be changed more than once within a title. A single title can consist of text strings made up of different fonts, colors, and sizes. This ability is useful to bring special symbols into the title and to highlight certain portions of the text. The default values for height and color are determined in a somewhat analogous fashion to the defaults for fonts described in Section 3.2.1.

The graph shown in this section was produced by the GSLIDE procedure with title statements containing different options for font, color, and size. We have included this example primarily to show how title options can be changed within a title statement. The following TITLE statements were used to produce the graph.

```
title1 'Figure 3.2.2';
title2 h=3 font=swissb 'swissb' color=red f=cartog 'J K L M N';
title3 h=1 f=simplex 'H1' h=2 'H2' h=4 'H4';
```

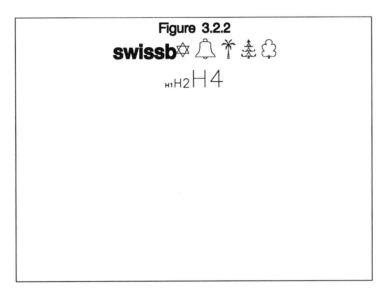

Figure 3.2.2

MORE INFORMATION:
> *SAS/GRAPH Software: Reference*, p. 454 - Additional information on the options HTITLE=, HTEXT=, CTITLE=, and CTEXT= can be found in the section on using graphics options.

3.2.3 Splitting title lines using the JUSTIFY= option

The option used to justify text (to the left, center, and right) can also be used to split a single title among two or more lines. In Figure 3.2.3 the first title appears on three different lines. You can split a title line by using the JUSTIFY= option two or more times with the same value in the same title. When this is done, the second and successive text strings each start on separate lines.

The following TITLE statements produce two titles on four lines :

```
title1 h=1.5 justify=left 'Figure 3.2.3'
       justify=l    'second line on left which is a long segment'
       j=l          'third line on title1'
       j=center     'fourth center top'
       j=c          'fifth in conflict with second'
       j=right      'sixth top right';
title2 'This is the second title';
```

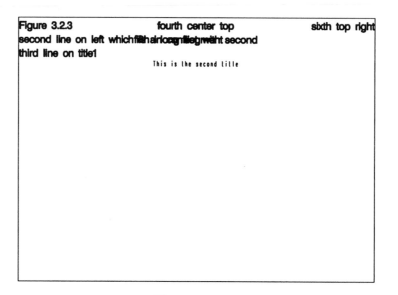

Figure 3.2.3

As is demonstrated in Figure 3.2.3, when JUSTIFY= is used to split titles and footnotes, SAS/GRAPH does not check to see if text strings are written on top of each other.

3.2.4 Changing text orientation with ROTATE= and ANGLE=

It is often very useful to be able to place axis labels next to the vertical axis of a scatter plot. The ROTATE= option applies to individual letters while ANGLE= applies to the entire string. You can also use these options in the AXIS statement to further control text orientation.

A title or a footnote can be placed along either axis by using the ANGLE= option. When ANGLE=90, the title is written along the vertical border on the left side (ANGLE=-90 writes to the right side). Footnotes move in the opposite direction.

Orienting text in a title

The use of the ANGLE= and ROTATE= title and footnote options in the
following code produce text lines along the vertical borders of the plot:

```
goptions htext=2;
proc gplot data=vol1.ca88air;
plot o3 * month;
title1 '1988 Air Quality Data - Ozone';
title2 angle=90 'OZONE levels at three locations';
title3 angle=90 ' ';
footnote1 angle=-90 rotate=90 'Figure 3.2.4a';
run;
```

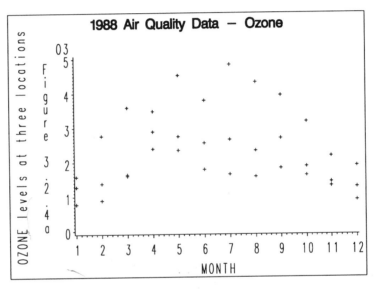

Figure 3.2.4a

In this code, TITLE and FOOTNOTE statements which utilize ANGLE= and
ROTATE= options are used with a PROC GPLOT. Notice that TITLE2 reads
from the bottom to the top while FOOTNOTE1 reads top to bottom. TITLE3 is
used to create a space between TITLE2 and FOOTNOTE1.

Orienting text in an axis

Axis labels can also be produced using the AXIS statement, and the ANGLE=
and ROTATE= options behave in a similar fashion in this statement as they do in
the TITLE and FOOTNOTE statements. The following code will produce axis
labels very similar to those shown in Figure 3.2.4a:

```
axis1
label = (f=simplex angle=90 ' '
         j=c angle=90 h=1.1 'Ozone levels at three locations'
         j=c angle=-90 rotate=90 'Figure 3.2.4b' );

proc gplot data=vol1.ca88air;
plot o3 * month / vaxis=axis1;
title1 h=1.5 f=simplex '1988 Air Quality Data - Ozone';
run;
```

The LABEL= option is used to define label text within the AXIS statement. Within the parentheses the options and text strings are arranged as they are for titles and footnotes.

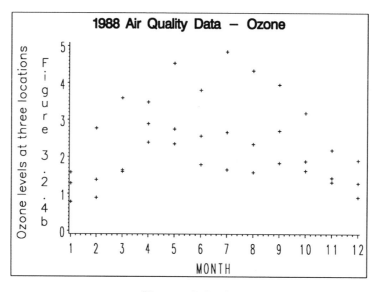

Figure 3.2.4b

MORE INFORMATION:

SAS/GRAPH Software: Reference, pp. 446-462 - See the section on TITLE Statement options for several examples of the use of ANGLE= and ROTATE=.

SEE ALSO:

Section 3.3 - Describes additional options and capabilities of the AXIS statement.

3.2.5 Creating subscripts and superscripts

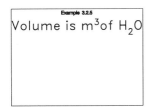

You can create subscripts and superscripts by changing text size and by using the MOVE= option in the TITLE, FOOTNOTE, and NOTE statements. The MOVE= option displaces the specified text from either the lower left corner of the graph (absolute displacement) or from the last position that text was written (relative displacement). The units of displacement can be specified as part of the MOVE= option (valid unit choices are CELLS, CM, IN, or PCT), on the graphic option GUNIT=, or left as the default, which is CELLS.

Usually when you create a subscript or superscript, the letter or number to be offset will immediately follow another character. Its placement is therefore relative to the placement of the preceding character and the appropriate MOVE= option will use relative displacement.

The form of the option is MOVE=(x,y), where x is the number of horizontal units to move (displace) and y is the number of vertical units. When a plus sign (+) or minus sign (-) precedes the x or y then the displacement is relative. When the plus and minus signs are absent, moves using absolute displacement are made. Just to confuse matters a bit more, both absolute and relative displacements can be made within the same MOVE= option.

Subscripts and superscripts generally should be about two-thirds the size of the other text and offset by between a third and a half of the text's height. Usually, subscripts are not moved as far down as superscripts are moved up. However, a superscript for a capital letter may need to be raised more than for a lowercase letter.

The process for creating a subscript, therefore, is to change the character height, move to a new position, write the subscript, move back to position, and reset the height. In this example MOVE= is used to rewrite "Volume is m^3 of H$_2$O" using both a subscript and a superscript.

```
title1 'Figure 3.2.5';
title2 f=duplex
       h=6 'Volume is m'
       h=4 move=(+0,+2) '3'
       h=6 move=(+0,-2) 'of H'
       h=4 move=(+0,-2) '2'
       h=6 move=(+0,+2) 'O';
```

The plus signs (+) and minus signs (-) are used here to make the position changes relative to the text string just written.

Figure 3.2.5

Experimentation is often needed to get the right combination of movement and size. In this example, the movement is two cells, which is a third of the text height. This superscript would probably look low on a capital letter.

MORE INFORMATION:

Cassidy, 1994 - This article contains several helpful ideas on the use of the MOVE= option.

SAS/GRAPH Software: Reference, pp. 362-363, 462 - Examples of subscripts and superscripts can be found at the end of chapters 14 and 17.

SEE ALSO:

Figure 3.3.1a - The title has an exponent.

Figure 3.3.3c - The NOTE statement uses the MOVE= option to place text on the graph.

Figure 5.7.7 - The title uses a subscript.

Section 6.3.7 - The MOVE= option is used to place titles on a template panel.

3.2.6 Using BY and macro variables in titles

Although it has been possible to place macro variables in titles and footnotes for quite awhile, Releases 6.07 (VMS, CMS, and MVS) and later (for other platforms) also include the ability to place BY variable names and values of BY variables in titles and footnotes as well. These options are documented in SAS Technical Report P-222, *Changes and Enhancements to Base SAS Software, Release 6.07*. Although these are not SAS/GRAPH options and they can be used in any TITLE or FOOTNOTE statement, their value should not be underestimated when producing graphs.

The names of BY variables and BY variable values are inserted into titles using #BYVAR and #BYVAL. Since it is common to have more than one variable in the BY statement, it is necessary to be able to have a way to associate the request with the correct variable. This is done in one of two ways. For the following BY statement

```
by station month;
```

#BYVAR2 or #BYVAR(MONTH) could both be used to place the text MONTH in a title. More useful is #BYVAL which places the *value* of the BY variable in the title.

In the following code, the GPLOT procedure produces one plot for each value of STATION.

```
options nobyline;

goptions htext=2;
proc gplot data=vol1.ca88air nocache;
by station;
plot o3 * month;
title1 '1988 Air Quality Data - Ozone';
title2 h=2 f=simplex 'Plots separated by #byvar1';
title3 h=2 f=simplex 'OZONE levels at #byval(station)';
footnote1 j=l h=2 f=simplex 'Figure 3.2.6';
run;
```

In this example, there is only one BY variable and it has been identified in TITLE2 with #BYVAR1, which could also have been written #BYVAR(STATION). This code produces three plots (one for each station). The second of these is shown in Figure 3.2.6.

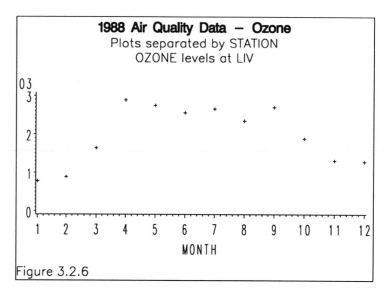

Figure 3.2.6

The NOBYLINE system option is placed in an OPTIONS statement and can be used to turn off the BYLINE, which is otherwise automatically produced. It is necessary to use this option for some base SAS and SAS/STAT procedures.

NOCACHE is an undocumented GPLOT statement option that must be used with GPLOT in Release 6.08 to correct a SAS bug. If it is not used, #BYVAL will always display the last value.

MORE INFORMATION:

SAS Technical Report P-222, pp. 44-45 - The syntax for the #BYVAR, #BYVAL, and #BYLINE options are shown with the title statement.

SAS Technical Report P-222, p. 88 The BYLINE system option is described.

SAS Technical Report P-222, pp. 159-162 - The #BYVAR, #BYVAL, and #BYLINE options are introduced with examples.

SAS Guide to Report Writing: Examples, pp. 29-34 - Example 5 uses the #BYVAL specification and discusses the NOBYLINE system option.

Westerlund, 1994 - This short article contains an example of a GPLOT with a title and footnote using #BYVAL and #BYVAR.

SEE ALSO:

Example 4.3.3e - Titles use a macro variable and the #BYVAL option.

3.3   Customizing Axes Using the AXIS Statement

The AXIS statement is used to control the appearance and scaling of the axes on a plot. This statement can be used in any procedure within SAS/GRAPH that produces an axis (except the G3D procedure). Unlike SYMBOL and PATTERN statements, the AXIS statement is self contained and is not additive.

The examples contained in the SAS/GRAPH documentation are quite extensive. However, a few options that are used in scientific graphs at times seem to cause confusion.

MORE INFORMATION: The reference information on creating and modifying axes has been greatly improved in the Release 6.06 documentation.

> *SAS/GRAPH Software: Reference*, Chapter 9 - This chapter is devoted to the AXIS statement.
> *SAS/GRAPH Software: Usage*, Chapter 51 - This chapter is devoted to the AXIS statement.

SEE ALSO:
> Many of the examples in Sections 4.3 and 4.4 utilize the AXIS statement.

3.3.1 Using the logarithm options

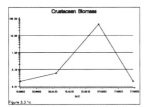
Figure 3.3.1c

Generally speaking, axes tend to have equally spaced major and minor tick marks. When data are highly skewed to the right (a few observations with very large values) or to the left (a few observations with very small values), linearly scaled plots will not show enough detail for a majority of the observations.

One approach to this type of problem is to use the logarithmic transformation on the data. This may show the detail, but the resulting graph is not scaled in the original units. Logarithmic scales do not have equally spaced minor tick marks, and while the major tick marks are equally spaced, the difference in value between them is not constant. The AXIS statement contains two options that allow the user to plot actual values against a logarithmic scale.

Demonstrating LOGBASE and LOGSTYLE
The two options that allow logarithmic scaling are LOGSTYLE and LOGBASE. LOGSTYLE is used to select a tick mark and spacing style for the axis and LOGBASE is used to select the logarithmic base.

LOGSTYLE=EXPAND   results in the unequally spaced minor tick marks.

LOGSTYLE=POWER   plots the exponent rather than the actual value. This results in a plot similar to what you would expect if the logarithmic transformation had been used.

LOGBASE=   selects any base $\geq$ 1, base e (E), or a base equal to π (PI).

The following code generates some logarithmic data and demonstrates what happens when it is plotted with and without using the AXIS options LOGSTYLE and LOGBASE.

```
data logdata;
do x = -1 to 3 by .1;
  y= 10 ** x;
  output;
end;

axis1 logstyle=expand logbase=10;

proc gplot data=logdata;
plot y * x;
plot y * x / vaxis=axis1;
symbol1 v=none i=join l=1;
title1 'Y = 10' move=(+0,+.5) 'X';
footnote1 j=1 h=2 'Figure 3.3.1a';
run;
```

The same data are plotted twice with different options for the vertical axis.

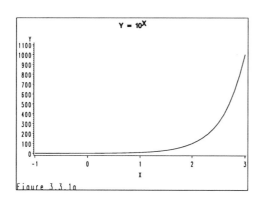
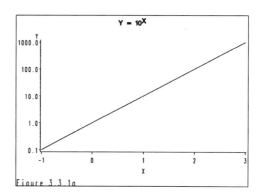

Figure 3.3.1a

Creating LOG graph paper
This example expands on the use of these same two AXIS statement options by using them to create logarithmically spaced graph paper. Several other AXIS

options are also used. These include:

minor = (n=5 h=1)   specifies five minor tick marks of a length of one cell unit.

label = none   blanks out the label for this axis.

major = (n=6 h=1.5)   requests six major tick marks each with a length of 1.5 cells.

value = none   blanks the values associated with the major tick marks.

In the following code:

- The %LET statement is used to allow a change in the logarithmic base by changing the value of the macro variable.

- The range of the vertical scale is changed by adjusting the minimum (MIN) and maximum (MAX) values.

- The horizontal lines are created by defining three horizontal points for each line. These take on the values of 1 (left-most horizontal value), 2 (right-most horizontal value), and missing, which breaks the line during plotting.

- The two styles of horizontal lines (major and minor) are designated using the variable LINETYPE, which is linked to the two SYMBOL statements through the PLOT statement.

```
* define the base as a macro variable;
%let base = 10;
* the variables min and max define the range of the Y axis;
%let min = -1;
%let max = 2;

* create a set of points to plot;
data logdata;
* loop defines major ticks;
do power = &min to &max by 1;
  y= &base ** power;
  linetype=1;                  * major ticks get solid line;
  h=1; output;                 * define the left and right;
  h=2; output;                 * points for each horizontal line;
  h=.; output;                 * missing value breaks line;
  linetype=2;                  * minor ticks get dashed line;
  hold=y;
  do j = 2 to 9;               * loop defines minor ticks;
     y=hold*j;
     h=1; output;
```

```
      h=2; output;
      h=.; output;
    end;
end;
run;

* horizontal axis statement;
axis1 minor = (n=4 h=1)
      label = none
      major = (n=6 h=1.5)
      value = none;

* vertical axis statement;
* note n=8 for minor ticks (not 9);
axis2 logstyle=expand logbase=&base
      minor = (n=8 h=1)
      major = (h=1.5)
      value = (f=simplex h=1.5)
      label = none;

proc gplot data=logdata ;
plot y * h = linetype / skipmiss
                        nolegend
                        haxis=axis1
                        vaxis=axis2
                        href=1.0 1.2 1.4 1.6 1.8 2.0;
symbol1 v=none i=join l=1 c=black;
symbol2 v=none i=join l=2 c=black;
title1 "Log Paper (Base &base)";
footnote1 j=1 h=1.5 f=simplex 'Figure 3.3.1b';
run;
quit;
```

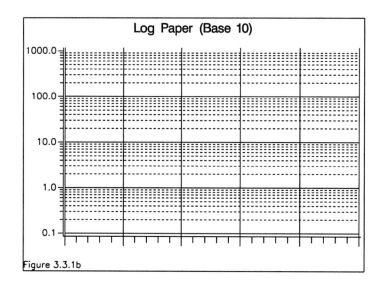

Figure 3.3.1b

Plotting data on logscale paper

The logscale graph paper generated in the previous section can be used as background to a plot of actual data. When this is done the horizontal bounds of the graph paper will depend on the limits of the data to be plotted.

In the following code the horizontal variable will be DATE, and the minimum and maximum values of DATE are stored in the data set MINMAX:

```
data bio (keep=date bmcrus linetype)
     minmax (keep=mindate maxdate);
set vol1.biomass (keep=date bmcrus station) end=eof;
retain mindate 999999 maxdate 0 linetype 3;
where station='D3350-25';
output bio;
mindate = min(mindate, date);
maxdate = max(maxdate, date);
if eof then output minmax;
run;
```

The step that generates the logscale graph is similar to that used in the previous example, except the horizontal bounds are now data driven.

```
* create a set of points to plot;
* the variables min and max define the range of the Y axis;
data logdata;
set minmax;
* loop defines major ticks;
do power = &min to &max by 1;
  y= &base ** power;
  linetype=1;               * major ticks get solid line;
  date=mindate; output;        * define the left and right;
  date=maxdate; output;        * points for each horizontal line;
  date=.;       output;    * missing value breaks line;
  linetype=2;             * minor ticks get dashed line;
  hold=y;
  do j = 2 to 9;          * loop defines minor ticks;
    y=hold*j;
    date=mindate; output;
    date=maxdate; output;
    date=.; output;
  end;
end;
run;
```

The two data sets, BIO and LOGDATA, are combined and plotted, as shown in Figure 3.3.1c.

```
data pltdata;
set logdata (rename=(y=bmcrus)) bio;
run;
```

```
* vertical axis statement;
* note n=8 for minor ticks (not 9);
axis1 logstyle=expand logbase=&base
      minor = (n=8 h=1)
      major = (h=1.5)
      value = (f=simplex h=1.5)
      label = none;

axis2 value = (f=simplex h=1.5);

proc gplot data=pltdata ;
plot bmcrus * date = linetype / skipmiss
                        nolegend
                        vaxis=axis1
                        haxis=axis2;
symbol1 v=none i=join l=1 c=black;
symbol2 v=none i=join l=2 c=black;
symbol3 v=dot  i=join l=1 c=black;
title1 "Crustacean Biomass";
footnote1 j=l h=1.5 f=simplex 'Figure 3.3.1c';
run;
```

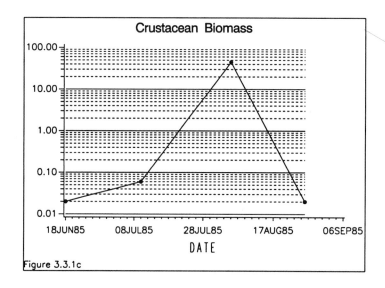

Figure 3.3.1c

MORE INFORMATION:

SAS/GRAPH Software: Reference, pp. 222-223, 256-258 - These pages contain syntax and an example of the LOGSTYLE and LOGBASE options.

SAS/GRAPH Software: Usage, pp. 705-707 - This section gives an example of AXIS statements with and without using the LOGSTYLE and LOGBASE options.

3.3.2 Working with tick mark text strings

It is at times useful to replace the tick mark numbers on one or both of the axes with textual information. Without using the ANNOTATE facility there are a couple of ways that this can be accomplished.

- User-defined formats

- VALUE= option in the AXIS statement.

Defining and using formats is fairly easy, and it was the only choice prior to the introduction of the AXIS statement. It is more difficult to fine tune the final graph when you use formats, because there is little or no font, size, or color control. This example shows you how to control the tick mark labels using the AXIS statement where these options are available.

By using the AXIS statement you can define labels for each major tick mark as well as for the axis itself. The VALUE= option on the AXIS statement allows specific text strings to be associated with specific values and increased control is achieved by using font and size options.

Primary control in the VALUE= axis option is exercised by identifying the tick mark number. Usually this implies that the user has specified the number of major tick marks, for example, major=(n=12) or order=(1 to 12), or knows how many tick marks there will be. The tick mark is designated with the T= option. Attributes for a specific tick mark will immediately follow the appropriate T= option. You can independently control the font, size, and color of the text for each tick mark.

In the following code the first AXIS statement (AXIS1) uses t=3 to identify the tick mark number which will have the text string "Alert" instead of its value (which would have been 2). The AXIS2 statement defines a default font and height for the axis (h=1.5 f=simplex) and also changes these two options for the fourth and fifth tick marks (Apr and May).

```
* define the vertical axis ;
axis1 label = (f=duplex h=1 a=90 'Ozone Level')
      order = (0 to 3 by 1)
      minor = (n=1)
      value = (t=3 h=1 'Alert');
```

```
* define the horizontal axis ;
axis2 label = (f=duplex h=1 'Monthly Average')
      minor = none
      value = (h=1.5 f=simplex t=1 'Jan'  t=2  'Feb' t=3  'Mar'
                              t=4 f=swissb 'Apr'
                              t=5 f=swissb 'May'
                              t=6  'Jun' t=7  'Jul' t=8  'Aug'
                              t=9  'Sep' t=10 'Oct' t=11 'Nov'
                              t=12 'Dec');


proc gplot data=vol1.ca88air;
where station='SFO';
plot o3 * month / vaxis=axis1
                  haxis=axis2
                  vref=2;
title1 '1988 Air Quality';
title2 h=1.5 f=simplex 'Assigning tick mark text';
footnote1 h=1.5 j=l f=simplex 'Figure 3.3.2';
run;
```

In the resulting graph we have placed the word Alert on the vertical axis (replacing the 2) and have changed the font and size for the two months of particular interest.

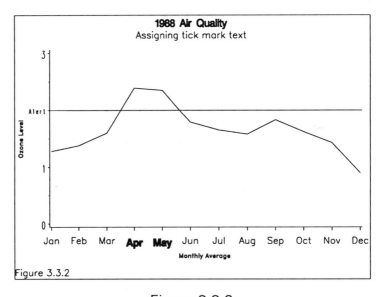

Figure 3.3.2

Controlling the characteristics of tick marks in the VALUE= statement is positionally dependent. In this example the AXIS2 statement has a fairly complicated VALUE= option statement. The default values of height (h=1.5) and font (f=simplex) are established by making the specification *before any* of the T= options. As soon as the first T= option is specified, other options such as H= and F= will apply to the tick mark designated by the preceding T= option. Thus, the font can be changed for T=4 and T=5 without changing the default font for the other tick marks.

MORE INFORMATION:
> *SAS/GRAPH Software: Reference*, pp. 227-229 - Syntax for the VALUE=
> option.
> *SAS/GRAPH Software: Usage*, pp. 686-688, 699-700 - Examples
> demonstrate the use of the VALUE= option.

3.3.3 Dealing with dates

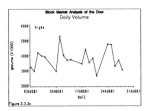

SAS dates and dates in general can present unique
problems when used to define points on an axis. SAS
dates are stored as the number of days since the
beginning of time in the SAS world (January 1, 1960). The
date April 5, 1978, for example is stored as 6,669 and July
4, 1776, is stored as -67,019.

When an unformatted variable containing SAS dates is used to define an axis
(usually the horizontal axis), the displayed values are essentially uninterpretable.
The following code plots the Dow Jones Average for a one-month period. For
illustrative purposes the DATE7. format associated with the horizontal variable
DATE has been removed.

```
goptions htext=1.5;

axis1 label=(h=1.5 a=90 'Volume (X1000)');

proc gplot data=vol1.dow;
plot volume*date=1 / vaxis=axis1;
symbol1 v='V' f=simplex l=1 i=join c=black;
format date 6.;
title1 'Stock Market Analysis of the Dow';
title2 h=2 f=simplex 'Daily Volume';
footnote1 j=l h=1.5 f=simplex 'Figure 3.3.3a';
run;
```

This code generates the following graph. Note the values used for DATE on the
horizontal axis.

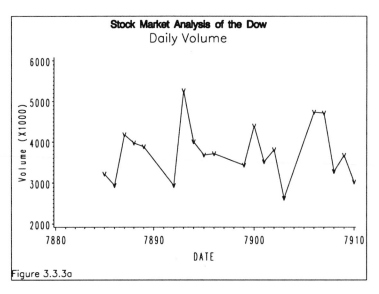

Figure 3.3.3a

Even if a format such as DATE7. is used, the resulting tick mark values are of little use. Because months do not have an equal number of days, the resulting axis may contain dates that add little meaning to the graph. The following graph repeats the previous plot with the DATE7. format associated with the horizontal variable.

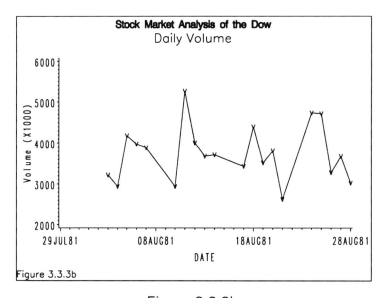

Figure 3.3.3b

For most graphs, major tick marks are equally spaced. However, on axes representing dates, you may want to have the tick marks represent something like the first of each month. This means that the major tick marks will have unequal spacing. For example, if the first major tick mark is on 01April, 01May will be 30 days later, and 01June will be 31 days after that.

Fortunately, the ORDER= option in the AXIS statement can be used to address issues associated with SAS dates. The ORDER= option is used to determine which values are to receive major tick marks. In the axis defined in the following code, major tick marks start on June 1 and continue on the first of each month through September.

```
axis1 order=('01jun85'd to '01sep85'd by month);
```

The AXIS2 statement in the following code will assign a date value for Monday of each week (03AUG81 is known to be a Monday).

```
goptions htext=1.5;

axis1 label=(h=1.5 a=90 f=swiss 'V' f=simplex 'olume (X1000)');
axis2 order=('03aug81'd to '31aug81'd by week)
      value=(h=1.5);

proc gplot data=vol1.dow;
plot volume*date=1 / vaxis=axis1 haxis=axis3;
symbol1 v='V' f=simplex l=1 i=join c=black;
format date date7.;
title1 'Stock Market Analysis of the Dow';
title2 h=2 f=simplex 'Daily Volume';
note move=(20,30)pct 'Volume';

footnote1 j=l h=1.5 f=simplex 'Figure 3.3.3c';
run;
```

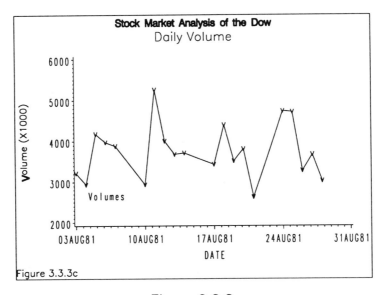

Figure 3.3.3c

On the horizontal axis, date is ordered by week. You can also set the increments to any of the valid arguments for the INTCK and INTNX functions. These include increments for DATE intervals (DAY, WEEK, MONTH, QTR, and YEAR), DATETIME intervals (DTDAY, DTWEEK, DTMONTH, DTQTR, and DTYEAR), and TIME intervals (HOUR, MINUTE, and SECOND).

MORE INFORMATION:

Easter, 1993 - A short example showing the use of dates with a PROC GCHART.

Kalt and Redman, 1993a - This article details the use of the AXIS statement with SAS dates.

SAS Technical Report P-222, pp. 4-9 - This section discusses date intervals and documents several new INTCK and INTNX intervals.

SAS/ETS User's Guide, pp. 70-77 - This section discusses, with numerous examples, the handling of SAS dates including the INTCK and INTNX functions.

SAS/GRAPH Software: Reference, pp. 224-226 - See these pages for syntax for the ORDER= option when using dates.

SAS Language: Reference, pp. 558-560 - These pages describe and give arguments for the INTCK and INTNX functions.

SEE ALSO:

Figure 5.7.6b - This figure also plots these data using the PLOT2 statement.

3.4 Creating Legends

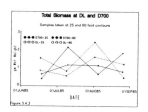

Figure 3.4.3

You can use the LEGEND statement to create customized legends for plots and charts. It is similar to the AXIS statement in its general characteristics and options. However, it is used to provide information concerning symbols or patterns that are not associated with just one axis. The LEGEND statement is well documented in the SAS System reference documentation, and the topics discussed in this section are included because they are somewhat problematic.

SEE ALSO:

Example 4.3.3e - Utilizes two different LEGEND statements on the same plot.

3.4.1 Positioning a legend

The legend created by the LEGEND statement may be placed anywhere within the graphic area. The default position is centered below the graph.

Default legend

When the LEGEND statement is not specified, most of the graphics procedures will create a legend if it is needed. In the following code PROC GPLOT creates a default legend (since no LEGEND statement is given).

```
axis1 order=('01jun85'd to '01sep85'd by month)
      value=(f=simplex h=1.5);

axis2 label= (h=1.5 a=90 'gm Wet Weight')
      value=(f=simplex h=1.5);

proc gplot data=vol1.biomass;
plot bmtotl * date = station / haxis = axis1 vaxis=axis2;
where station in ('DL-25', 'DL-60', 'D700-25', 'D700-60') ;
symbol1 v=dot    i=join l=1  c=black;
symbol2 v=dot    i=join l=2  c=black;
symbol3 v=circle i=join l=1  c=black;
symbol4 v=circle i=join l=2  c=black;
title1 'Total Biomass at DL and D700';
title3 h=1.5 f=simplex 'Samples taken at 25 and 60 foot contours';
footnote1 j=l h=1.5 'Figure 3.4.1a';
run;
```

Notice that the legend is centered below the graph *outside* the axis area.

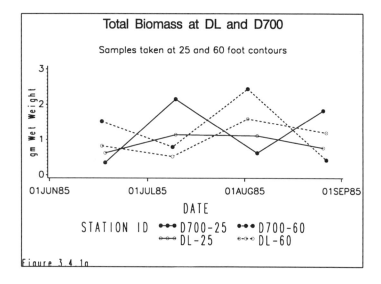

Figure 3.4.1a

There are three LEGEND statement options that deal directly with positioning.

- POSITION=   places the legend in a general area on the graph.

- OFFSET=   adjusts the legend placement relative to the POSITION= area.

- ORIGIN=   explicitly places the legend using coordinates of the entire graphic output area.

Using the POSITION= and OFFSET= options

The POSITION= option allows you to select one of eight locations outside the axis area or nine locations within the axis area. These locations are designated by a combination of TOP, MIDDLE, BOTTOM, and LEFT, CENTER, RIGHT with either INSIDE or OUTSIDE.

The following code uses the POSITION= option to center the legend at the top of the graphics area:

```
legend position=(center top)
       across=2
       label=none;

proc gplot data=vol1.biomass;
plot bmtot1 * date = station / legend=legend1
                               haxis = axis1 vaxis=axis2;
where station in ('DL-25', 'DL-60', 'D700-25', 'D700-60') ;
symbol1 v=dot    i=join l=1  c=black;
symbol2 v=dot    i=join l=2  c=black;
symbol3 v=circle i=join l=1  c=black;
symbol4 v=circle i=join l=2  c=black;
title1 'Total Biomass at DL and D700';
title3 h=1.5 f=simplex 'Samples taken at 25 and 60 foot contours';
footnote1 j=l h=1.5 f=simplex 'Figure 3.4.1b';
run;
```

The POSITION selected in the code is (CENTER TOP), which by default is outside the axis area. The OFFSET= option can be used to fine tune the placement of the legend within the selected position.

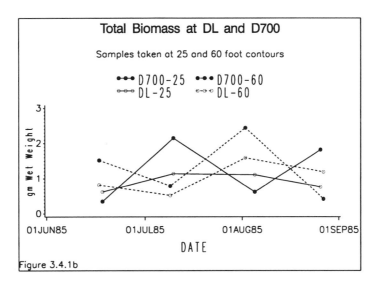

Figure 3.4.1b

Using the ORIGIN= option

You can also position the legend with the ORIGIN= option. This option allows the specific placement of the legend anywhere on the graph by the use of coordinates based on the lower left-hand corner. The default units are in percentage of the graphic area, but they can also be in inches and the other standard units. The ORIGIN= option is often used in conjunction with the MODE= option, which controls whether the legend can share space (overlay) with the graph.

In this example, since MODE=SHARE the legend can be written inside the axis area. With MODE=SHARE, care must be taken on the placement, since the legend and the graph can become jumbled.

Replacing the LEGEND statement in the previous example with this one using the ORIGIN= option produces the graph shown in Figure 3.4.1c.

```
legend origin=(10 pct, 65 pct)
       mode=share
       across=2
       label=none;
```

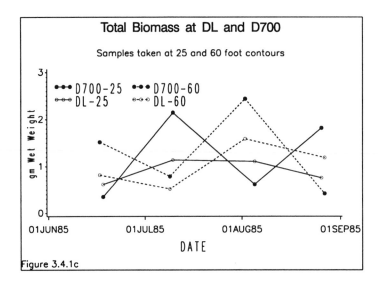

Figure 3.4.1c

The LABEL=NONE removes the label for the plot variable (STATION ID) and the ACROSS=2 option limits the number of legend entries to two per row.

MORE INFORMATION:
> *SAS/GRAPH Software: Reference*, p. 310 - See this page for syntax for the MODE= option.
> *SAS/GRAPH Software: Reference*, pp. 333-334 - These pages give locations for positioning the legend.

3.4.2 Controlling text for legend entry labels

In the legend the default text associated with each plot symbol is the value of the plotted variable. You can easily change this text by using the VALUE= and TICK= options in the same way as they are used in the AXIS statement.

The following code modifies the text of one of the four values of the variable STATION:

```
legend origin=(10 pct, 65 pct)
       mode=share
       across=1
       label=none
       value=(f=simplex h=1.2
              t=1 h=1.2 f=swissb 'D700 at 25 feet')
       ;
proc gplot data=vol1.biomass;
plot bmtotl * date = station / legend=legend1
                               haxis = axis1 vaxis=axis2;
where station in ('DL-25', 'DL-60', 'D700-25', 'D700-60') ;
```

```
symbol1 v=dot    i=join l=1  c=black;
symbol2 v=dot    i=join l=2  c=black;
symbol3 v=circle i=join l=1  c=black;
symbol4 v=circle i=join l=2  c=black;
title1 'Total Biomass at DL and D700';
title3 h=1.5 f=simplex 'Samples taken at 25 and 60 foot contours';
footnote1 j=l h=1.5 f=simplex  'Figure 3.4.2';
run;
```

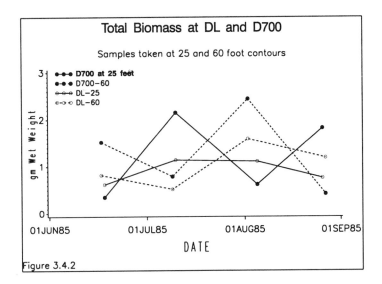

Figure 3.4.2

SEE ALSO:
Section 3.3.2 - Changes tick mark values in the AXIS statement using the VALUE= option.

3.4.3 Adjusting the legend entry symbol size

Control of the size of the symbols in the legend often becomes important. The size of the symbols may need to be adjusted when the graph is

- reduced in size through photocopying

- placed in a less than full-size template panel

- loaded into a word processor figure

- projected in a large room.

The shape and size of the symbol portion of the legend is controlled through the

SHAPE= option. For PROC GPLOT this option usually takes the form of SHAPE=SYMBOL(*width,height*), where *width* is the size of the symbol area (the default is 5) and *height* is the height of the symbol. Reducing the width will crowd the symbols together (as will increasing the height without increasing the width). Usually the SHAPE= option is used in conjunction with the VALUE= option to control all the size aspects of the text and symbols in the legend.

The following code increases both the width and height of the symbols in the legend. The LEGEND statement used is

```
legend origin=(10 pct, 65 pct)
       mode=share
       across=2
       label=none
       value=(f=simplex h=1.2)
       shape=symbol(8,2)
    ;
```

This LEGEND statement produces Figure 3.4.3.

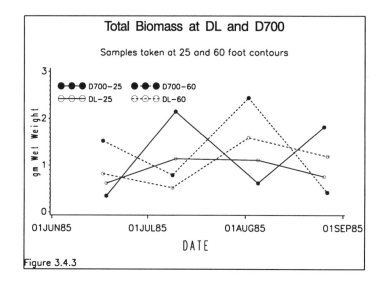

Figure 3.4.3

4 Customizing Graphs

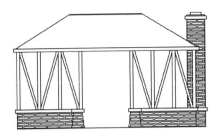

Extending the Structure

4.1   Introduction

In this chapter, you will learn a broad variety of techniques that can customize your graphics output. Customized graphs are produced when you extend the usual presentation graphics procedure by taking advantage of any of a number of options or features in SAS/GRAPH. For many users, the creation of customized graphics displays is synonymous with the use of the ANNOTATE facility. Others seem to avoid SAS/GRAPH altogether simply because they do not know how to use ANNOTATE. Both of these extremes fail to take full advantage of the capabilities of SAS/GRAPH when producing customized graphs. While ANNOTATE does add a large array of capabilities, SAS/GRAPH can generate a wide variety of graphs without using ANNOTATE, and these techniques are presented in this chapter.

Techniques that you can use to customize your graphs range from simple to complex. Included in this chapter are examples that show you

●   how to use the OVERLAY option

●   data manipulation techniques to create error bars, broken scale histograms, multiple axis plots, butterfly plots, box-whisker plots, and cluster scatter plots

- methods to control the scaling of axes

- how to create and use a GFONT to produce a sunflower plot.

4.2   Using Symbols with the OVERLAY Option

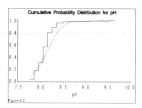

Overlaying two or more plots to form a single graph is accomplished in the GPLOT procedure in much the same way as in the PLOT procedure. The PLOT statement is used to define two or more plots, and the OVERLAY option is used to place them onto a single graph. Control of the appearance of the individual plots is accomplished with the SYMBOL statement. Each plot definition is tied to a specific SYMBOL statement by using the form $y*x=z$, where the z is either the SYMBOL definition number or a variable whose values are used to distinguish the SYMBOL definitions.

You must be careful to correctly associate the desired symbols with the correct plot. Because it is not intuitively obvious which SYMBOL statement will be used for each plot request, it is important for you to understand how and when each SYMBOL statement is selected. Although not obvious, the topic of symbol selection is not necessarily difficult once the rules are established.

This example plots the observed cumulative probability distribution of pH values in a water quality study and overlays the plot with the cumulative normal distribution with the same mean and variance. The data set that is plotted contains three variables: the pH rounded to the nearest tenth (PHROUND), the observed cumulative probability for that pH (PHCUML), and the normal cumulative probability value for the same pH (PHNORM).

The following code contains two plot requests and the use of the OVERLAY option:

```
* plot the cumulative distributions;
proc gplot data=pltdata;
plot phcuml * phround = 1
     phnorm * phround = 2 / overlay
                          vaxis = 0 to 1 by .2
                          haxis = 7.5 to 10 by .5;
label phround = 'pH'
      phcuml  = 'Cumulative Probability';
symbol1 v=none i=stepcj l=1  c=black;
symbol2 v=none i=join   l=2  c=black;
title1 'Cumulative Probability Distribution for pH';
footnote1 j=l h=1.5 f=simplex 'Figure 4.2';
run;
```

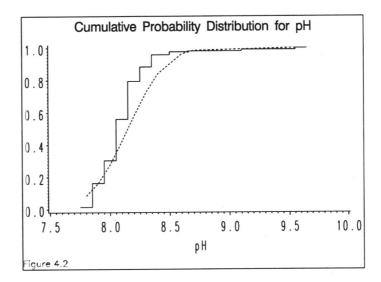

Figure 4.2

The 1 in the plot request

        phcuml * phround = 1

ties the plot to the first symbol definition, which in this case is SYMBOL1. The INTERPOL option (abbreviated as `i`) requests that the points be joined using a step function and, to allow visual interpolation, requests that each step be centered on the point.

The 2 in the plot request

        phnorm * phround = 2

ties this plot to the second symbol definition which is *not* necessarily defined by SYMBOL2. It is a *feature* of the SYMBOL statement that when colors (C=) are not specified, the set of colors will be exhausted before using the next SYMBOL statement. The set of colors is device dependent; for example, a monochrome device would only have one color in the set of colors. If the COLOR= option had not been set to a specific color (in this case black) for a device that supports multiple colors, both lines would have been drawn using different colors based on the SYMBOL1 statement i.e. LINE=1 and INTERPOL=STEPCJ. The second SYMBOL statement would not have been used, because the second symbol definition would have been satisfied by the first SYMBOL statement using its second color. You can test this by removing the `c=black` from the SYMBOL1 statement.

MORE INFORMATION:
> *SAS/GRAPH Software: Reference*, p. 418 - Syntax and example for the
> I=STEP SYMBOL statement option.
> *SAS/GRAPH Software: Usage*, pp. 261-270 and especially pp. 266-267 -
> Discusses the use of SYMBOL definitions in the context of
> overlaid plots.

SEE ALSO:
> Figure 2.3.2b - Example using the OVERLAY option in PROC PLOT.

4.3 Creating Customized Specialty Graphs Using Data Manipulation

Because PROC GPLOT produces scatter plots based on data set observations, you can manipulate data and generate plots that seem to be outside of the capabilities of SAS/GRAPH without using ANNOTATE. The techniques demonstrated in this section enable you to create graphs and charts with GPLOT that are customized to your needs and for which there are no standardized options.

In each of the examples in this section, observations (data points) are added to the data to be plotted. These additional points cause GPLOT to create the selected graph. The methods used in these examples are not the only way, or perhaps even the best way, to construct these graphs. However, they are to be used as examples of the technique of data manipulation.

These techniques allow you to use GPLOT to create:

- plots with error bars

- histograms with broken axes and uneven groupings

- scatter plots with multiple axes

- butterfly plots

- box-whisker plots

- cluster scatter plots.

MORE INFORMATION:
> Carpenter, 1989 and 1994b - Papers deal with various data-manipulation
> techniques including several techniques shown in Section 4.3.

4.3.1 Generating error bars

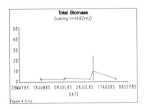

Error bars can be generated directly by using the interpolation option in the SYMBOL statement, but there are some disadvantages to this approach. The statement `i=std2mjd` requests that the scatter plot be placed so that for each value of the horizontal variable, a vertical line should be drawn two standard errors above and below the mean and that the means should be joined. Although the data will not be plotted, they are used to determine the vertical axis.

Error bars generated with the INTERPOL= option

The following code generates Figure 4.3.1a using the INTERPOL= option (i=)in the SYMBOL statement:

```
proc gplot data=vol1.biomass;
plot bmtotl* date;
symbol1 v=none i=std2mj  c=black l=1;
title1 'Total Biomass';
title2 f=simplex '(using i=std2mj)';
footnote1 j=l h=1.5 f=simplex 'Figure 4.3.1a';
run;
```

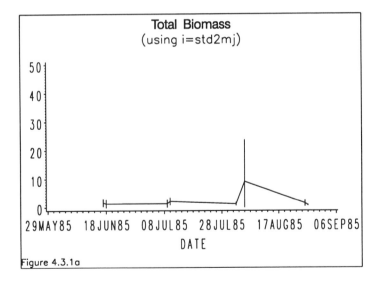

Figure 4.3.1a

The upper vertical axis is much too high; it has been scaled to accommodate a single large unplotted point. The lower axis values do not allow the printing of the complete error bars because there were no biomass values less than zero. It is also not possible to place symbols at the ends of the error bars.

Creating error bars with generated data points

The following example corrects the scaling problems shown in Figure 4.3.1a and allows symbols to be added to the plot at the mean and at the ends of the error bars.

Figure 4.3.1b shows means with two standard errors. The mean and standard error are both statistics that you can easily calculate by using PROC SUMMARY (or any of several other univariate summary procedures). In this case, the data are summarized for each date.

The results of the summary procedure are saved in a data set so that there will be one observation containing the mean and standard error for each horizontal value (DATE). You can then manipulate each of these observations to construct four observations that are plotted.

In this example, PROC SUMMARY creates the data set of selected statistics with one observation for each date. For each date, the following code outputs an observation for the vertical variable (mean biomass) then adds two standard errors and outputs the second observation. The second and third (mean minus two standard errors) become the end points of the error bars. The fourth observation is a repeat of the first and returns the line to the mean so that successive means can be joined. A SYMBOL statement defines the line and plot symbols. This technique also allows you to place symbols on the joined line, as shown in Figure 4.3.1b.

```
proc sort data=vol1.biomass
          out=biosort;
by date;
run;

* determine the summary statistics;
proc summary data=biosort;
by date;
var bmtotl;
output out=stats mean=mean stderr=se;
run;

* create the observations to be plotted;
data all(keep=date biomass);
set stats;
* for each observation create four;
biomass=mean;          output;
biomass=mean+ 2*se;  output;
biomass=mean- 2*se;  output;
biomass=mean;          output;
run;

proc gplot data=all;
plot biomass * date;
symbol1 v=dot i=join  c=black l=1;
title1 'Total Biomass';
footnote1 j=l h=1.5 f=simplex 'Figure 4.3.1b';
run;
```

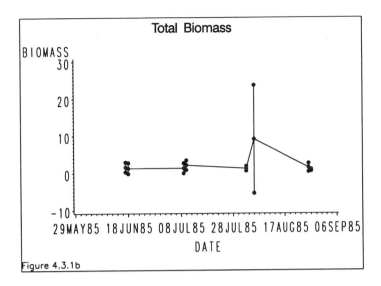

Figure 4.3.1b

MORE INFORMATION:

SAS/GRAPH Software: Reference, pp. 437-440 - discusses handling of data that is out of range.

SAS/GRAPH Software: Reference, p. 438 - MODE=INCLUDE and MODE=EXCLUDE can be used to adjust the error bars by including or excluding data.

4.3.2 Creating histograms using GPLOT

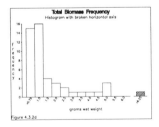

PROC GCHART does not always provide the flexibility required when generating histograms. GPLOT, on the other hand, has a great deal of flexibility but is not designed to generate histograms. The SYMBOL statement option INTERPOL=STEP will create steps but not a histogram. Through data manipulation, however, you can use GPLOT to create histograms that

- control the fill pattern according to some criteria

- vary the width of the bars

- break the horizontal axis

- vary the grouping criteria according to a format

- allow uneven spacing between the bars.

Figures 4.3.2a and 4.3.2b were created using GCHART on the BIOMASS data. The grouping variable (BMTOTL) takes on values less than 6, except for one value of 44. When the full range is charted in the first histogram (Figure 4.3.2a), all the meaningful information on the distribution of biomass is lost. The distribution of biomass can be shown, as in Figure 4.3.2b, but only by eliminating the largest value.

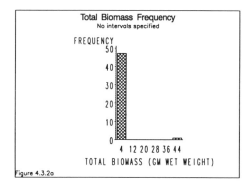

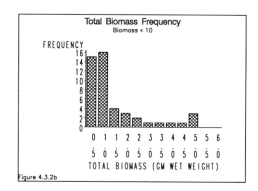

Figure 4.3.2a   Figure 4.3.2b

GCHART can specify irregular intervals by specifying the midpoints that are to be used. The following PROC GCHART creates Figure 4.3.2c, a histogram with all of the data:

```
proc gchart data=vol1.biomass;
vbar bmtotl / midpoints = .5 to 6 by .5, 30
              raxis=axis1
              maxis=axis2;
title1 'Total Biomass Frequency';
title2 h=1.5 f=simplex 'Using uneven midpoints';
footnote1 j=1 h=1.5 f=simplex 'Figure 4.3.2c';
run;
quit;
```

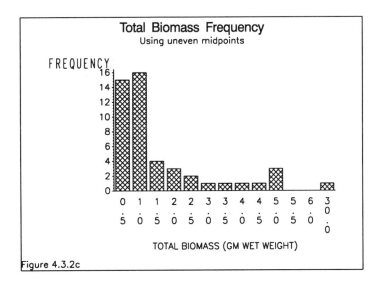

Figure 4.3.2c

Figure 4.3.2c has three intervals that have different widths from the other intervals (0.5, 6.0, and 30.0). These are not, however, easily distinguished by a casual reader. It is possible to produce a meaningful histogram with all of the information by using GPLOT and data manipulation.

You can create a histogram such as the one shown in Figure 4.3.2d by using PROC GPLOT rather than GCHART. Features of the techniques shown in this example include

●   the vertical bars and the split horizontal axis were created using data manipulation techniques

●   shading is accomplished with the AREAS= option.

The data are grouped into categories and summarized. Then, each observation is used to define the four corners of the vertical bar. The split horizontal axis was also constructed by specifying the end points of the two segments. Similar techniques can create bars with variable spacing.

For continuous variables, the first step is to define a midpoint variable. The ROUND function is used in this example to create groups spaced at .5 units. Logic is then added to combine any observations that fall on the extremes, creating two groups with unequal width.

```
* Group the observations into buckets;
data group (keep=group bmtotl);
set vol1.biomass (keep=bmtotl);
group = round(bmtotl,.5);
* Combine 0-.25 with .25-.75;
if group=0 then group=.5;
* combine all groups > than 6.25 into one bucket;
group = min(7, group);
run;
```

PROC SUMMARY or some other summarization technique is used to summarize the data. This step and the previous step would have been done automatically by GCHART. GROUP will be the horizontal plot variable and FREQ will be the vertical plot variable.

```
* determine the observation count for each bucket;
proc summary data=group;
by group;
var group;
output out=count n=freq;
run;
```

The default axis must be suppressed and an artificial one built if a split horizontal axis is desired. The new axis is simply created by drawing two horizontal line segments with appropriately selected endpoints and eliminating the actual horizontal axis. Temporary variables hold the original values of GROUP and FREQ. When AREAS=n is used in the PLOT statement, this line cannot take on the minimum value and still show, so it has been given a small positive offset.

```
tgroup = group;
tfreq = freq;

*Create a broken horizontal axis;
if _n_=1 then do;
   pltvar=1;
   freq=0.02;
           group=0;   output;
           group=6.4; output;
   pltvar=2;
           group=6.6; output;
           group=7.4; output;
end;
```

The variable PLTVAR is used to distinguish the SYMBOL and PATTERN selections. In this example, the first two values are assigned to the horizontal axis. Because the AREAS= option is used, the lowest lines are plotted first and should, therefore, have the lowest values of PLTVAR. The other two values of PLTVAR distinguish the two types of histogram bars.

```
* separate the count in the largest group;
if tgroup le 6 then pltvar=3; else pltvar=4;
```

The summarized data usually have one observation for each bar on the histogram. This observation then defines each of the four corners of that bar. This example takes the midpoint (TGROUP) of each bar and establishes the corners at +/- .25 units. Because the width of each bar is now the same as the width of the group, the bars are next to each other. Bars with space between them can be created simply by adjusting the amount added and subtracted from TGROUP.

```
group = tgroup - .25;  freq =       0; output;    *lower left corner;
                       freq = tfreq; output;    *upper left corner;
group = tgroup + .25;                 output;    *upper right corner;
                       freq =       0; output;    *lower right corner;
```

The remainder of the job is a straightforward GPLOT. The AXIS statement suppresses the default horizontal axis and its tick marks, and a format created with PROC FORMAT provides the horizontal axis labels.

```
* Horizontal axis ;
axis1 order= 0 to 7.5 by .5
      style=0
      major=none
      minor=none
      label=(h=2 f=simplex)
      value=(h=1.5 f=simplex a=55)
      offset=(0cm);
* Vertical axis ;
axis2 offset=(0 cm)
      order=0 to 16 by 2
      value=(h=1.5 f=simplex)
      minor=none;

* define fill patterns (1 & 2 used for horiz. axis);
pattern1 v=me c=black;
pattern2 v=me c=black;
pattern3 v=me c=black;
pattern4 v=m1x45 c=black;

symbol1 i=join c=black l=1;
symbol2 i=join c=black l=1;
symbol3 i=join c=black l=1;
symbol4 i=join c=black l=2;

proc gplot data=plot;
plot freq*group=pltvar / areas=4
                        haxis=axis1
                        vaxis=axis2
                        nolegend;
format group grp5.;
```

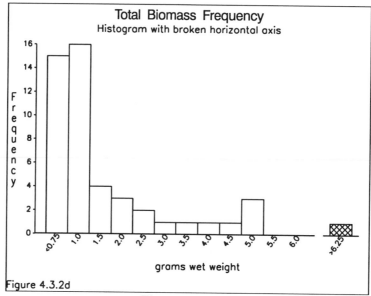

Figure 4.3.2d

Hewlett-Packard Graphics Language (HP-GL) files with filled areas, as with the AREAS= option, do not always transfer well into word processors. This example required the use of the CGMWPCA device driver, which is user created and is described in SAS Technical Support Document TS252G. When transferring to WordPerfect, SAS Institute recommends the use of one of the CGMWPxx drivers over the HPGL drivers that were used in most of the examples in this book.

MORE INFORMATION:

Carpenter, 1989, 1994b - Contain similar examples to those shown in Section 4.3.2.

SAS/GRAPH Software: Reference, p. 418 - I=STEP syntax.

SAS Technical Support Document TS252G - Discusses drivers for use with WordPerfect.

SEE ALSO:

Section 5.3 - Problems specific to word processing programs are discussed.

4.3.3 Creating multiple axes

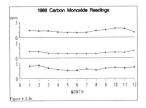

Generally, you place more than one plot on a page by using templates (see Section 6.3). The process, however, can be tricky if the template changes the aspect ratio of the plot itself or if certain elements such as axes of the individual graphs need to be aligned. When you find that using templates in these situations creates more problems than are solved, you may wish to generate multiple plots without using templates.

The examples in Section 4.3.2 create a horizontal axis by defining the endpoints of horizontal line segments. Line segments can also be used to create a series of complete axes.

Multiple plots using one vertical axis

Figure 4.3.3a contains a single plot of three stations. Often, when several lines are overlayed on one graph, the graph can become cluttered and difficult to read. When this happens, it may be necessary to separate the individual plots for easier reading.

Although the three stations shown in Figure 4.3.3a are fairly easy to distinguish, the figure serves as an example for the techniques discussed in this section.

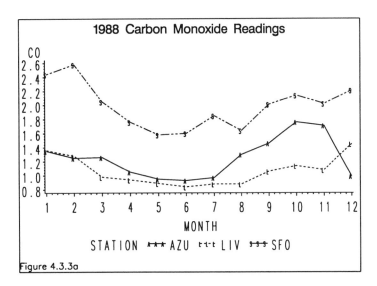

Figure 4.3.3a

Creating multiple axes

The plots of each of the stations shown in Figure 4.3.3a can be separated so that each station has its own set of axes. The vertical and horizontal axes in Figure 4.3.3b were generated through the use of line segments, and the data have been separated by using a vertical offset. Presented together, the plots of the three stations appear to have been separated.

The dummy axes are created first, and as was done in the histogram example in the previous section, the variable PLTVAR is used to identify segments and associate these segments with SYMBOL statements. In this example, the vertical range for each station is known. In actual practice the positioning of the axes will usually be dynamic. For each axis, four points are defined. The first three define the endpoints and the origin, and the fourth has a missing value. When coupled with the SKIPMISS option, the missing value separates the axes into distinct segments.

```
* Create dummy axes for each station;
* Allow three vertical units for each axis with one unit between
* each plot.;
if _n_=1 then do;
   pltvar=1;
   * axis for SFO;
   yvar=0; month=12; output;
           month=0;  output;
   yvar=3;           output;
   yvar=.;           output;
   * axis for LIV;
   yvar=4; month=12; output;
           month=0;  output;
   yvar=7;           output;
   yvar=.;           output;
   * axis for AZU;
   yvar=8; month=12; output;
           month=0;  output;
   yvar=11;          output;
   yvar=.;           output;
   month=tmon;
end;
```

The temporary variable TMON is used to hold the true value of MONTH, which is needed for plotting.

The data values for two of the stations (AZU and LIV) are offset vertically from the true origin by a fixed amount. This amount, which is specified in the OFFSET variable, causes the data for these two stations to be higher on the vertical scale. A distinct PLTVAR value is also used for each station so that different SYMBOL definitions can be applied.

```
if first.station then do;
    * The data for each station is offset vertically to fit
    * with the dummy axes.;
    if station = 'AZU' then do;
        offset=8;
        pltvar=2;
    end;
    else if station = 'LIV' then do;
        offset=4;
        pltvar=3;
    end;
    else do;
        offset = 0;
        pltvar=4;
    end;
end;

yvar = co + offset;
output;
run;
```

Primary axis and symbol control is maintained through the use of the AXIS and SYMBOL statements. The line for both axes is turned off (STYLE=0) and the first letter of the station name is designated as the plot symbol.

```
* Control the vertical axis;
axis1 order = 0 to 11 by 1
      label = (h=1.15 f=simplex 'ppm')
      minor=none
      style=0;
* Control the horizontal axis;
axis2 minor=none
      style=0;

* Define the symbols for each subplot;
* SYMBOL1 controls the axes;
symbol1 v=none c=black l=1 i=join;
symbol2 v='A'  c=black l=1 i=join f=simplex;
symbol3 v='L'  c=black l=1 i=join f=simplex;
symbol4 v='S'  c=black l=1 i=join f=simplex;
```

The default tick-mark values for the vertical axis are replaced with meaningful numbers, which are supplied through the use of a user-generated format (VERT.).

```
* Define a format for the vertical axis;
proc format;
value vert 0,4,8  = '0'
           3,7,11 = '3'
           other  = ' ';
run;
```

The actual PROC GPLOT is fairly straightforward with PLOT statement options to turn off the legend, select the axis statements, and invoke the SKIPMISS option.

```
* Plot the data;
proc gplot data=air1;
plot yvar*month=pltvar / nolegend
                         skipmiss
                         vaxis=axis1
                         haxis=axis2;
format yvar vert.;
title1 '1988 Carbon Monoxide Readings';
footnote1 j=1 h=1.5 f=simplex 'Figure 4.3.3b';
run;

quit;
```

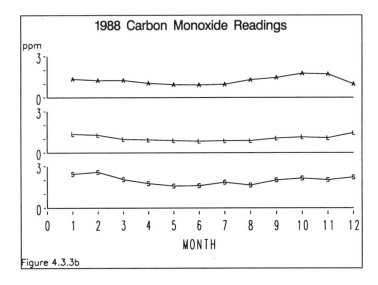

Figure 4.3.3b

This technique can have the disadvantage of compressing the vertical axis and in this case, removing much of the *character* of the graph.

Separating three variables on a single vertical axis

The plots in Figure 4.3.3b were separated using the variable STATION. It is also possible for you to make separate plots of three different variables using similar techniques and the OVERLAY option.

The following code produces Figure 4.3.3c:

```
* Plot the data;
proc gplot data=vol1.biomass;
where station = 'D700-60';
plot bmothr*date ='O'
     bmcrus*date ='C'
     bmpoly*date ='P' / overlay
                        vaxis=axis1 haxis=axis1;
symbol1 v='O' c=black f=swiss;
symbol2 v='C' c=black f=swiss;
symbol3 v='P' c=black f=swiss;
```

```
title1 'Biomass at D700-60';
title2 h=1.5 f=swiss 'C' f=simplex 'rustacean  '
             f=swiss 'P' f=simplex 'olychaete  '
             f=swiss 'O' f=simplex 'ther';
footnote1 j=l h=2 f=simplex 'Figure 4.3.3c';
run;
```

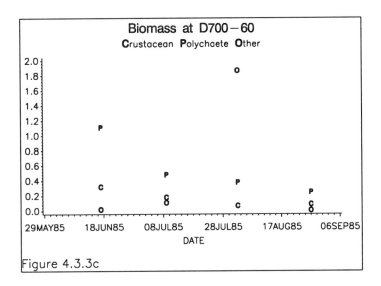

Figure 4.3.3c

The biomass readings for the three taxonomic groups are quite different and a separation might make it easier to see trends. The code used is similar to that used to produce Figure 4.3.3b. The primary difference is in how the three variables are separated. In the following code, three observations, one for each variable of interest, are created from each data observation:

```
* The data for each taxa is offset vertically to fit
* with the dummy axes.;
* BMOTHR there is no offset;
    pltvar=2;
    yvar = bmothr;
    output;
* BMPOLY is placed in the middle axis ;
* the offset is .75;
    pltvar=3;
    yvar = bmpoly + .75;
    output;
* BMCRUS is placed in the upper axis;
* the offset is 1.50;
    pltvar=4;
    yvar = bmcrus + 1.50;
    output;
run;
```

The AXIS and SYMBOL statements and the format VERT are tailored for this data set. The GPLOT is straightforward.

```
* Control the vertical axis;
axis1 order = 0 to 2 by .25
        label = (h=1.5 f=simplex a=90 'gm wet weight')
        value=(h=1.5 f=simplex)
        minor=none
        major=none
        style=0;
* Control the horizontal axis;
axis2 minor=none
        order= '15jun85'd, '01jul85'd, '15jul85'd,
                '01aug85'd, '15aug85'd, '01sep85'd
        label=(h=1.5 f=simplex)
        value=(h=1.5 f=simplex)
        style=0;

* Define the symbols for each subplot;
* SYMBOL1 controls the axes;
symbol1 v=none c=black l=1 i=join f=;
symbol2 v='O'  c=black l=1 i=join f=swiss;
symbol3 v='P'  c=black l=1 i=join f=swiss;
symbol4 v='C'  c=black l=1 i=join f=swiss;

* Define a format for the vertical axis;
proc format;
value vert 0.0, 0.75, 1.5 = '0'
           0.5, 1.25, 2.0 = '.5'
           other = ' ';
run;

* Plot the data;
proc gplot data=bio1;
plot yvar*date =pltvar / nolegend
                         skipmiss
                         vaxis=axis1
                         haxis=axis2;
format yvar vert.;
title1 'Biomass at D700-60';
title2 h=1.5 f=swiss 'C' f=simplex 'rustacean  '
             f=swiss 'P' f=simplex 'olychaete  '
             f=swiss 'O' f=simplex 'ther';
footnote1 j=l h=2 f=simplex 'Figure 4.3.3d';
run;
quit;
```

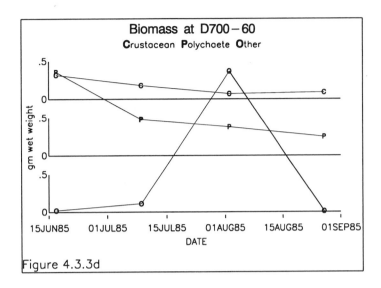

Figure 4.3.3d

In Figure 4.3.3d, two of the values are outside of the range of the three small axes. Because the scales are set on the actual vertical axis, all of the values are placed correctly. If templates had been used, the scale of BMOTHR would not have been preserved.

Using the PLOT2 statement

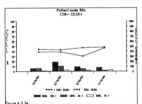

A second vertical axis can also be generated by using the PLOT2 statement. The second vertical axis can be used to provide additional control over various aspects of the plot.

Figure 4.3.3e has a number of interesting aspects and displays a lot of information in a single location. The data used in this example are from a study on lymphocytes in the blood of a patient (50x) with a compromised immune system. Both the absolute counts and the relative percentages of certain types of immune cells are displayed (plot portion) along with measurements taken from another assay at three concentrations (histogram portion). Because it is only the relative height at different concentrations that conveys the important information, the original values of the histograms have not been preserved. The height of the histograms have been scaled in a data step so that they appear below the plots. For plotting purposes, the histogram portion is tied to the left axis.

Both axes represent the values of the plot portion of the graph, the percent values on the left, and the absolute counts on the right. Using two vertical axes (the PLOT2 statement generates the right axis) allows us to generate and use two different LEGEND statements in the same plot. The histograms were generated by using the methods covered in Section 4.3.2, and they were filled by using the AREAS= option on the PLOT statement.

Unlike the previous example, this example program has been generalized to accommodate data sets with different dependent variables and a different number of horizontal data points. This was done by implementing it using a macro and macro calls.

The variable SYMNUM is used to control the SYMBOL statement usage. In this example, one observation is used to generate all three vertical bars for each date. The center of the three bars (HOLDPT) is used as the reference point for the generation of all three, hence the changing displacements. POINT is the horizontal plot variable and CONC is the vertical plot variable. The variable PTYPE distinguishes between the two types of plots.

```
* the variables symnum and symnum2 point to SYMBOL statements;
* ptype separates points to be plotted on PLOT or PLOT2;
conc = .; symnum=3; ptype='2';
symnum2=4; conc2 = &pervar*10; ptorder+1; output conc;
symnum2=5; conc2 = &var;         ptorder+1; output conc;

* create pseudo points for the histograms;
* histograms plotted using PLOT statement;
conc2 = .; symnum2=5; ptype='1';
holdpt = point;
* three vertical bars: conc100, conc30, and conc10;
* create the four corners of each of the three bars for each
POINT;
* conc100;
symnum = 1;
point=holdpt-.375; conc=0;         ptorder+1; output conc;
                   conc=conc100;   ptorder+1; output conc;
point=holdpt-.125;                 ptorder+1; output conc;
                   conc=0;         ptorder+1; output conc;
* conc30;
symnum = 2;
point=holdpt-.125; conc=0;         ptorder+1; output conc;
                   conc=conc30;    ptorder+1; output conc;
point=holdpt+.125;                 ptorder+1; output conc;
                   conc=0;         ptorder+1; output conc;
* conc10;
symnum = 3;
point=holdpt+.125; conc=0;         ptorder+1; output conc;
                   conc=conc10;    ptorder+1; output conc;
point=holdpt+.375;                 ptorder+1; output conc;
                   conc=0;         ptorder+1; output conc;
point=holdpt;
```

The dates on the horizontal axis are written at an angle of 55 degrees. This prevents the dates from running together as the number of dates increases.

The number of dates is determined from the data and stored in the macro variable &TOTPTS.

```
* gplot axis and legend statements;
axis1 major = none
      offset = (0,0)
      label = none
      minor = (n=1 h=1)
      value = (h=1 f=simplex angle=55   ' '
        %do i = 1 %to &totpts;
          "&&date&i"
        %end;  ' ')
      order = (0 to &axpts by 1);
```

The PROC GPLOT call contains both a PLOT and a PLOT2 statement. This is required for a couple of reasons. First, there are two different types of legends to display, and the LEGEND statement can only do one type of legend at a time. Second, the AREAS= option used with the PLOT statement complicates the graph.

The real trick is coordinating the SYMBOL statement calls and definitions. This is done by using two separate variables (SYMNUM and SYMNUM2) to hold the definition request number.

The BY statement is also included, but it is used only to invoke the #BYVAL title option. Obviously, the order in which the points are placed onto the plot is very important, and PTORDER ensures that they stay in proper sequence.

```
goption hby=0;
proc gplot data=conc;
by patient;
plot conc * point = symnum / areas=3
                             skipmiss
                             legend=legend1
                             vaxis=axis2
                             haxis=axis1;

plot2 conc2*point = symnum2/ vaxis=axis3
                             legend=legend2
                             skipmiss;

symbol1 v=none c=black i=join l=1;
symbol2 v=none c=black i=join l=1;
symbol3 v=none c=black i=join l=1;
symbol4 v='U'  c=black i=join l=1 f=marker  h=.5;
symbol5 v='U'  c=black i=join l=1 f=markere h=.5;

pattern1 v=solid c=black;
pattern2 v=m2x45 c=black;
pattern3 v=empty c=black;

label conc2 = 'COUNT'
      conc  = '%';
title1  f=duplex h=1.5 'Patient code #byval(patient)';
title2  f=simplex h=1.5 "&varstrg";
```

```
footnote h=1.5 j=l f=simplex 'Figure 4.3.3e';
run;
```

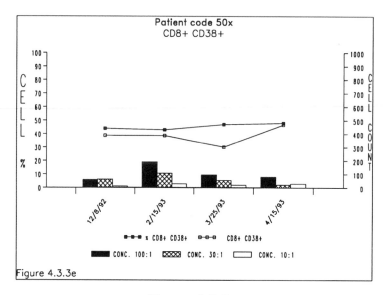

Figure 4.3.3e

MORE INFORMATION:

Carpenter, 1989, 1994b - Contains similar examples to those shown in Section 4.3.3.

Kalt and Redman, 1993b - A short example that plots three variables on a single vertical axis with three scales.

Mendelson, 1994 - Discusses the use of the LENGTH= and ORIGIN= AXIS statement options to place multiple plots on a page.

SAS/GRAPH Software: Reference, pp. 1120-1129 - Syntax and examples of the PLOT2 statement.

Westerlund, 1994 - This short article contains an example of a GPLOT with a title and footnote using #BYVAL and #BYVAR.

SEE ALSO:

Section 3.2.6 - Covers the use of the #BYVAL and #BYVAR title options.

Section 3.3 - Examples and discussion of the AXIS statement.

Section 3.4 - Additional detail is given for the LEGEND statement.

Section 5.7.6 - Discusses problems associated with non-aligned axes.

4.3.4 Drawing shapes (butterfly plots)

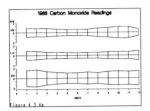

Butterfly plots can be used as a variation of a scatter plot when there is only one y value for each x value. The first example shown in this section contains the same information as was presented in the first two graphs of the previous section (Figures 4.3.3a and 4.3.3b), however, the butterfly plots can be much more expressive, and can retain more of the plot's character.

Using one variable to distinguish plots

A number of similarities exist between the code used to generate the first multiple axis plot in the previous section (Figure 4.3.3b) and the butterfly plots shown. Both create dummy axes, but the shape generated in a butterfly plot is centered on the horizontal axis. As a consequence, four statements are needed to define each axis.

```
tmon=month;

* Create dummy axes for each station;
* Allow six vertical units for each axis with one unit between
* each plot.;
if _n_=1 then do;
   pltvar=0;
   * axis for SFO;
   yvar=0; month=0;  output;
   yvar=6;           output;
   yvar=3;           output;
           month=12; output;
   yvar=.;           output;
   * axis for LIV;
   yvar=7; month=0;  output;
   yvar=13;          output;
   yvar=10;          output;
           month=12; output;
   yvar=.;           output;
   * axis for AZU;
   yvar=14;month=0;  output;
   yvar=20;          output;
   yvar=17;          output;
           month=12; output;
   yvar=.;           output;
   month=tmon;
end;
```

The OFFSET for each station is assigned, as is a variable (PLT) that counts the stations. Because PLT is inside the FIRST.STATION DO loop, it is incremented once for each new station.

```
if first.station then do;
   plt+1;
   * The data for each station is offset vertically to fit
   * with the dummy axes.;
   if station = 'AZU' then offset=17;
   else if station = 'LIV' then offset=10;
   else offset = 3;
end;
```

The butterfly plot for each station is made of three lines; the upper and lower bounds and a vertical line joining the bounds at each horizontal value. Each of these lines has its own unique value of PLTVAR for each station. The current value of PLTVAR is a function of the station number (PLT), the number of stations (3), and the type of line.

Some butterfly plots do not include the vertical line for each horizontal value (MONTH). In this example, the center points of the vertical lines are connected along the dummy horizontal axis. This, in effect, abrogates the need for drawing the dummy horizontal axis for each station. The vertical line for each month consists of three segments (four points). Plotted by themselves, these segments would look very much like the error bars created in Section 4.3.1. The segment end points are added starting and ending at the center line so that they can be connected from month to month. The missing value technique could have been used to provide a break between months if you would rather not have them connected.

```
* Each butterfly plot is made up of three sets of lines
* with a common SYMBOL statement;
* Upper line;
pltvar = plt*3-2; yvar = offset + co; output;
* Lower line;
pltvar = plt*3-1; yvar = offset - co; output;
* Hilo line;
pltvar = plt*3  ; yvar = offset      ; output;
                  yvar = offset - co; output;
                  yvar = offset + co; output;
                  yvar = offset      ; output;
run;
```

The axis statements and PROC GPLOT are very similar to those in Figure 4.3.3b, although PROC FORMAT has been somewhat altered.

```
* Define a format for the vertical axis;
proc format;
value vert 0,7,14  = '3'
           6,13,20 = '3'
           3,10,17 = '0'
           4       = 'SFO'
           11      = 'LIV'
           18      = 'AZU'
           other   = ' ';
run;
```

```
* Plot the data;
proc gplot data=air1;
plot yvar*month=pltvar / nolegend
                         skipmiss
                         vaxis=axis1
                         haxis=axis2;
format yvar vert.;
title1 '1988 Carbon Monoxide Readings';
footnote1 j=l h=1.5 f=simplex 'Figure 4.3.4a';
run;
```

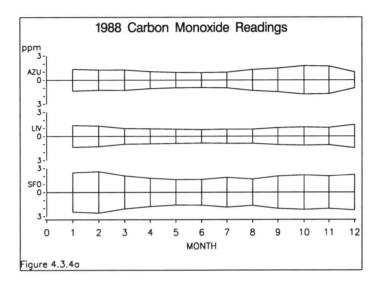

Figure 4.3.4a

Using the mean statistic to determine the plot width

In the previous example, the three stations are separated by using the different values of the variable STATION. Similar results can be achieved when the information is contained in separate variables. It is also possible to use a summary statistic such as the mean or variance to determine the width of the butterfly at any given value.

The first step is to create the dummy axes. The variables MNPOLY, MNMOLL, and MNOTHR contain the mean biomass for each taxonomic group averaged across stations for each date. In this plot, each of the small vertical axes is one unit high with a .25 unit separation.

```
* Create dummy axes for each taxa;

* Allow one vertical units for each axis with .25 units
* between each plot.;
if _n_=1 then do;

    * hold the current value of date ;
    tdte = date ;
```

```
      pltvar=1;
      * axis for MNPOLY;
      yvar=0;      date='15jun85'd;  output;
      yvar=1;                        output;
      yvar=.5;                       output;
                   date='01sep85'd;  output;
      yvar=.;                        output;
      * axis for MNMOLL;
      yvar=1.25; date='15jun85'd;    output;
      yvar=2.25;                     output;
      yvar=1.75;                     output;
                   date='01sep85'd;  output;
      yvar=.;                        output;
      * axis for MNOTHR;
      yvar=2.50; date='15jun85'd;    output;
      yvar=3.50;                     output;
      yvar=3.00;                     output;
                   date='01sep85'd;  output;
      yvar=.;                        output;
      date = tdte;
   end;
```

The three parts of the butterfly (top, bottom, and vertical) are then constructed for each variable. The mean (MNPOLY, MNMOLL, and MNOTHR) is used to establish the vertical width of the butterfly. The axes, format and GPLOT statements are similar to those used to produce Figure 4.3.4a.

```
* Each butterfly plot is made up of three sets of lines
* each with a common SYMBOL statement;
* the horizontal value for each point is date;

* BMPOLY (centered vertically on .5);
* Upper line;
pltvar = 2; yvar =   .5  + mnpoly/2; output;
* Lower line;
pltvar = 3; yvar =   .5  - mnpoly/2; output;
* Hilo line;
pltvar = 4; yvar =   .5  + mnpoly/2; output;
            yvar =   .5  - mnpoly/2; output;
            yvar =   .;              output;

* BMMOLL (centered vertically on 1.75);
* Upper line;
pltvar = 5; yvar = 1.75 + mnmoll/2; output;
* Lower line;
pltvar = 6; yvar = 1.75 - mnmoll/2; output;
* Hilo line;
pltvar = 7; yvar = 1.75 + mnmoll/2; output;
            yvar = 1.75 - mnmoll/2; output;
            yvar =  .;              output;

* BMOTHR (centered vertically on 3.00);
* Upper line;
pltvar = 8; yvar = 3.00 + mnothr/2; output;
* Lower line;
pltvar = 9; yvar = 3.00 - mnothr/2; output;
* Hilo line;
pltvar =10; yvar = 3.00 + mnothr/2; output;
            yvar = 3.00 - mnothr/2; output;
            yvar =  .;              output;
```

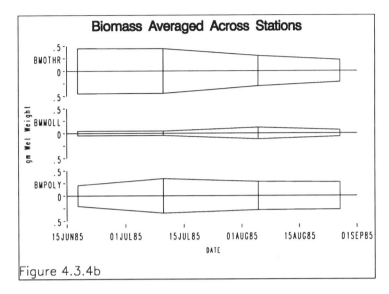

Figure 4.3.4b

MORE INFORMATION:
Carpenter, 1989 and 1994b - Papers include examples of butterfly plots.

4.3.5 Generating box-whisker plots

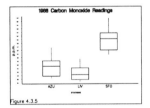

Beginning with Release 6.06, the SYMBOL statement option INTERPOL= can be set to BOX. This option generates box-whisker plots and has several variations. When the available options are not sufficient, such as when you want to change the thickness of the box lines, box plots can be generated using the same techniques as shown in the previous section on butterfly plots.

Selected statistics such as the median and various percentiles can be calculated using PROC UNIVARIATE and added onto the graph. Extensions of the box-whisker plots shown here are easily created using these techniques.

The box plot generated in this section is a fairly simple representation of one of a variety of box plots that can be generated using these methods. In this example, the median, quartile range, first quartile, and third quartile are calculated and saved through PROC UNIVARIATE.

```
* determine the median, and quartile statistics for each station;
proc univariate data=caair noprint;
by station;
var co;
output out=stats median=median
                 q1=q1 q3=q3 qrange=qrange;
run;
```

The length and end points of the whiskers are determined by the quartile range. Some box plots use 1.5 times the quartile range (QRANGE) as the maximum length for how far the whiskers can extend above and below the box. In this example, the length is extended to the most extreme point that falls within this distance. This requires an additional pass of the data, which saves the high and low end points (HIGHPT & LOWPT). These two variables are added to the summary statistics generated by UNIVARIATE.

```
* Determine the whisker endpoints;
* Whisker endpoints are the most extreme data values that are
* within 1.5*qrange of the quartiles.;
data stats2;
merge stats caair;
by station;
retain lowpt highpt;
drop co;
if first.station then do;
  lowpt=.; highpt=.;
end;

* does this point determine the whisker end point?;
if q1-1.5*qrange <= co <= q3+1.5*qrange then do;
    * look for the smallest value that is between
    * q1-1.5*qrange and q1;
    if lowpt=. then lowpt = co;
    * look for the largest value that is between
    * q3+1.5*qrange and q3;
    if highpt=. then highpt = co;
    else highpt=max(highpt,co);
end;

if last.station then output;
run;
```

The data set STATS2 has all of the information needed to build the boxes. However, one of the advantages of the box plot is to show outliers. To show outliers, the original data are merged with the statistics to determine which, if any, observations extend past the ends of the whiskers (There are none in this example). Outliers (points between 1.5 and 3.0 times the quartile range from the quartile) are noted by receiving a PLTVAR code of 3. Extreme outliers (greater than 3 times the quartile range from the quartile that defines the box edge, i.e. Q1 or Q3) receive a different value of PLTVAR and are plotted with a different symbol.

The box and whiskers plots are built using the point addition method used in the previous example. The whiskers are assigned a PLTVAR of 1, which will be matched to a dotted line in a SYMBOL statement. The solid lines of the box are assigned through the second SYMBOL statement accessed with PLTVAR=2. Notice the missing values to prevent upper and lower whiskers and adjacent boxes from being joined. STACNT adjusts the positions of the boxes horizontally by counting the stations. Therefore, this step will automatically accommodate any number of stations.

```
* combine the stats with the data and retain extreme points;
data both;
merge stats2 caair;
by station;
if first.station then do;
    * Build the box and whiskers from the summary stats;
    stacnt + 1;

    * Whiskers are dotted lines;
    pltvar=1;
    * start at the top whisker;
    xvar=stacnt   ; yvar=highpt        ;  output;
                    yvar=q3            ;  output;
    xvar=.        ;                       output;
    xvar=stacnt   ; yvar=lowpt         ;  output;
                    yvar=q1            ;  output;
    xvar=.        ;                       output;

    * The box is a solid line;
    pltvar=2;
    xvar=stacnt+.3; yvar=q3            ;  output;
                    yvar=median        ;  output;
    xvar=stacnt-.3;                       output;
    xvar=stacnt+.3;                       output;
                    yvar=q1            ;  output;
    xvar=stacnt-.3;                       output;
                    yvar=q3            ;  output;
    xvar=stacnt+.3;                       output;
    xvar=.        ;                       output;

end;

* plot outliers;
xvar=stacnt;
yvar=co;

* Determine where this point falls;
* Extreme outliers;
if co < q1-3*qrange or co > q3+3*qrange then do;
    pltvar=4;
    output;
end;
else if co < q1-1.5*qrange or co > q3+1.5*qrange then do;
    pltvar=3;
    output;
end;
run;
```

The GPLOT is once again the straightforward part of the graph. Axis statements dress up the plot.

```
* Control the vertical axis;
axis1 label=(h=1.5 f=simplex a=90 'p.p.m.')
       value=(h=1.5 f=simplex);

* Control the horizontal axis;
axis2 label=(h=1.5 f=simplex 'STATIONS')
       order=(0 to 4 by 1)
       major=none
       minor=none
       value= (h=1.5 f=simplex
               t=1 ' ' t=2 'AZU' t=3 'LIV' t=4 'SFO' t=5 ' ');

* Define the symbols;
symbol1 v=none c=black l=2 i=join;
symbol2 v=none c=black l=1 i=join;
symbol3 v=circle c=black;
symbol4 v='P' f=marker c=black;


* Plot the data;
proc gplot data=both;
plot yvar*xvar=pltvar / nolegend
                        skipmiss
                        vaxis=axis1
                        haxis=axis2;
title1 h=2 '1988 Carbon Monoxide Readings';
footnote1 j=1 h=2 f=simplex 'Figure 4.3.5';
run;
```

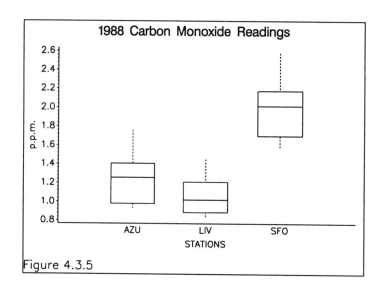

Figure 4.3.5

Variations of the box plot include caps on the whiskers, notches in the boxes, and adjustable box width to indicate the number of observations.

MORE INFORMATION:

Benoit, 1985 - Although the article is primarily on ANNOTATE, there are examples on box-whisker plots.

Friendly, 1990 - Includes some discussion of box plots.

Friendly, 1991, pp. 294-305 - Provides several examples of box plots and includes a macro that uses the ANNOTATE facility.

McGill, 1978 - Discusses and gives examples of a number of variations of box plots, which are further discussed in Friendly, 1990 & 1991, and Olmstead, 1985.

Olmstead, 1985 - Includes a very detailed discussion and motivation for building box plots.

SAS/GRAPH Software: Reference, p. 411, pp. 436-437 - Syntax and example of the use of the I=BOX SYMBOL statement option.

SAS Language and Procedures: Usage 2, pp. 329-339 - Description of UNIVARIATE's box plots.

4.3.6 Cluster scatter plots

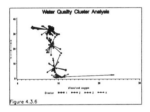

Figure 4.3.6

Although plots are not generated directly by the clustering procedures, the FASTCLUS procedure in SAS/STAT allows the cluster information to be saved for later plotting. The graphical presentation of cluster analysis results can be extremely important, if not critical, in determining the cohesion and isolation of clusters.

Usually, the determination of the number of natural clusters, the variables that define those clusters, and cluster membership criteria is a process that may include several trials. Scatter plots of the proposed clusters can be used as an aid to decide on the final clustering criteria.

In this example, PROC GPLOT plots the water quality data in four possible clusters. The two selected plot variables are SALINITY and DO (dissolved oxygen). Each line segment is drawn from the data point to the center of the cluster by creating a second observation for each data point.

First, the cluster analysis is performed using the FASTCLUS procedure, and the two output data sets are saved. The MEANCLUS data set contains the cluster summary information, and the OUTCLUS data set contains each observation's cluster membership.

```
proc fastclus data=vol1.h2oqual
    mean=meanclus
    out=outclus
    maxclusters=4
    noprint
    ;
var depth temp ph do cond salinity;
run;

* sort the cluster mean data;
proc sort data=meanclus;
by cluster;
run;

* sort the raw data with the cluster assignments;
proc sort data=outclus;
by cluster;
run;
```

The two data sets are brought together, and the cluster summary information is used to define the center of each cluster. This has been done inside a macro that allows you to plot any pair of variables easily.

```
%macro pltclus(xvar, yvar);
* create a macro to plot any two data variables;

* Combine the cluster means with the rawdata;
* Select two plotting variables;
data both (keep=cluster &xvar &yvar);
set meanclus (keep= cluster &xvar &yvar)
    outclus  (keep= cluster &xvar &yvar);
by cluster;
retain xmean ymean;
* the first value for each cluster contains the summary info;
if first.cluster then do;
   xmean= &xvar;
   ymean= &yvar;
   output;
end;
else if &xvar>. and &yvar>. then do;
   * for each point output two observations that form the line
   * segment from the centroid to the data point;
   output;
   &xvar = xmean;
   &yvar = ymean;
   output;
end;
```

The GPLOT is straightforward and uses the SYMBOL statements to assign unique symbols to each cluster.

```
* graph the clusters using GPLOT;
proc gplot data=both;
plot &yvar * &xvar = cluster;

symbol1 line=1 i=join c=black v=square;
symbol2 line=1 i=join c=black v=circle;
symbol3 line=1 i=join c=black v=triangle;
symbol4 line=1 i=join c=black v=star;
symbol5 line=1 i=join c=black v=diamond;
```

```
title1 'Water Quality Cluster Analysis';
footnote h=2 f=simplex j=l 'Figure 4.3.6';
%mend pltclus;

%pltclus(do  , salinity)  run;
```

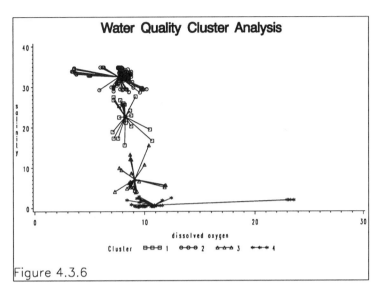

Figure 4.3.6

Figure 4.3.6 indicates that SALINITY does a good job of separating clusters, but dissolved oxygen (DO) by itself does not.

MORE INFORMATION:
> Larus, 1987 - Includes more detailed plots, discussion of clustering, and a three-dimensional plot of Fisher's Iris Data.

4.4   Controlling Scales on Axes

The automatic scaling of GPLOT axes is easy to use and is usually adequate, but when customized axes are required, the AXIS statement is available to greatly extend the range and flexibility for axis control. However, this section discusses several scaling issues that are not handled completely by the AXIS statement.

SEE ALSO:
> Section 3.3 - Discusses the use of the AXIS statement and several of its options.

4.4.1 Creating non-linear axes (probability/quantile plots)

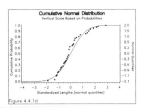

Figure 4.4.1d

Although you can create non-linear logarithmic scales directly by using the LOGSTYLE axis option (Section 3.3.1), other non-linear scales must be programmed. This is not an intuitive task, and is, therefore, often not attempted. This section shows you, through the use of formats and probability functions, how to create the non-linear scales used in probability and quantile plots.

Probability scales are some of the most often required non-linear scales. Normal probability paper utilizes one such scale. You can use probability or quantile plots to graphically identify deviations from a hypothesized probability distribution. Because of a lack of scaling alternatives, these plots are generally created using linear scales. However, non-linear scaling is often desirable.

Probability plots (Figures 4.4.1b and 4.4.1d) plot the cumulative probability on the vertical axis, while quantile plots (Figures 4.4.1c and 4.4.1e) use the quantile value. Both types of plots convey the same information. The quantile plot may be easier to work with, however, as the standard to which the comparisons will be made is a straight line.

Using a histogram to show a distribution
The following histogram, Figure 4.4.1a, shows the distribution of the lengths of fish caught in a study using a Lampara net. This type of graph is often used to determine if the lengths are normally distributed.

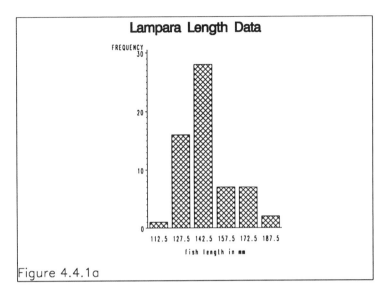

Figure 4.4.1a

Quantile plots assist the researcher's evaluation of the distributional aspects of data. Although examples shown in this section look at the question of the distribution's normality, other distributions can be easily substituted by changing the probability functions.

In this example, the researcher may be interested in determining if the lengths of the captured fish are distributed normally. Comparison of a sample distribution to a known distribution can be accomplished through the use of probability and quantile plots. The methods used to generate probability and quantile plots are shown next, first on artificially generated data and then using the length data shown in Figure 4.4.1a.

Probability and quantile plots on artificial data

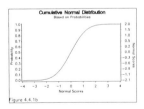

Figures 4.4.1b (probability plot) and 4.4.1c (quantile plot) both show the cumulative normal probability distribution and were plotted using a linear scale on the left and a non-linear scale on the right. These two plots show the same information and appear to be different only because the vertical axis has been transformed. For demonstration purposes, we have set the example up so that the left axis on the probability plot is the same as the right axis on the quantile plot.

The non-linear scales are created by the use of a user-defined format that assigns the transformed values to the major tick marks of a linear scale.

The normal quantile values (X) and their associated cumulative probabilities (Y) are generated in a DO loop in a DATA step. The probabilities are calculated using the PROBNORM function. Distributions other than the normal could be used by replacing the PROBNORM function with the function appropriate to the desired distribution, and by adjusting the quantile values (X). The duplicate variables X2 and Y2 are used in the plotting process for the second axis.

```
* Generate normal probabilities (y) and two data sets
* that can be used to generate formats.;
data norm (keep= x x2 y y2)
     f1 (keep=fmtname start label)
     f2 (keep=fmtname start label fuzz);
length start label $12;
retain fuzz .05;
do x = -4 to 4 by .1;
  x2 = x;
  y = probnorm(x);
  y2 = y;
  output norm;
```

The non-linear scale for the right-hand vertical axis is generated by plotting the vertical variable used in the PLOT statement twice, the second time with a user defined format. The data sets used to create the formats (PRNORM. and PROBIT.) are generated from the same DATA step that creates the normal data. PRNORM. converts normal quantiles to probabilities and PROBIT. converts normal probabilities to quantiles.

The formats are constructed directly from the data sets F1 and F2 using PROC FORMAT and the CNTLIN= option. Data sets that create formats are expected by PROC FORMAT to have specific variables. These include

- FMTNAME   name of the format to be created
- LABEL   formatted value
- START   defines the start of the label's range or its unique value

The values of the three variables are assigned and then written to data sets.

```
* Prepare to generate a format (PRNORM.) to convert
* normal values to probabilities;
fmtname = 'prnorm';
start = put(x,4.1);
label = put(y,8.3);
output f1;

* Prepare to generate a format (PROBIT.) to convert
* probabilities to normal values;
fmtname = 'probit';
start = put(y,9.7);
label = put(x,4.1);
output f2;
end;
label x = 'Normal Scores';
run;
```

```
* create the two formats from the control data sets;
proc format cntlin=f1;
proc format cntlin=f2;
run;
```

The two plots are each generated in a separate PROC GPLOT step. The AXIS statement disables the axis labels, which are actually provided by the third and fourth TITLEs (using the A= option). The two vertical plot variables Y and Y2 are actually identical and are both used so that the format PROBIT. can be assigned to Y2. Because the transformation from probabilities to quantiles is not linear, the scale appears to be non-linear when the format is applied.

The probability plot uses the PROBIT. format to scale the right axis.

```
axis1 label=none;
      value=(h=1.5 f=simplex);
axis2 label=(h=1.5 f=simplex)
      value=(h=1.5 f=simplex);

proc gplot data=norm;
plot y*x / vaxis=axis1 haxis=axis2;
plot2 y2*x / vaxis=axis1;
symbol1 v=none l=1 i=join c=black r=2;
format y2 probit.;
title1 'Cumulative Normal Distribution';
title2 h=1.5 f=simplex 'Based on Probabilities';
title3 h=1.5 f=simplex a=90 'Probability';
title4 h=1.5 f=simplex a=-90 'Normal Scores';
footnote1 h=2 f=simplex j=l 'Figure 4.4.1b';
run;
```

The probability plot shows the distinctive S shape of the cumulative normal distribution. The probability scale on the left is linear, while the scale for the normal scores on the right is not linear.

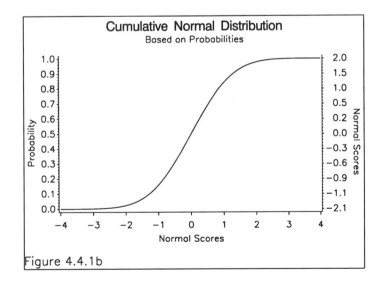

Figure 4.4.1b

The quantile plot uses the PRNORM. function to scale the right axis.

```
proc gplot data=norm;
plot x*x / vaxis=axis1 haxis=axis2;
plot2 x2*x / vaxis=axis1;
symbol1 v=none l=1 i=join c=black r=2;
format x2 prnorm.;
title1 'Cumulative Normal Distribution';
title2 h=1.5 f=simplex 'Vertical Scale Based on Normal Scores';
title3 h=1.5 f=simplex a=90 'Normal Scores';
title4 h=1.5 f=simplex a=-90 'Probability';
footnote1 h=2 f=simplex j=l 'Figure 4.4.1c';
run;
```

The quantile plot places the normal scores on the left axis with a linear scale, while the probabilities are non-linear on the right axis.

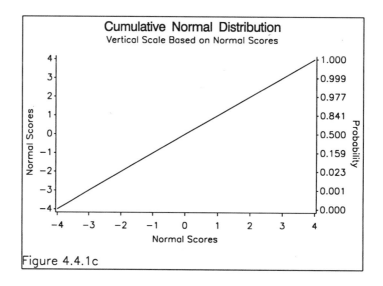

Figure 4.4.1c

Probability and quantile plots with actual data

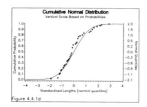

The techniques developed to produce the probability and quantile plots shown in Figures 4.4.1b and 4.4.1c can be modified to be used with actual data. The distribution of lengths in the Lampara data (shown in the histogram in Figure 4.4.1a) is compared to the normal distribution in the following two graphs (Figures 4.4.1d and 4.4.1e). The formats and standard normal curves are generated in the same way as in the previous example that uses artificial data. The variables X2 and Y2, which are used in the above example to define the second axis, are replaced with variables associated with the real data.

The data are standardized to a normal (0,1) distribution by using the STANDARD procedure. This is necessary because the quantiles and the formats are based on this distribution. The quantiles from any other distribution could have been used. It is only necessary that the two data sets contain data that are comparable.

```
* convert the length information to standard normal;
proc standard data=vol1.lampara
               out=standard
               mean=0 std=1;
   var length;
   run;
```

Once normalized, the cumulative probabilities are calculated. The percentages can be calculated by PROC FREQ and then summed in a DATA step. The data set containing the percentages (PERCENT) and the normal curve data (NORM) are concatenated for plotting. The data from NORM is used in the PLOT2 statements to produce the normal curves. The cumulative probabilities for the data are calculated using the PROBIT function that converts probabilites to normal quantiles.

```
* Determine the length frequencies for the lampara data;
proc freq data=standard noprint;
   table length / out=percent;
   run;

* Calculate the cumulative length probabilities;
data cumulpr (keep= length cumulpr cumnorm x y);
   set percent (in=inper) norm ;
   if not inper then do;
      length = x;
      cumulpr = .;
   end;
   else do;
      cumulpr + (percent/100);
      cumnorm = probit(cumulpr);
   end;
   label length  = 'Standardized Lengths (normal quantiles)'
         cumulpr = 'cumulative probabilities'
         cumnorm = 'normal quantiles';
   run;
```

The plots are generated in a similar fashion to those in the previous example, but because the vertical variables are not actually the same, the ORDER= option *must* be used in the AXIS statements. The same AXIS statement is used for both the left and right axis, and the values in the ORDER= option are for the unformatted left axis.

```
* Axis and symbol definitions;
* Axis1 used to plot probabilities;
axis1 order= 0 to 1 by .1
      value=(h=1.5 f=simplex)
      label=none;
* Axis2 used to plot normal quantiles;
axis2 order= -4 to 4 by 1
      value=(h=1.5 f=simplex)
      label=none;
axis3 label=(h=1.5 f=simplex)
      value=(h=1.5 f=simplex)
```

```
* symbol1 is used with the data;
symbol1 v=dot c=black;
* symbol2 is used to control the normal line;
symbol2 i=join v=none l=1 c=black;
```

The probability plot is generated using CUMULPR as the vertical axis variable.

```
* Plot the probabilities with the second axis
* formatted to normal quantiles;
proc gplot data=cumulpr;
plot cumulpr*length=1 / vaxis=axis1;
plot2 y*length=2 / vaxis=axis1;
format y probit.;
title1 'Cumulative Normal Distribution';
title2 h=1.5 f=simplex 'Vertical Scale Based on Probabilities';
title3 h=1.5 f=simplex a=90 'Cumulative Probability';
title4 h=1.5 f=simplex a=-90 'Normal Quantiles';
footnote1 h=2 f=simplex j=l 'Figure 4.4.1d';
run;
```

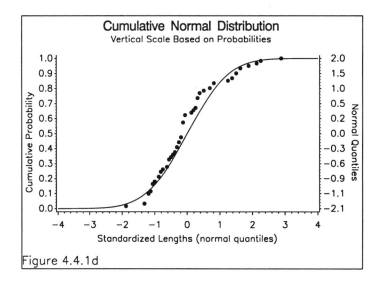

Figure 4.4.1d

The quantile plot uses the CUMNORM variable to define the vertical axis.

```
* Plot the normal scores with the second axis
* formatted to probabilities;
proc gplot data=cumulpr;
plot cumnorm*length=1 / vaxis=axis2 haxis=axis3;
plot2 x*length=2 / vaxis=axis2;
format x prnorm.;
title1 'Cumulative Normal Distribution';
title2 h=1.5 f=simplex 'Vertical Scale Based on Normal Quantiles';
title3 h=1.5 f=simplex a=90 'Normal Quantiles';
title4 h=1.5 f=simplex a=-90 'Probability';
footnote1 h=2 f=simplex j=l 'Figure 4.4.1e';
run;
```

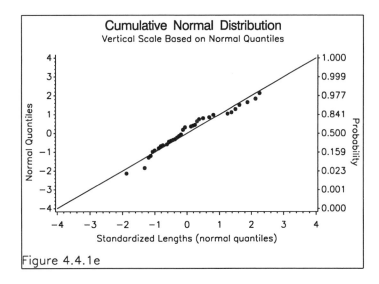

Figure 4.4.1e

It is likely that in a quantile plot such as the one shown in Figure 4.4.1e, only one of the vertical scales would be used. Both are shown in this example for demonstration purposes.

MORE INFORMATION:

Friendly, 1991, pp.118-141 - Includes discussion on the creation of similar and related plots, as well as detailed explanations on their use and interpretation.

Latour and Johnson, 1992 - Short example discusses the techniques associated with generating normal probability plots based on UNIVARIATE output.

SAS/GRAPH Software: Usage, p.689 - Brief example of the OFFSET= option.

SAS/GRAPH Software: Usage, pp. 703-707 - Example using the LOGBASE= and LOGSTYLE= options.

SAS Procedures Guide, pp. 300-302 - Discusses the use of SAS data sets to construct user-defined formats.

SEE ALSO:

Section 3.3 - Discusses the use of the AXIS statement.

4.4.2 Creating equally scaled X and Y axes

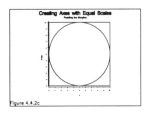

SAS/GRAPH scales the two axes independently and the physical length of each axis is dependent on the available space in the graphics area. Because the graphics area for most devices is not square even if both axes have the same range, e.g. from 0 to 10, the physical distance for a given number of units in the horizontal direction will probably be different than for the same number of units in the vertical direction. This can cause problems when you need to create a graph in which equal graphical distances relate to equal physical distances on the page. If it is not corrected, squares appear as rectangles and circles appear as ovals.

Figure 4.4.2a is a plot of a square with an inscribed circle. Although the range for both axes is the same (0 to 10), the circle and square appear distorted because the X axis is physically longer and its scale is therefore stretched.

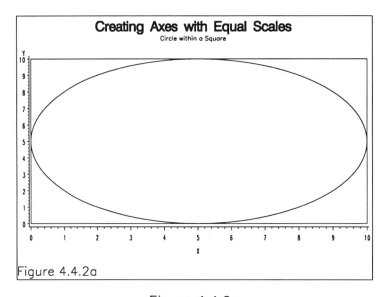

Figure 4.4.2a

Controlling physical and graphical distances

There are several controllable factors that influence the relationship between the physical and graphical distances. Any one of these can be manipulated to produce equally scaled axes. Some of these factors are easier to apply than others, and several may involve a trial-and-error approach. These include

- physical length of the axis

- axis offset

- graphical page size (HSIZE and VSIZE specifications)

- space used by titles, labels, and axis labels

- range of values covered by the axis.

Ultimately, the scales are equal if the lengths of the axes and their ranges are proportional. This can be expressed as

$$\frac{\text{length y axis}}{\text{length x axis}} = \frac{\text{range y axis}}{\text{range x axis}}$$

The length of the axes is indirectly affected by the size of the graphical page and the space taken up by titles and labels.

Controlling the physical length of the axes

The physical length of the axis can be adjusted directly. The relationship shown in the previous section can be solved for the length of the axis to be adjusted, and the LENGTH= option in the AXIS statement can be used to set the length of the axis. When Figure 4.4.2a was first plotted, the horizontal axis had a length of 19.5 cm, the vertical had a length of 9.5 cm, and both axes had a range of 10. [Note: the graph was resized when it was included in the book.] To create equal scales, the length of the horizontal axis would be

```
x_length= (x_range) * (y_length) / (y_range)

       = (10) * (9.5) / (10)

       = 9.5
```

This calculation suggests the following AXIS statement:

```
axis1 length=9.5 cm;
```

This should be the easiest and most direct method to control axis scales. In practice, the LENGTH= option does not always work because on some devices the distance on the LENGTH= option is not always translated to the same distance on the graph. This seems to be especially true when the

TARGETDEVICE= option is used as it only controls relative appearances, not exact appearances. If the LENGTH= option does not produce the desired length, use it for both axes. At least you should be able to control the proportions.

This method usually produces axes with equal scales. Try this method first, and if it works for your device then use it! If not, then one of the methods that follow may be useful.

The OFFSET= option in the AXIS statement should also be capable of adjusting the scale but often has the same problem as the LENGTH= option. Again, using the same numbers as before, the horizontal axis is 10 cm too long (19.5 - 9.5), so 5 cm could be trimmed from each end by using the following axis statement:

```
axis1 offset=(5,5)cm;
```

Both of these methods are worth a try and can be made to work, even if trial-and-error process is required. Also, the use of percent (PCT) rather than CM as the GUNIT often helps.

Manipulation of page size
Manipulation of the physical page size also usually involves a trial-and-error process. The space available to the graph is physically limited by using the HSIZE and VSIZE options. The following code replots Figure 4.4.2a with a reduced HSIZE

```
goptions hsize=5;
proc gplot data=design;
plot y*x=pltvar / nolegend;
symbol1 v=none i=j l=1 c=black r=2;
title1 'Creating Axes with Equal Scales';
title2 h=1 f=simplex 'Adjusting the HSIZE GOPTION';
footnote1 h=2 f=simplex j=2 'Figure 4.4.2b';
run;
```

For this device, the default HSIZE is 9.8 inches (Figure 1.4.1) and the default VSIZE is 7.1 inches. Taking into consideration the space used by the titles, footnotes, and labels, we estimate that a HSIZE of 5 inches is about correct. This results in the following graph:

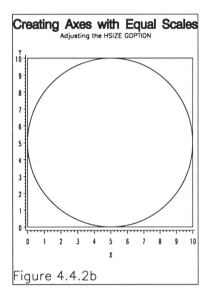

Figure 4.4.2b

One of the drawbacks of this method is the change in the overall shape of the graph. It no longer has the same width and height as the other graphs in this book.

Using titles and labels
The default length of the axes is dependent on the amount of space delegated to the graphics area. The graphics area is the space available to the plot after the titles and footnotes have been defined. In Figure 4.4.2a, the horizontal space is too large, and it could be reduced by placing a large blank title along the left and right margins (title option A=-90 and A=90, respectively). A label on the vertical axis created by the AXIS statement can also be used.

In this example, a large blank space is on each side of the graph, and the vertical axis has been given a label. By placing the titles on both sides, the graph remains centered.

```
axis1 label=(h=1.5 f=simplex a=90 'Y axis')
      value=(h=1.5 f=simplex);

axis2 label=(h=1.5 f=simplex 'X axis')
      value=(h=1.5 f=simplex);

proc gplot data=design;
plot y*x=pltvar / nolegend vaxis=axis1;
symbol1 v=none i=j l=1 c=black r=2;
title1 'Creating Axes with Equal Scales';
title2 h=1.5 f=simplex 'Padding the Margins';
title3 h=10.9 f=simplex a=-90 '  ';
title4 h=10.9 f=simplex a= 90 '   ';
footnote1 h=2 f=simplex j=l 'Figure 4.4.2c';
run;
```

The selection of the size of the blank space used in TITLE3 and TITLE4 depends on the graph being generated. Selection of the correct size can be a time consuming trial-and-error process. Because the size of the vertical axis depends on the size and number of titles and footnotes, a change in one of these could require a readjustment of the size of the blanks.

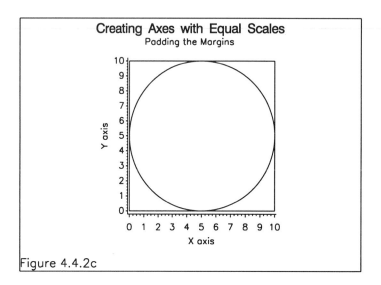

Figure 4.4.2c

Controlling the range of the axes

In axes with equal scales, the ratio of a variable's range of values to the physical distance used by the axis to plot that range is equal for both axes. When a scale is stretched (as is the horizontal axis in the first graph in this section, Figure 4.4.2a), its ratio is too low. The ratio of a stretched axis can be adjusted by increasing its range. Because the horizontal axis is stretched, increasing its range decreases the scale. The new range for X can be calculated by solving the equation for the horizontal range and by using the same values as were used earlier:

```
x_range = (y_range) * (x_length) / (y_length)

        = (10) * (19.5) / (9.5)

        = 20.5
```

A range of 20 ought to be close enough, and if we use end points of -5 to 15 the graph is still centered. This range could be handled in the data by adding dummy observations, but it is usually much cleaner to use the ORDER= option in the AXIS statement. The following code uses this method to adjust the horizontal axis in Figure 4.4.2d:

```
* Select the range of the longer axis such that:
* range = (range_short)*(length_long)/(length_short);
axis1 order= -5 to 15 by 5
        value=(h=1.5 f=simplex)
        label=(h=1.5 f=simplex)
        minor=(n=4);

axis2 value=(h=1.5 f=simplex)
        label=(h=1.5 f=simplex) a=90 'Y Axis');

axisproc gplot data=design;
plot y*x=pltvar / nolegend haxis=axis1;
symbol1 v=none i=j l=1 c=black r=2;
title1 'Creating Axes with Equal Scales';
title2 h=1.5 f=simplex 'Adjusting the Axis Range';
footnote1 h=2 f=simplex j=l 'Example 4.4.2d';
run;
```

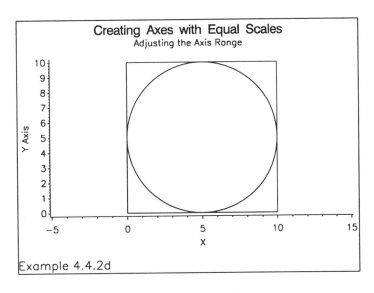

Figure 4.4.2d

MORE INFORMATION:

SAS/GRAPH Software: Reference, p. 224 - Syntax for the OFFSET= option.

SEE ALSO:

Section 3.3 - Provides additional information and examples dealing with the AXIS statement.

4.5   Using Fonts as Graphic Symbols

Any of the symbols or characters available with SAS/GRAPH can be used to designate a point on a graph. Additionally, user-defined symbols may be generated using the GFONT procedure. User-defined fonts can be simple characters, complex designs such as logos, or even complete graphs.

The selection of the font character can add more to the graph than merely cosmetic enhancement. Specially constructed fonts that are based on the data can convey additional information.

The two examples in this section use the input data to construct the graphics font and to add the symbols to the graph. PROC GFONT creates the font symbols by assigning coordinates to a series of points (observations) that are then connected. Because this is analogous to the data manipulation techniques used to construct plots and histograms in Section 4.3, you can also build font symbols using the same techniques. The data are used to construct the symbol by connecting the data points. Each symbol is assigned a name, and the font is saved for use later.

A typical scatter plot displays the values of two variables. The display of additional dimensions is often useful, and Section 5.7 demonstrates several commonly seen, although not necessarily recommended, techniques for increasing the dimensionality of a plot. When using techniques such as these, be careful not to get too carried away with the technique and end up forgetting the message of the graph itself.

MORE INFORMATION:

SAS/GRAPH Software: Reference, pp. 168-174 - Lists the standard fonts available through SAS/GRAPH.

SAS/GRAPH Software: Reference, p. 421 - Table contains the special graphics symbols available in the default graphics font.

SAS/GRAPH Software: Reference, Chapter 26 - This chapter explains the syntax and use of the GFONT procedure. Several examples are included.

SAS/GRAPH Software: Usage, Chapter 41 - The process of creating a logo using PROC GFONT is discussed in detail.

4.5.1 Histograms as points

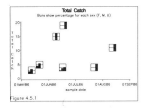

Figure 4.5.1

The scatter plot shown in Figure 4.5.1 plots the total catch of fish on each sample date. You may also wish to know the distribution of SEX for each date. This could be done in a separate graph with histograms. However, it is possible to combine the two into a single graph. In Figure 4.5.1, each data point has been plotted as a histogram showing the percent of the catch for each sex. The plot not only displays the total catch through time, but the relative abundance of each sex as well. The histograms are actually GFONT plot symbols that have been created using the data associated with that point.

The first step in constructing the individual histograms is to calculate the percentage of each value of SEX for each date. The result is stored in an output data set (PERCENT).

```
* Determine the cell frequencies for each dateXsex;
proc freq data=vol1.lampara;
by date;
table sex / noprint out=percent;
run;
```

The percentage for each SEX within each DATE is used to construct the histogram symbols in the same way as the histogram was constructed in Section 4.3.2, for example, each observation defines the four corners of the histogram bar. Because you want to leave space for bars with zero percentages, we need to make sure that the data contains an observation even if the catch was zero. The data set GROUP has been created to have one dummy observation for each possible combination of DATE and SEX. When merged with PERCENT, we can use the dummy observation as a guide to make sure that zero percent is assigned to the values of DATExSEX that were not in the data set PERCENT. In the same step the total catch (TOTCATCH), which is the vertical variable, is calculated. Because each date has its own unique font symbol, a new value of PLTVAR is saved for each date.

```
* Add a null value to dates without all three sex groups;
data groups (keep=date sex);
set percent (keep=date);
by date;
if first.date then do sex = 'F', 'M', 'U';
   output;
end;
run;
```

```
* Fill empty cells with a zero percent and
* count the total catch (data to be plotted);
data percent2 (keep=date sex percent)
      totcatch (keep=date totcatch pltvar);
merge percent (in=inper) groups;
by date sex;
* Add zero values for empty cells;
if not inper then do;
   percent=0;
   count=0;
end;
output percent2;
* Determine the total catch for each date;
if first.date then do;
   totcatch=0;
   pltvar+1;
end;
totcatch + count;
if last.date then output totcatch;
label totcatch = 'Total Catch';
run;
```

The font for the histogram symbols is created from a data set (FONTDATA). This data set is constructed from PERCENT2, which is built in the previous step. PROC GFONT expects certain variables to be present, and each variable has a specific meaning. X and Y correspond to a coordinate system (in percent) for the symbol. CHAR is the symbol name that is associated with a histogram and is used in the SYMBOL statement to include the appropriate histogram symbol into the plot. The variable SEX, which takes on the values 'F' (Female), 'M' (Male), and 'U' (Undetermined), is used to distinguish the three histogram bars.

```
data fontdata (keep=char seg x y lp ptype);
set percent2 (keep=date sex percent);
by date;
length char $1;
retain char ' ' ptype 'V';
if first.date then do;
  pltvar + 1;
  char = put(pltvar,1.);
  * define the outline;
  seg=1; lp='L';
  x=  0; y=  0; output;
         y=100; output;
  x=100;        output;
         y=  0; output;
         y= 50; output;
  x=  0;        output;
end;

* Draw the histogram bars;
* Bar height is determined by the data,
* the width coordinates (x) are F=0-33, M=33=66, and U=66-100;
seg=2; lp='P'; y=percent;
if sex = 'F' then do;
   x= 0; y=0;       output;
         y=percent; output;
   x=33;            output;
end;
```

```
else if sex = 'M' then do;
   x=33; y=percent; output;
   x=66;            output;
end;
else if sex = 'U' then do;
   x=66; y=percent; output;
   x=100;           output;
          y=0;      output;
   x=0;             output;
end;
run;
```

The font is created through PROC GFONT using this data set (FONTDATA).

When SAS searches for a font, it does not look in the WORK library but only searches in libraries associated with special librefs. One of these librefs, such as GFONT0, must be specified or the font will not be found. In this example, the font HISTO is written into a catalog (FONTS) in the library specified by the libref GFONT0.

```
* Define the gfont library;
libname gfont0 "<system specific path information>";

* Create the GFONT (HISTO);
proc gfont data=fontdata
          name=histo
          filled
          nodisplay;
run;
```

The GPLOT step is similar to those that we have seen already. The font containing the histograms is identified in the SYMBOL statement, and the variable PLTVAR corresponds to the SYMBOL definition and font character number (V=).

```
* Display the total catch using the user-defined font;
proc gplot data=totcatch;
plot totcatch*date=pltvar /
     nolegend
     vaxis= axis1
     haxis= axis2;
title1 'Total Catch';
title2 h=1.5 f=simplex
       'Bars show percentage for each sex (F, M, U)';
footnote1 h=2 j=l f=simplex 'Example 4.5.1';
symbol1 f=histo c=black h=3 v=1;
symbol2 f=histo c=black h=3 v=2;
symbol3 f=histo c=black h=3 v=3;
symbol4 f=histo c=black h=3 v=4;
symbol5 f=histo c=black h=3 v=5;
symbol6 f=histo c=black h=3 v=6;
symbol7 f=histo c=black h=3 v=7;
symbol8 f=histo c=black h=3 v=8;
run;
```

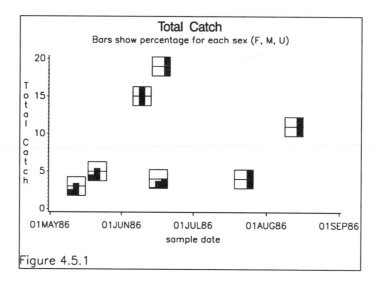

Figure 4.5.1

MORE INFORMATION:

> Buckner, 1988 - Contains an example of a plot that uses histograms as points.

4.5.2 Showing the magnitude of a third variable (Sunflower plots)

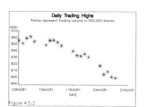

Sunflower plots can be used to indicate the magnitude of a third variable in a scatter plot or as a counter for the number of points that fall at a given combination of the X and Y variables. Essentially, this allows you to plot a third dimension on a scatter plot.

The advantage of the sunflower plot over other techniques such as the bubble plot (Section 5.7.7) is that rather than using area to show magnitude, the value is displayed by placing an increasing number of petals on the flower. Five petals can correspond to a value of five for the third dimension. Usually, a point is used at the center of the flower and for a size of one.

Although any number of petals can be included, more than 20 tend to create a symbol that appears blotchy and artificially dark. A data transformation or a format can be used (as was done in this example) to create twenty categories.

In this way, one sunflower font can be made to fit most any data set. In Figure 4.5.2, the stock market data is plotted for a one-month period. The vertical axis represents the Dow's daily high, and each petal represents a consistent volume (500,000) of shares traded.

As in the previous example (Section 4.5.1), the first step creates the data set from which the font is constructed. Unlike that example, however, this step is independent of the data to be plotted. For this example, we have chosen to create twenty sunflowers. The first will be a dot, and each of the remainder will have the number of petals associated with its number, i.e. sunflower number five will have five petals.

The filled circle or dot that is included at the center of each sunflower is made up of four arcs. PROC GFONT creates an arc by indicating the starting and ending points of the arc (PTYPE='v') before and after the arc's center point (PTYPE='c'). Our sunflowers are centered on x=50 and y=50, and the dot is constructed out of four quarter segments (fewer segments make a misshapen circle). LP='p' is used to indicate that we are making a filled polygon.

The following statements define the dot at the center of each sunflower. This code becomes part of a DATA step.

```
seg=0; lp='p';
ptype='w'; x =  0; y=100; output;
ptype='v'; x = 50; y= 60; output;
ptype='c'; x = 50; y= 50; output;
ptype='v'; x = 40; y= 50; output;
ptype='c'; x = 50; y= 50; output;
ptype='v'; x = 50; y= 40; output;
ptype='c'; x = 50; y= 50; output;
ptype='v'; x = 60; y= 50; output;
ptype='c'; x = 50; y= 50; output;
ptype='v'; x = 50; y= 60; output;
```

When creating the petals (symbols 2 through 20), the first is to be placed vertically and the remainder spaced equally around the circle. Since SAS uses radians to measure angles, the variable TWOPI is used to store the value of 2 times pi. The value of pi, π, is easily calculated as the arc cosine of -1. An angle of zero is horizontal to the right, so all angles need to be shifted by a quarter of a turn counter clockwise. Each petal is drawn as a line (LP='L') from the center of the symbol (50,50) with a length of 50 units. The font character name is stored in CHAR and will take on the first 20 letters of the alphabet.

```
* create the data used to create the font;
data fontdata(keep=char seg x y lp ptype);
length char $1;
retain char ' ';
```

```
twopi = 2*arcos(-1);
quarter = twopi/4;
do pltvar = 1 to 20 by 1;
  char = substr('ABCDEFGHIJKLMNOPQRSTUV',pltvar,1);
  * define the center point as a circle with radius 10;
  seg=0; lp='p';
  ptype='w'; x =  0; y=100; output;
  ptype='v'; x = 50; y= 60; output;
  ptype='c'; x = 50; y= 50; output;
  ptype='v'; x = 40; y= 50; output;
  ptype='c'; x = 50; y= 50; output;
  ptype='v'; x = 50; y= 40; output;
  ptype='c'; x = 50; y= 50; output;
  ptype='v'; x = 60; y= 50; output;
  ptype='c'; x = 50; y= 50; output;
  ptype='v'; x = 50; y= 60; output;

  * for pltvars > 1 include petals;
  lp='l';
  if pltvar>1 then do seg = 1 to pltvar;
    * Divide the circle into pltvar parts, draw a line for
    * each part.  Shift the angle by one quarter turn to
    * make the first vertical;
    angle = twopi/pltvar*(seg-1) + quarter;
    x= 50; y = 50;  output;
    x= 50*cos(angle)+50; y=50*sin(angle)+50; output;
    * for the very last point draw back to the center;
    if seg=pltvar then do;
      x= 50; y = 50;  output;
    end;
  end;
end;
```

The character used to identify the symbol should have a length of one.
Therefore, we need to translate the 20 numbers into letters. This is easily done
by using the SUBSTR function. When PLTVAR=5, the fifth character, 'E', is
selected. This is easier and quicker than a user-defined translation format.

The variable that we would like to plot (VOLUME) using sunflowers has more
than 20 values and ranges in the thousands. Therefore, it needs to be scaled to
accommodate the twenty-character range of our font. In this way, a mapping is
created such that

VOLUME		PETALS	PLTVAR	
0 - 500	→	dot	→	1
501 -1000	→	2 petals	→	2
1001-1500	→	3 petals	→	3
etc.				

This mapping can be accomplished with formats or with a numeric
transformation, as was done here. The following transformation creates the
variable PLTVAR which represents the number of shares traded in units of

500,000 shares. The CEIL function returns the smallest integer greater than the quotient.

```
data dow;
set vol1.dow;
pltvar = ceil(volume/500);
output;
```

As is mentioned in Section 4.2, it is not necessarily true that SYMBOL5 is used when PLTVAR=5. For a given value of PLTVAR, we need to know which of the sunflowers is used. If PLTVAR only takes on the values of 1, 2, and 4, SYMBOL3 will be used for PLTVAR=4. This is clearly unacceptable and can be remedied by making sure that all of the SYMBOL statements are associated with the correct value of PLTVAR even if all twenty values of PLTVAR are not used. This is accomplished by generating 20 dummy unplotable points with PLTVAR varying from 1 through 20. Unplottable points have either the x or y variable equal missing.

```
data dow;
set vol1.dow;
pltvar = ceil(volume/500);
output;

* Each of the twenty symbol statements must be requested
* even if all are not used on the plot.  PLTVAR=n points to
* the Nth activated symbol statement, not just SYMBOLn.;
* Create 20 points that will not be plotted, but will activate
* each of the 20 symbol statements;
if _n_=1 then do pltvar=1 to 20;
  high=.;
  output;
end;
run;
```

The PROC GPLOT step is fairly straightforward and only requires the addition of the 20 SYMBOL statements.

```
* Display the closing high;
proc gplot data=dow;
plot high*date=pltvar /
     vaxis=axis1 haxis=axis2
     nolegend;
title1 'Daily Trading Highs';
title2 'Petals represent trading volume in 500,000 shares';
footnote1 h=1 j=l f=simplex 'Example 4.5.2';
symbol1  f=sunflwr c=black h=2 v=A;
symbol2  f=sunflwr c=black h=2 v=B;
symbol3  f=sunflwr c=black h=2 v=C;
symbol4  f=sunflwr c=black h=2 v=D;
symbol5  f=sunflwr c=black h=2 v=E;
symbol6  f=sunflwr c=black h=2 v=F;
symbol7  f=sunflwr c=black h=2 v=G;
symbol8  f=sunflwr c=black h=2 v=H;
symbol9  f=sunflwr c=black h=2 v=I;
symbol10 f=sunflwr c=black h=2 v=J;
symbol11 f=sunflwr c=black h=2 v=K;
symbol12 f=sunflwr c=black h=2 v=L;
```

```
symbol13  f=sunflwr  c=black  h=2  v=M;
symbol14  f=sunflwr  c=black  h=2  v=N;
symbol15  f=sunflwr  c=black  h=2  v=O;
symbol16  f=sunflwr  c=black  h=2  v=P;
symbol17  f=sunflwr  c=black  h=2  v=Q;
symbol18  f=sunflwr  c=black  h=2  v=R;
symbol19  f=sunflwr  c=black  h=2  v=S;
symbol20  f=sunflwr  c=black  h=2  v=T;
run;
```

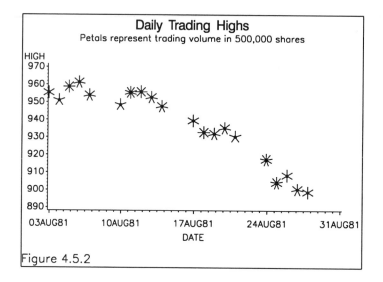

Figure 4.5.2

The creation and use of user-defined fonts can be simplified, and the problems associated with the use of the SYMBOL statements can be eliminated by placing the symbols with ANNOTATE.

MORE INFORMATION:

Benoit, 1985 - Although the article is primarily on ANNOTATE, a
sunflower example shows how to calculate angles for the petals.
Cleveland, 1984b - First proposed use of the sunflower plot to indicate
the number of points that were plotted at a given location.
Friendly, 1991 - Two examples of sunflower plots and the included SAS
code is generalized with macros.

SEE ALSO:

Section 4.2 discusses the use of the SYMBOL statement in conjunction
with the use of a third plot variable.

5 Helpful Details for Presenting Your Graphs

Finishing Touches

5.1   Introduction

As you prepare your graphic for presentation, you may find that the little details of the preparation cause some of the largest delays. Delays often happen because the final presentation and production of a graph involves more than just the manipulation of SAS code. The graph must be presented, either as hardcopy or in a presentation. Often, the graph must be incorporated into a word processing document, and at times the graph itself needs to be edited or presented using tools that are not a part of the SAS System.

This chapter discusses the following assortment of tools and techniques that should prove helpful as the graph is prepared for presentation:

- the selection and use of plotter interfaces

- importing the graph into Word and WordPerfect word processing programs

- editing a SAS/GRAPH object using a graphics editor other than the one included with SAS/GRAPH

- when to use or not to use the ANNOTATE facility

- graphics techniques and options that can cause problems.

5.2   Using Device Drivers

Every graphics device, whether it is a plotter, printer, or graphics terminal, requires certain types of commands before it can generate a graph. The commands are different from device to device. Although some devices share command languages, most are specific to a particular device. Graphics device drivers convert the internal SAS/GRAPH commands to the language that is appropriate for a particular device.

When you specify a driver with the DEVICE= graphics option, SAS/GRAPH generates the appropriate commands based on information contained in the catalog SASHELP.DEVICES (other customized device driver catalogs can be created). This catalog contains the setup information, including defaults for the specified device. You can change these defaults through the use of PROC GDEVICE. However, if the SASHELP.DEVICES catalog is shared, it is usually best to create a separate customized catalog and make the changes there.

Most of the parameters stored in the DEVICES catalog can also be controlled in the GOPTIONS statement. Some, such as color, font, and size, can also be changed in the statements that cause their use. It is not usually wise to change the DEVICES catalog, unless the new default is desired for all SAS applications. Task by task, changes should be handled in the appropriate job by the use of the GOPTIONS statement rather than through PROC GDEVICE.

At times it may be desirable to create or modify device drivers. Although SAS Institute has developed drivers for most of the hardware devices that you are likely to use, it is possible to customize drivers to suit your particular needs. User-defined drivers, such as the one used in Example 4.3.2d, are stored in a catalog called DEVICES in a library with the *libref* GDEVICEx (where x is a number such as 0, 1, 2, and so on).

MORE INFORMATION:
> *SAS/GRAPH Software: Reference*, Chapter 4 - Discusses device drivers, their parameters, and how these parameters are accessed.

SAS/GRAPH Software: Reference, Chapter 25 - Specifics on the
GDEVICE procedure.
SAS Technical Support Document TS252 - This series of documents
discuss the generation of CGM drivers tailored for various word
processing packages.

5.3   Incorporating Your Graphs into Word Processing Programs

SAS/GRAPH can create an output file that you can store and plot later or import
into a number of different word processing programs. This section covers Word
and WordPerfect, two of the more popular word processing programs. Some of
the techniques are general enough that you should be able to apply them to
other word processing programs as well.

MORE INFORMATION:
SAS Technical Support Document TS-252$_i$ - A series of Technical Support
documents are available that detail the creation and use of CGM
drivers designed specifically for over 20 word processing and
graphics packages. TS-252 covers most of the packages in
general, while TS-252$_i$ covers individual packages in greater detail.
SAS Technical Support maintains extensive up-to-date information
on this topic.

SEE ALSO:
Chapter 6 discusses the GREPLAY procedure as it is used to reproduce
graphs.

5.3.1 Creating a graphics stream file
The first step in either delaying the plotting of a graph or in transferring a graph
to a word processor is to create a graphics stream file (GSF) that can be saved
for later use. Most hardware devices and word processing programs accept
one or more types of GSFs. Select the type of GSF you want to create with the
DEVICE= graphics option.

The GOPTIONS statement controls several aspects of the file that are to be
transferred to the word processor. Graphics options of particular interest in this
context include BORDER/NOBORDER, DEVICE, GSFNAME, and GSFMODE.

The following code shows these options in a GOPTIONS statement. The
quoted string in the FILENAME statement is dependent on the operating

system being used (Release 6.08 of the SAS System under Windows was used in this sample code).

```
* using the FILENAME statement to identify the GSFNAME file;
filename fileref '\myplots\xyplt.hpg';

goptions noborder
         gsfname=fileref
         device=hp7475a
         gsfmode=replace noprompt;
```

The previous code uses the options discussed in this section to create a Hewlett-Packard Graphics Language, HP-GL, file. HP-GL is a fairly standard file transfer format for graphic files. Other GSF files are created using these same options. Although fairly universal and usually reliable, the HP-GL drivers are not SAS Institute's recommended choice for the creation of GSFs that are to be exported to WordPerfect and other word processors. The Technical Support Document TS252 discusses the creation of the recommended drivers.

DEVICE= - The type of file created is specified by the device driver named in the DEVICE= option. The device driver for the HP7475A plotter creates a standard HP-GL file. Although this type of file is recommended by WordPerfect and is generally adequate, SAS Institute recommends the use of Computer Graphics Metafiles, CGM, which are created by specific drivers. Using the CGM drivers minimizes problems associated with transferring GSF files between software packages. SAS maintains a CGM driver list that is updated regularly. Contact SAS Technical Support for the latest driver information. The Technical Support Documents (TS252) described earlier in this section are especially useful.

NOBORDER - When you use the BORDER option, the size of the graph (HSIZE and VSIZE) is the same as the page because HP-GL commands are specified that include the border, the space between the border and the graph, and the graph itself. When NOBORDER is specified, the HP-GL file only contains the commands needed to draw the graph and does not contain any instructions about the space on the page that surrounds the graph.

GSFMODE= - This option controls whether the graphics commands are appended (GSFMODE=APPEND) to the file or replace (GSFMODE=REPLACE) the contents of the file.

GSFNAME= - This option is used to route the graphic stream file to a file specified for the operating system. GSFNAME= requires the use of a *fileref* or, on some host systems, an actual file specification.

5.3.2 Importing your graphs into a word processor

All recent versions of both WordPerfect and Word, as well as many other word processing programs, accept several types of graphics files. For any given graph there is more than one way to import it. Specifics on the methods to import a graph are constantly changing, and it is impractical to incorporate all the specific steps into this book. If you need help incorporating graphs, the series of documents in the Technical Support Documents TS252 also provides word-processor-specific commands used to import graphs. These documents are updated by the SAS Technical Support staff and should be very helpful. A few specifics for WordPerfect and Word are included in this section.

WordPerfect

Graphs can be loaded directly into the WordPerfect document. It is also possible to just point to a system file that contains the graph.

WordPerfect has the ability to add borders to a figure that has been imported. In most of the figures in this book, the borders were generated strictly by SAS/GRAPH using the BORDER option. A WordPerfect figure border was not added. Figures 5.3.2a and 5.3.2b demonstrate the difference in how WordPerfect loads two simple GSLIDE graphs that were created using the BORDER and NOBORDER options. Unlike other figures in this book, Figure 5.3.2b is outlined by WordPerfect (dotted border).

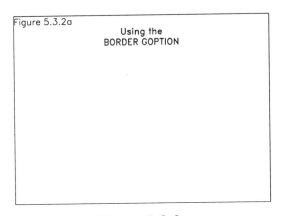

Figure 5.3.2a

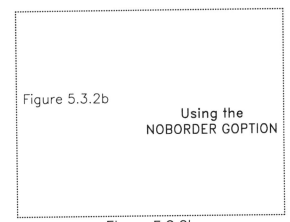

Figure 5.3.2b

Notice that the figure generated with the NOBORDER option has

- expanded (larger) type

- vertical centering

- lost horizontal centering.

With the exception of this figure, all of the graphs in this book have had their borders generated using the BORDER graphics option.

Microsoft Word

Word 5.0, and later versions accept several types of graphics files, as does Word Perfect. The steps required to import graphs into Word are highly dependent on the version of Word being used.

The graph cannot be resized and edited when using Word for DOS.

Importing HP-GL files into Word can result in a truncated image if the page size of the device is larger than the margins allowed in the Word document. The problem can easily be corrected by

- changing the HSIZE and VSIZE options

- selecting a DEVICE with the appropriate page size

- adjusting the default page dimensions for the DEVICE selected.

MORE INFORMATION:

Griffin, 1994 - Provides additional detail regarding the process of importing SAS/GRAPH graphs into WordPerfect.

SAS Technical Support Documents TS252B and TS252L - Discuss the generation of CGM drivers specifically tailored to Microsoft Word for Windows, Versions 5 and 6, respectively.

SAS Technical Support Document TS252G - Discusses the generation of drivers specifically tailored to WordPerfect.

SAS Technical Support Document TS252P - Covers WordPerfect in detail.

Wind, 1993 - Discusses a method to move SAS/GRAPH maps to WordPerfect.

SEE ALSO:

Section 4.3.2c - Uses a CGM driver recommended in TS252G.

5.4   Editing Your SAS/GRAPH Object under Windows

Under Windows, you can use SAS/GRAPH to create an image that is used directly by Windows. This allows you to use SAS/GRAPH to create icons (.ICN), logos, or other bitmapped files (.BMP). You can select all or just a portion of a graph and pass it through the paste buffer to almost any Windows program that accepts pasted input. The Windows Paintbrush accessory provides specific tools for editing and storage and is a part of Windows.

The following steps create a bitmapped file using the Windows Paintbrush accessory:

1   Create and display a graph using SAS/GRAPH.

2   Select all or a portion of the graph by pressing and holding the left mouse button, LMB, and dragging the mouse.

3   On the tool bar, select the COPY icon.

4   From the Windows Program Manager, initiate the Paintbrush accessory (or other graphics editor).

5   Using the LMB, select EDIT and from the pulldown window, select PASTE. The SAS graph now appears in the Paintbrush window where it can be edited and saved.

6   Files saved as .PCX files can be loaded into WordPerfect (Section 5.3.2).

Once copied to the paste buffer, most Windows programs, including WordPerfect for Windows, also allow the graph to be pasted directly without creating an intermediate PCX file.

5.5   When to Use and Not to Use the ANNOTATE Facility

As is demonstrated elsewhere in this book, SAS/GRAPH can produce very sophisticated graphs without the use of the ANNOTATE facility. On the other hand, virtually all of the graphs in this book could be made with ANNOTATE.

The question then becomes when to use, and when not to use, the ANNOTATE facility.

ANNOTATE can be used with

- SAS/GRAPH procedures that produce graphical output

- selected graphical procedures in SAS/QC and SAS/OR.

Many of the functions of ANNOTATE can also be accomplished using other methods within SAS/GRAPH such as

- placing text and symbols on a graph using TITLE, FOOTNOTE, and SYMBOL statements

- creating labels using TITLE, FOOTNOTE, and NOTE statements

- creating legends and titles using the LEGEND and TITLE statements.

ANNOTATE can more efficiently do things such as

- drawing shapes and figures, for example, polygons, arcs, and lines.

If you do not know how to use ANNOTATE and find yourself going to great lengths to accomplish tasks such as those shown in this book, it might be wise to consider the ANNOTATE alternative. If the techniques shown in this book are adequate and easily adapted for use in your application, you may not yet need to learn ANNOTATE. It is important to remember that when the topic is SAS/GRAPH, there is almost always more than one way to solve a problem. If your solution seems overly complicated, then there is probably an easier solution.

MORE INFORMATION:
> *SAS/GRAPH Software: Usage*, Chapter 54 - Discusses various aspects of adding text to graphs using ANNOTATE.
> *SAS/GRAPH Software: Reference*, Chapter 18 - Introduces the ANNOTATE facility.
> Carpenter, 1991, 1992, 1994a - Introduces the ANNOTATE facility and the ANNOTATE data set.

5.6   Graph Construction; Things to Think about

It is often not sufficient to simply know the SAS programming statements to create a good graph. The graph must be designed to convey the proper information, and not all of the various tools available within SAS are appropriate for any given plot or chart. You must design a graph that makes sense of the data, and you must utilize the appropriate graphic elements.

MORE INFORMATION:
> Corning, 1994a,b,c - Very good articles on various aspects of effective graphics design and production.
> Tufte, 1983 - This book is full of interesting examples of both good and bad graphical displays.
> Wainer, 1984 - Article highlighting a number of techniques that do a poor job of displaying data.

5.6.1 Making a graph make sense

Graphs are used to convey information, but the best method of presenting this information is not always apparent. This means that all too often plots and charts are created that do not convey the intended information. The human eye often *sees* what is not anticipated by the person designing the graph. Perhaps you are familiar with common examples of optical illusions. What many programmers overlook is that many popular graphical charts and techniques create their own kind of optical illusion.

Several considerations should be taken into account when designing a graph. The design process includes the use of graphical elements, such as position, scale, direction, length, area, volume, curvature, shading, and color. The human eye and mind can process the information contained in some of these elements better than others. Consequently, a graph utilizing the correct combination of graphic elements is more likely to convey the intended information.

The layout and design of a graphic presentation can be crucial to the successful conveyance of the graphical content. We encourage you to consult Dr. Friendly's book, which has a very good summary of the proper use of graphical elements (Friendly, 1991). A great deal of the research into the perception of graphic presentations has been done by William Cleveland. His paper is easily read and highly recommended (Cleveland, 1984a). Cleveland concludes that there are six group of graphics elements, and he orders them by how likely the graphical information is to be successfully absorbed:

1	Position along a common scale
2	Position along nonaligned scales
3	Length, direction, and angle
4	Area
5	Volume and curvature
6	Shading and color saturation

Positions along common scales (axes) are easily and successfully compared, while comparisons of values through the use of shadings and color saturation are much less likely to be successful.

When designing a graph, consider using length (bar chart) before area (pie chart) to accurately convey information. Readers of a graph are more likely to successfully compare two points on a single axis (1) than two areas (4). Color can be used to highlight aspects of a graph, but since we do a poor job of distinguishing shadings it might not be wise, for example, to use increasing color saturation to indicate increasing density (6).

MORE INFORMATION:
> Bessler, 1994a - Contains a number of very useful things to think about when designing graphs.
> Cleveland, 1984a - Discusses a variety of problems associated with the construction of graphs.
> Corning, 1994a - Includes a number of examples as well as a discussion covering these and other considerations.
> Friendly, 1991 - Includes very good examples and discussion of the creation of graphs using SAS.

SEE ALSO:
> Section 5.7 - Examples of common graphics techniques that produce less than the desired results.

5.6.2 Use of color

Color is a powerful tool for the presentation of information. While the eye is not good at comparing shading and color saturation, color can be very effective when used to distinguish portions or elements of a graph. When properly applied, color can be very beneficial.

The use of color is limited more by the hardware generating the graph than by SAS/GRAPH. Graphs generated by the base product are constrained to black and white. SAS/GRAPH, however, has the ability to utilize the full color capabilities of any attached monitors, plotters, and color-capable printers.

In many workplaces, quality color plotters or printers are not generally available or are not practical for a particular task. Color plotters tend to be expensive both to purchase and to operate, and their production throughput is usually slower than their black-and-white counterparts. Some plotters and printers, especially those with pens and ribbons, may also have problems with the consistency of color hue. These considerations become especially important when large numbers of graphs are to be produced.

5.6.3 Using color on black-and-white plots

Although color graphs have distinct advantages, color is not always a production option as many graphical applications are constrained to the use of black and white. This is especially true for reports that are created or produced on printers, such as LaserJet printers, or that are reproduced on a black-and-white photo copier.

When the final graph is to be produced in black and white and you wish to distinguish portions of the graph using shadings, gray scales (discussed in Section 5.6.4) can be very useful. Unfortunately, many plotters and some printers cannot produce gray scales. When this is the case, the following alternative can sometimes be used.

Color can at times be used to advantage on plots that are reproduced (photocopied) in black and white because not all colors reproduce with the same intensity when copied using a black-and-white photocopier. Blue and red both tend to fade, and blue and yellow may even disappear altogether. This feature can be used to advantage to highlight or de-emphasize areas or lines.

If you have a color plotter, try generating a figure such as the one shown in Section 5.6.4 using as many colors as possible instead of gray scales. Photocopy the graph in black and white, and determine which colors appear to fade. Use this technique as an alternate to the gray-scales shown in Section 5.6.4.

MORE INFORMATION:
SAS/GRAPH Software: Usage, pp. 727-750 - Chapter 53, "Selecting Patterns".

5.6.4 Using gray-scales

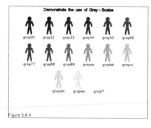

Figure 5.6.4

If you have a printer that can handle it , an excellent alternative to black-and-white cross-hatching and to color is that of gray scale. Shades of gray allow noncolor reproduction while maintaining a formal appearance. In many work places, it is easier to find laser printers that do well with shades of gray than it is to find quality color plotters. Because of speed and cost considerations, this becomes especially important when large quantities of graphs are to be produced.

Gray-scale plots also avoid several of the problems of inconsistent color hues that are associated with some hardware. These problems include pens and ribbons that run low on ink, partially clogged ink jets, and differences among plotter types.

Gray scales are used by specifying GRAYxx as the color, where the value of xx is the lightness of the gray and is given as a hexadecimal number in the range from 00 (gray00 is black) to ff (grayff is white). This allows 256 levels on the gray-scale. Shades of gray about one-third of the way from 00 to ff (that is, gray4c) would be seen as dark gray.

The following code creates a graph showing 15 figures in various shades of gray:

```
proc gslide;
title1 h=2 f=swiss j=c 'Demonstrate the use of Gray-Scales';
note h=10 c=gray00 j=c f=marker 'Q' c=gray22 'Q' c=gray33 'Q'
                    c=gray44 'Q' c=gray55 'Q' c=gray66 'Q';
note j=c h=1.8 f=simplex
            c=gray00 'gray00        gray22         gray33'
            '             gray44         gray55         gray66';
note h=10 c=gray77 j=c f=marker 'Q' c=gray88 'Q' c=gray99 'Q'
                    c=grayaa 'Q' c=graybb 'Q' c=graycc 'Q';
note j=c h=1.8 f=simplex
            c=gray00 'gray77        gray88         gray99'
            '             grayaa         graybb         graycc';
note h=10 c=graydd j=c f=marker 'Q' c=grayee 'Q' c=grayff 'Q';
note j=c h=1.9 f=simplex
            c=gray00 'graydd        grayee         grayff';
footnote j=l h=2 f=simplex 'Figure 5.6.4';
run;
```

This code produces Figure 5.6.4, which demonstrates a fifteen-shade progression. Notice that the fifteenth shade (grayff or white) does not show up because the background is also white.

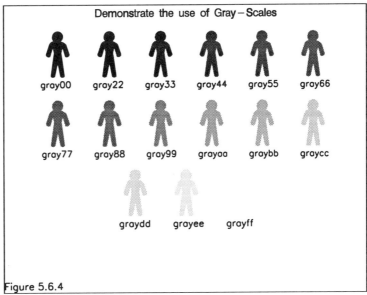

Figure 5.6.4

Use of gray-scales requires a gray-scale-capable driver and printer (or monitor). As with any other graphs produced by SAS/GRAPH, the graph can be generated immediately or exported to a file for printing later. The driver used in this example, CGMWPGA, is designed to create gray-scale CGM files that are to be imported into WordPerfect.

Gray-scale-capable drivers for other software packages are discussed in the series of Technical Support Documents that contain the designation TS252 in their title. These documents can be obtained directly from the Technical Support Division.

MORE INFORMATION:
> *SAS/GRAPH Software: Reference*, p. 183 - A very brief description of the use of gray scales.
>
> SAS Technical Support Documents TS252 - This series of documents discusses the creation of hardware specific drivers that allow the use of gray-scales.

SEE ALSO:
> Section 5.2 - The creation and use of drivers is discussed. Discussion also includes plotter interfaces and some information on customized device drivers.

5.7   Graphics Options and Techniques to Avoid

Several available graphics options produce graphs and charts that are either misleading or do not convey the information intended by the creator of the graph. This section discusses a few of these graphs and their pitfalls. Section 5.6.1, "Making a graph make sense," discusses your reader's ability to distinguish and interpret graphs that contain many of the graphical elements shown in the following sections.

Please note that just because a technique has been brought up as an example in one of the following sections does not mean that you should never use that technique. If you are aware of the problems that can be associated with a particular technique, then you should be able to make an informed decision about when and how to use it.

MORE INFORMATION:
> Corning, 1994a,b,c - Very good articles on various aspects of effective graphics design and production. Many of the topics covered in this section are also reviewed in these papers. The third article (1994c) makes a very thorough comparison of various techniques and when each should be used.

SEE ALSO:
> Section 5.6.1 - Discusses graphical elements in more detail.

5.7.1 Stacked bar charts

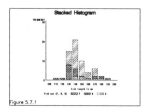

Figure 5.7.1

Stacked bar charts show the values of two or more variables (or categories) on each bar. Both the CHART and GCHART procedures allow the use of the SUBGROUP= option to easily create this kind of graph. The problem with this type of chart is that the stacked values are perceived as being on a common scale, when actually the scales are nonaligned. Not only are they nonaligned, all of but the first set of vertical values do not have a common base.

The following code produces a histogram with stacked subgroups:

```
proc gchart data=vol1.lampara;
title 'Stacked Histogram';
footnote j=1 h=2 f=simplex 'Figure 5.7.1';
vbar length / subgroup=sex
              midpoints = 100 110 120 130 140 150
                          160 170 180 190 200;
pattern1 value=l1 c=black;
```

```
pattern2 value=x1 c=blue;
pattern3 value=r1 c=green;
run;
```

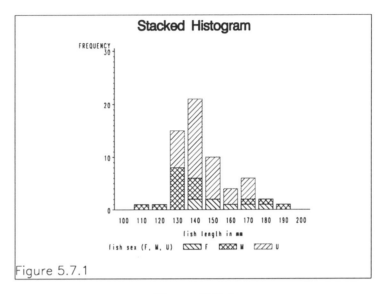

Figure 5.7.1

Because the stacked segments do not have a common base, it is difficult to compare values such as the number of Males in the 130mm category and the number of Undetermineds in the 150mm category. You may want to avoid a stacked bar chart if you want to compare the relative size of subgroups across bars, but it can still provide valuable information, depending on what you want to show.

The GROUP= option provides an alternative to the stacked subgroups. This option shows the same information. However, all of the subgroups are plotted with a common base. Although also not without problems, the BLOCK charts discussed in Section 5.7.3 can be used to display this type of information. The use of the SUBGROUP= option can be useful if the primary emphasis of the graph is to show a rough approximation of the relative contribution of the subgroup *within* the vertical bar.

MORE INFORMATION:
> Redman, 1993 - The segments are reordered by size so that the largest is always on the bottom.

5.7.2 Plots in layers

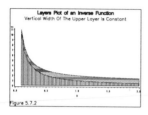

Figure 5.7.2

The PROC GPLOT equivalent to the stacked values discussed in Section 5.7.1 uses the AREAS= option in the PLOT statement. Unlike the stacked histogram segments, the AREAS= option is designed to plot two or more variables that always take on monotonically greater-than values. That is, for any value of the horizontal variable, $y1 < y2 < y3$ and so on. While this provides a vertically and horizontally aligned scale, the eye perceives a nonaligned scale.

The following code generates two variables (Y1 and Y2) with a constant vertical difference. These variables are then plotted using the AREAS= option.

```
data inverse;
do x = .10 to 2 by .05;
   y1 = 1/x;
   y2 = 1/x + 1;
   output;
end;

proc gplot data=inverse;
footnote j=l h=2 f=simplex 'Figure 5.7.2';
title 'Layers Plot of an Inverse Function';
title2 h=2 j=c f=simplex
        'Vertical Width Of The Upper Layer Is Constant';
plot y1*x y2*x / overlay haxis = 0 to 2 by .5
                 areas=2;

symbol1 i=join v=none l=1;
symbol2 i=join v=none l=2;

pattern1 value=m3n90 color=black;
pattern2 value=m3n0 color=red;
run;
```

The use of the AREAS= option (aggravated by the choice of PATTERNs) makes it very difficult to see the constant difference of Y1 and Y2. The eye sees the horizontal difference between the two lines as well, thereby totally hiding the constant vertical difference.

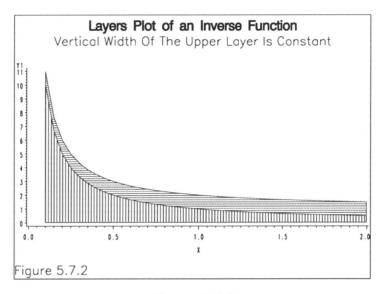

Figure 5.7.2

5.7.3 Block charts

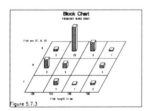

Block charts are a form of a histogram and are created by using the BLOCK statement in PROC GCHART. Block charts show a series of pseudo three-dimensional towers, each with the height representing the value of a selected variable. When two classification variables are selected, as in this example, the towers are arranged like a small city of skyscrapers.

The following code generates a block chart in two dimensions (fish length and sex). The height of each tower represents the number of observations that fall into each category.

```
proc gchart data=vol1.lampara;
title1 'Block Chart';
footnote j=l h=2 f=simplex 'Figure 5.7.3';
block length / group=sex
               midpoints = 120 140 160 180;
run;
```

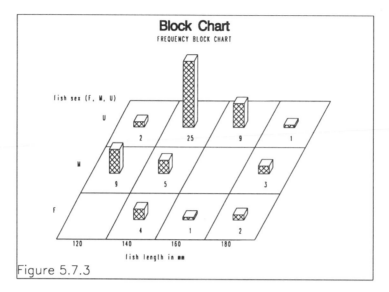

Figure 5.7.3

In addition to being a problem of nonaligned scales, the eye wants to see a three-dimensional picture and will attempt to use perspective where none has been added. Because the eye wants to see towers in the back row as being farther away, a tower in the back row appears taller than one of equal height in the front row. For some readers, the tower for the 120mm Males appears shorter than the one representing the 160mm Undetermineds, even though the towers are the same height. Notice also that the parallel grid lines running from the front to the back seem to diverge. This an optical illusion and is also an artifact of the eye trying to put the graph into perspective.

Block charts can be useful to show rough estimates of relative height.

SEE ALSO:
Figure 1.4.3b - A block chart is produced.

5.7.4 Optical illusion and the pattern statement

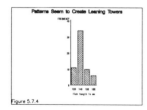

Some combinations of lines and especially patterns just do not complement each other. When placed together, some patterns seem to clash, and some even form the optical illusions of histogram bars that appear to lean. Patterns formed by increasing density, such as shades of gray (Section 5.6.4), are much less likely to be discordant. Patterns formed with lines of alternating or changing angles are much less likely to be successful. As you design your graph and choose your fill patterns, you must guard against creating charts such as the one shown in this example.

The following code generates a histogram with specified patterns. The patterns are selected with the VALUE= option in the PATTERN statement.

```
proc gchart data=vol1.lampara;
title 'Patterns Seem to Create Leaning Towers';
footnote j=1 h=2 f=simplex 'Figure 5.7.4';
vbar length / patternid=midpoint
              midpoints = 120 140 160 180 ;
pattern1 value=l1 color=black;
pattern2 value=r1 color=black;
pattern3 value=l1 color=black;
pattern4 value=r1 color=black;
run;
```

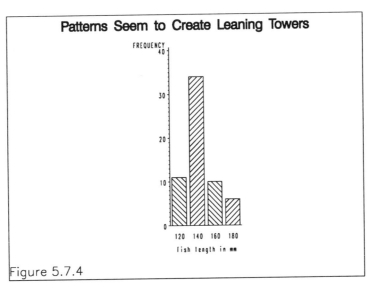

Figure 5.7.4

Although the vertical bars are parallel and equally spaced, they appear to be leaning toward or away from their neighbor. The selected patterns clash with each other.

5.7.5 Pie chart

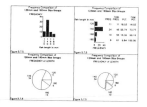

The pie chart is one of the classic graphical alternatives to the histogram (bar chart). While the histogram is good for showing relationships between groups, the pie chart is especially useful for making comparisons of contributions to the total. Pie charts can be very useful for showing overall contributions, but they are less useful when the sizes of two sectors need to be compared. The programmer (and wouldn't it be nice, the user of the graph) needs to be aware that the eye can more accurately distinguish the lengths of bars with a common scale than it can distinguish the area of a circular sector.

The following code generates four graphs of the same data; two histograms and two pie charts:

```
proc gchart data=vol1.lampara gout=chpt5;
title1 'Frequency Comparison of';
title2 h=2 j=c f=duplex '120mm and 160mm Size Groups';
footnote j=l h=2 f=simplex 'Figure 5.7.5';
vbar length / midpoints = 120 140 160 180 name='vbar';
hbar length / midpoints = 120 140 160 180 name='hbar';
pie  length / midpoints = 120 140 160 180 name='pie1';
pie  length / midpoints = 120 140 160 180 explode=160 name='pie2';
```

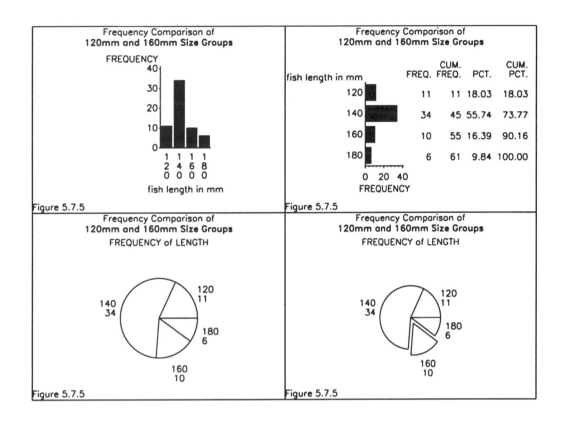

Figure 5.7.5

Although the frequency counts for the size classes of 120mm and 160mm are close, it is fairly easy to distinguish which is larger in the two histograms (they have an aligned scale). It is much more difficult to determine the larger group by inspecting the two pie diagrams (comparison of area). The pie chart is useful when the purpose of the graph is to show percentages of the total. For example, each of these charts shows that the 140mm size class accounts for about half of the total. This is much more apparent in the pie charts than in the histograms.

Exploded pie charts (EXPLODE= option in the PIE statement) can be more problematic because they trick the eye into seeing too much area. Some readers perceive the exploded sector (160mm) to be larger than the 120mm section when, in fact, it is not. Exploded sectors are good for focusing the reader's attention but should not be used when the size of the exploded sector is to be compared with another sector.

5.7.6 Nonaligned axes

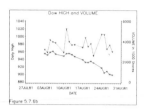

The PLOT2 and BUBBLE2 statements in PROC GPLOT allow you to specify a second vertical axis when overlaying two variables with a common horizontal axis. Regardless of whether these two axes have values in common, the eye tends to compare the magnitude of two values by looking at their height above the horizontal axis rather than by seeking out their true values on the axis.

The following code creates a scatter plot with two vertical axes. The PLOT statement is used to plot ozone (O3) concentration and the PLOT2 statement plots carbon monoxide (CO).

```
proc gplot data=vol1.ca88air;
plot o3 * month = 'O';
plot2 co * month = 'C';
where station='SFO';
title1 '1988 Air Quality Data - SFO';
title2 h=2 f=simplex 'Two Non-aligned Axes';
footnote1 j=l h=2 'Figure 5.7.6a';
run;
```

This scatter plot has two non-aligned vertical axes. That is, values on one axis in no way correspond to those on the other axis. This makes it difficult to compare concentrations of ozone and carbon monoxide.

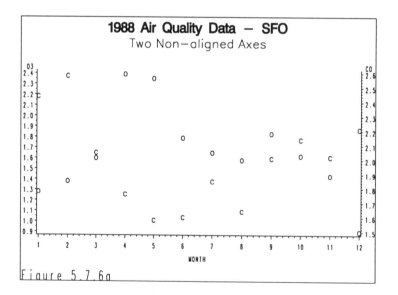

Figure 5.7.6a

In September (month=9), it first appears that the O3 concentration is greater because it is higher on the plot. Closer inspection, however, shows that O3 was equal to about 1.85, while CO was over 2.0. Because the axes are nonaligned, there is a danger that the user will misinterpret the values.

Figure 5.7.6a is especially easy to misinterpret because both axes have similar ranges. The problem could be easily corrected by plotting both variables using one vertical axis, or by using the same ORDER= option in an axis statement for each of the two axes. Either of these two methods would have eliminated the problem of the nonaligned axis scales.

There are times when nonaligned scales are useful and not misleading. Plots like this are best used when the magnitude of the two scales is very different and when the following precautions are taken:

- plot symbols are clearly associated with the appropriate axis

- the symbols associated with each axis are plotted in separate portions of the graph (minimizing overlap helps to minimize confusion)

- the intended audience is sophisticated enough to properly interpret the graph

- text accompanying the graph should alert the reader to the axis scales.

The following code also produces a plot with non-aligned axes. However, more care has been taken to minimize problems of misinterpretation.

```
axis1 order=880 to 1040 by 20
      value=(h=1.5 f=simplex)
      label=(h=1.5 a=90 f=simplex 'Daily High');
axis2 order='27jul81'd to '31aug81'd by 7
      value=(h=1.5 f=simplex)
      label=(h=1.5 f=simplex 'DATE');
axis3 order=0 to 6000 by 2000
      value=(h=1.5 f=simplex)
      label=(h=1.5 a=-90 f=simplex 'VOLUME in 1000 Shares');

proc gplot data=vol1.dow;
plot high * date / vaxis=axis1
                   haxis=axis2;
plot2 volume*date/ vaxis=axis3;
title1 'Dow HIGH and VOLUME';
footnote1 j=l h=2 'Figure 5.7.6b';
symbol1 i=join v='H' f=simplex l=1 c=black;
symbol2 i=join v='V' f=simplex l=2 c=black;
run;
```

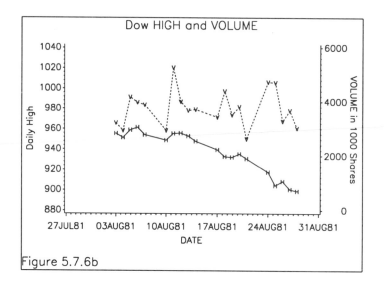

Figure 5.7.6b

5.7.7 Bubble plots

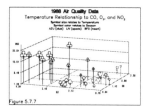

The BUBBLE and BUBBLE2 statements in PROC GPLOT and the SCATTER statement with the SIZE= option in PROC G3D can be used to produce symbols whose size represents the magnitude of another variable. As a general rule, most people find it difficult to accurately compare the size or area of two or more symbols. The problem is compounded when the comparison is between two different shapes.

At least with the BUBBLE and BUBBLE2 statements, comparisons are made among symbols that have the same shape. In a PROC G3D plot generated with the SCATTER statement, different shapes and even color add additional dimensions to the plot. As is shown in Figure 5.7.7, it is possible, but generally not wise, to create a plot with six dimensions of information. This figure attempts to display the following (although color is lost in the black-and-white reproduction of the graph):

- Y axis   O3 concentration

- X axis   CO concentration

- Z axis   NO3 concentration

- symbol size   ambient temperature

- symbol   station

- color   season

The variables for character shape (SHAPEVAR), color (COLORVAR), and temperature (SIZEVAR) are created in a DATA step.

```
data air; set vol1.ca88air;
if station='AZU' then shapevar='club';
else if station='LIV' then shapevar='spade';
else if station='SFO' then shapevar='heart';

if month in (3,4,5) then colorvar='yellow ';
else if month in (6,7,8) then colorvar='green  ';
else if month in (9,10,11) then colorvar='magenta';
else if month in (1,2,12) then colorvar='black  ';

* temperatures range from 40 to 80;
* create a scaled variable based on temperature
* (ranges from 0 to 3);
min=40; max=80;
sizevar = (tem-min)/(max-min)*3;
run;
```

The SCATTER statement in the G3D procedure step is used to identify the variables that will be used to determine character shape, color, and size.

```
proc g3d data=air;
scatter o3 * co = no3 / size=sizevar
                        shape=shapevar
                        color=colorvar
                        grid;
title1 h=2 f=swiss '1988 Air Quality Data';
title2 h=2 f=simplex 'Temperature Relationship to CO, O'
            h=1 move=(+0,-.5) '3'
            h=2 move=(+0,+.5) ', and NO'
            h=1 move=(+0,-.5) '3';
title3 h=1.2 f=simplex 'Symbol size relates to Temperature';
title4 h=1.2 f=simplex 'Symbol color relates to Season';
title5 h=1.2 f=simplex 'AZU (club)   LIV (spade)   SFO (heart)';
footnote j=1 h=2 f=simplex 'Figure 5.7.7';
run;
```

Unfortunately, the eye does not easily compare the volumes of a heart, spade, and club, and the problem is compounded by the pseudo three-dimensional effect discussed in Section 5.7.3.

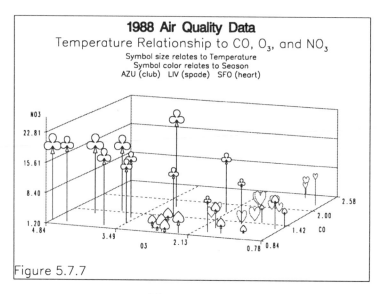

Figure 5.7.7

This type of plot can actually be useful when displaying the three data variables (CO, O3, and NO3). Even a categorical variable for different symbols (STATION) does not clutter the graph too much. The real problem of clutter and readability arises when the continuous variable (TEMP) drives the size of the plot symbol.

6 Displaying Graphs Using the GREPLAY Procedure

Presentation is Everything

6.1   Introduction
6.2   Saving and Replaying Graphs
6.3   Controlling Graphical Display with Templates

6.1   Introduction

It is not unusual for graphs to be produced at one time and actually displayed or plotted at some other time. Often, the generation of the graph itself takes quite a bit of time, time that may not be available during the presentation itself. In other cases, the output device may be shared and physically not available until later. Fortunately, SAS has the capability of saving graphics output generated by SAS/GRAPH in a catalog, and these graphs can then be reproduced by using the GREPLAY procedure.

You can use PROC GREPLAY to

- reproduce graphs that have been saved in a catalog

- manage all aspects of a catalog, including copying and deleting

- control various aspects of how a stored graph is to be displayed

- change the graphics device

- create and assign page layout using templates

- determine the order of the reproduction or presentation.

The examples on PROC GREPLAY in *SAS/GRAPH Software: Reference* and *SAS/GRAPH Software: Usage* are quite good and are not repeated here. Section 6.2 primarily serves as an introduction to the GREPLAY procedure, which is referenced in Section 6.3 on templates.

6.2 Saving and Replaying Graphs

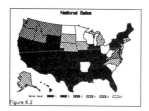
Figure 6.2

Prior to Version 6, graphs were stored in graphics catalogs. In Version 6, there are no longer different types of catalogs. Instead, graphs are now stored as GRSEG entries in a SAS catalog. You save a graph as a GRSEG entry from any SAS/GRAPH procedure that creates graphics output. These GRSEG entries can then be manipulated by the same tools that you use on other SAS catalogs. In addition, PROC GREPLAY has a number of tools that are designed specifically for use with GRSEG entries, and these tools are available in both batch and interactive modes.

Although you can use the GREPLAY procedure in batch mode, most of PROC GREPLAY's features are best accessed interactively. This allows the full-screen capabilities of PROC GREPLAY to assist with

- catalog management

- creation and management of templates

- graphic presentation.

The GREPLAY window is not necessarily opened under the display manager when PROC GREPLAY is executed. This can be useful when

- the templates and various other aspects of a presentation have been determined previously

- the user is ready to produce or present a series of graphic images that have been stored as GRSEG entries

• you want to perform the same operations on several of the GRSEG entries, and you don't want to perform these operations manually.

The following code creates a map of the United States that is redisplayed in Section 6.3.3. The GOUT=VOL1.CHAPT6 portion of the PROC GPLOT statement designates the name of the destination catalog where the graph is stored for replay later. The NAME= option in the CHORO statement provides a name for the graphic catalog member.

```
proc gmap map=maps.us
          data=vol1.salesmap
          gout=vol1.chapt6;
id state;
choro code / coutline=black
             name='salesmap'
             discrete;
pattern1 v=msolid c=black;
pattern2 v=m5x45  c=black;
pattern3 v=m1x45  c=black;
pattern4 v=m1n135 c=black;
pattern5 v=m1n45  c=black;
pattern6 v=empty  c=black;

title1 'National Sales';
footnote1 j=l h=2 f=simplex 'Figure 6.2';
run;
```

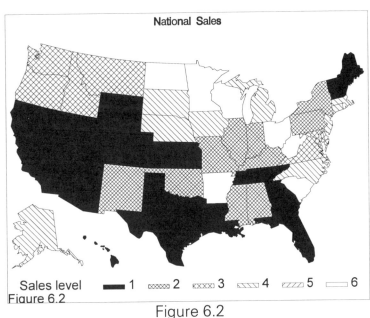

Figure 6.2

MORE INFORMATION:

Bessler, 1994b - Discusses various considerations for the use of GMAP in statistical presentations.

6.2.1 Using GREPLAY interactively

You access PROC GREPLAY interactively through the GREPLAY window. The following code opens for interactive use the GREPLAY window shown in Display 6.2.1:

```
proc greplay igout= vol1.chapt6;
```

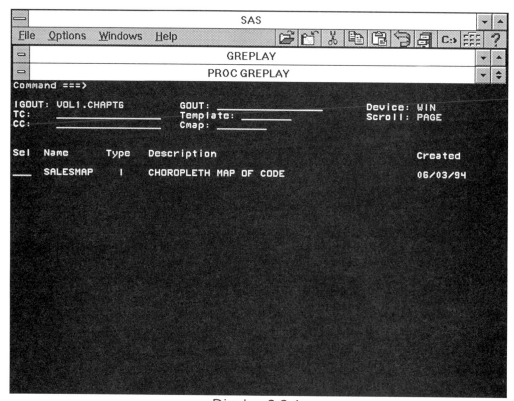

Display 6.2.1

The GREPLAY window (Display 6.2.1) shows you the graphics entries stored in the input catalog (IGOUT). From this window you can

- change the graphics device (DEVICE)

- specify graphics catalogs for input and output (IGOUT and GOUT)

- specify color mapping (CC and CMAP)

- name a template catalog (TC)

- select a template entry (TEMPLATE)

- select a catalog entry for replay (SEL)

- associate catalog entries with template panels (SEL).

MORE INFORMATION:
> *SAS/GRAPH Software: Reference*, pp. 1231-1245 - Introduction to the windows available through PROC GREPLAY.
> *SAS/GRAPH Software: Reference*, pp. 1244-1255 - Specific example and explanations of the use of the GREPLAY procedure window.
> *SAS/GRAPH Software: Usage*, pp. 782-790 - Simple example using the PROC GREPLAY and TEMPLATE DESIGN windows.

SEE ALSO:
> Section 6.3 discusses the creation and use of templates through PROC GREPLAY.

6.2.2 Executing the GREPLAY procedure in line mode

Line mode or batch execution of PROC GREPLAY is usually used to display or replay graphs that have been created previously. The NOFS option is used to deactivate full-screen processing and causes PROC GREPLAY to expect all input to be supplied by the procedure options and statements.

Each of the fields in the GREPLAY window shown in the previous section can be filled in interactively or specified through the use of PROC GREPLAY statement options or procedure statements. The code that generates the figure in the previous section designates the input graphics catalog by using the IGOUT= option in the GREPLAY statement. Alternatively, the IGOUT statement could have been used, as shown in the following code:

```
proc greplay  nofs;
igout vol1.chapt6;
replay salesmap;
run;
```

The NOFS option deactivates full-screen processing, and the REPLAY statement designates the GRSEG entries of the catalog to be displayed. Members to be selected may be designated by name or number, but using the name is preferred to ensure that the correct graph is displayed. Default names are a variation of the name of the procedure that generated the graph and are automatically assigned. Under Release 6.08, member names are unique and duplicate names are slightly altered automatically by SAS/GRAPH. Unless care is taken, this can cause difficulties in systems that are fully automated. As mentioned in Section 6.2, you can also explicitly name the entries by using the NAME= option when the graph is generated.

MORE INFORMATION:

> *SAS/GRAPH Software: Reference*, pp. 1202-1231 - Syntax and examples of the use of line-mode statements associated with PROC GREPLAY.
>
> *SAS/GRAPH Software: Usage*, pp. 774-781 - Discusses the use of line-mode access to templates.

6.3 Controlling Graphical Display with Templates

By default, the procedures that produce graphs plot one graph per page. However, templates may be used to create a graph consisting of one or more graphs and titles on one page. It is through PROC GREPLAY that SAS/GRAPH constructs, controls, and applies templates.

The template panels may be distinct, or they may overlap to the extent that they are completely overlaid.

Template panels can be used to

- display multiple graphs

- add graphics inserts such as legends

- provide banner style titles

- change the size, aspect ratio, and perspective of graphical displays.

Usually, panels are rectangular with approximately the same width-to-height ratio (ASPECT ratio) as the plot device. Panels with differing aspect ratios than were used to construct the graph can be used to flatten or elongate text and symbols. Panels that are not rectangular can be used to create the illusion of perspective.

Using the TEMPLATE DIRECTORY window

Although templates can be created through batch processing, you may find it easier to work with templates when using PROC GREPLAY interactively. Templates are stored in a catalog as TEMPLATE entries and are managed through GREPLAY's TEMPLATE DIRECTORY window. The TEMPLATE

DIRECTORY window is displayed by placing the name of the catalog in the field marked TC in the GREPLAY window and then entering a TC on the command line (Display 6.3a). In the GREPLAY window shown in Display 6.3a, the template catalog SASHELP.TEMPLT is being requested.

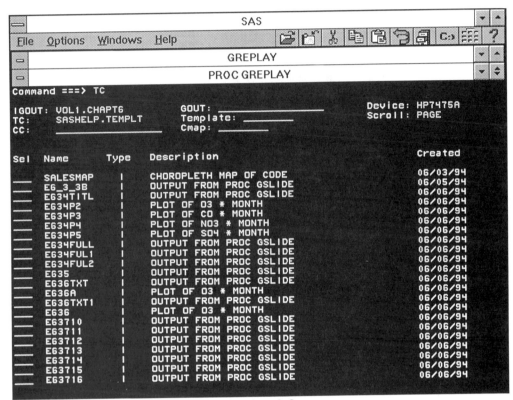

Display 6.3a

SASHELP.TEMPLT is an Institute-supplied catalog of useful templates. These templates are ready to use as provided or can be used as models when further customization is required.

The TEMPLATE DIRECTORY window shown in Display 6.3b is used to list all of the templates that have been created and stored as part of the catalog.

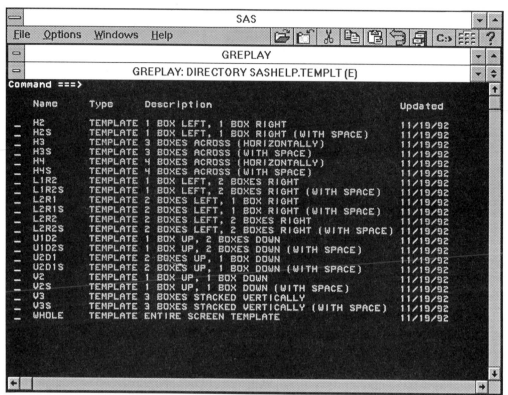

Display 6.3b

Using the Template Design window

Template entries are usually built through the use of the TEMPLATE DESIGN
window, which is accessed from the TEMPLATE DIRECTORY window. A
catalog of sample templates (SASHELP.TEMPLT) is included with SAS/GRAPH
and has been used in the examples in this section. Refer to *SAS/GRAPH
Software: Reference* for the details for building and maintaining templates. A
sample TEMPLATE DESIGN window is shown in Display 6.3c.

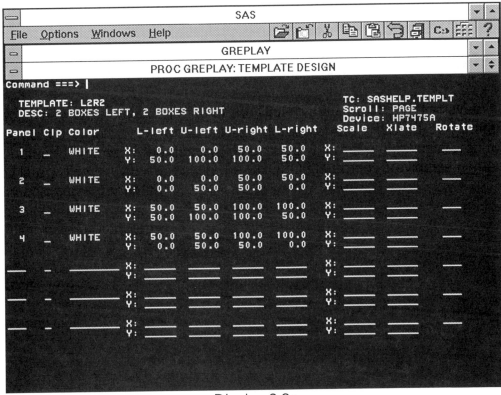

Display 6.3c

Template design is the first step in the creation of a graph using templates. Through the design of the template, you select the number of graphs, charts, and plots to be placed on a page as well as the layout of the page itself.

When designing the template you need to be aware of

- maintaining panel width-to-height ratio

- sizing panels

- sizing text within a panel

- arranging panels and graphs within panels

- resolution of the graphics device.

The Template Design window (Display 6.3c) contains each panel definition. Panels are always defined by their four corners: lower left (L-left), upper left (U-left), upper right (U-right), and lower right (L-right). These corners are defined by coordinates x and y, which are in percent, and refer to the graphics page. For example, x=0 and y=50 for the L-left define the lower left corner of the panel at (0,50) percent.

The various examples of Section 6.3 highlight a number of different template designs. One such design is shown in Display 6.3c, where the definition of the L2R2 template from the SASHELP.TEMPLT catalog is shown. In it, four panels have been defined. Therefore, this template could be used to display up to four graphs on a single page. Panel 1 will be in the upper left quadrant of this page, since its lower left corner, which is at x=0 and y=50, will be placed on the left side of the page and positioned half-way up. A graph placed in Panel 4 has its upper left corner placed at the center of the graphics page (x=50 and y=50), and occupies the lower right quadrant.

MORE INFORMATION:

Carpenter, 1990 - Discusses various aspects of the design of templates, including the use of templates to zoom, cut, and rotate graphs.

Kalt, 1986 - Good paper with a number of examples using GREPLAY and templates.

Rooth, 1987 - Examples of different ways to use templates.

SAS/GRAPH Software: Reference, pp. 1251-1257 - Syntax and limited examples for building and using templates.

SAS/GRAPH Software: Usage, pp. 771-790 - Chapter 55 discusses the use of templates to display multiple graphs per page.

SAS/GRAPH Software: Usage, pp. 772-774 - Introduces the elements of templates.

SASHELP.TEMPLT - The SAS System is delivered with a sample template catalog, which can be accessed through the SASHELP library.

SEE ALSO:

Section 2.3.3 - Places multiple plots per page without using SAS/GRAPH.

6.3.1 Controlling plot size with templates

A plot or graph need not fill the available space for the specified output device. Section 1.4.2 (HSIZE & VSIZE versus HPOS & VPOS) discusses two ways of controlling the physical size of the graph by using graphics options. The disadvantage of using these methods to control size is that the specified size is device dependent. When a graph is stored, the size settings are not saved as part of the catalog entry. By using templates to control the size of the graph, you can use whatever size constraints are either appropriate for the specific output device or are needed at the time the graph is replotted.

The following code produces a simple graph, which is used in several examples throughout the discussion on templates:

```
proc gslide gout=vol1.chapt6 name='e6_3_1a';
title1 f=simplex h=2 j=l 'upper' j=r 'upper';
title2 f=simplex h=2 j=l 'left' j=r 'right';
note f=brush h=6 j=c ' A B C';
footnote1 f=simplex h=2 j=l 'lower' j=r 'lower';
footnote2 f=simplex h=2 j=l 'left' j=r 'right';
run;
```

This code produces the following graph, which has each of its corners labeled:

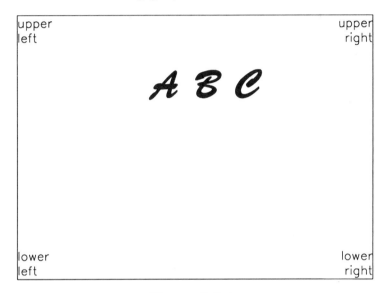

Figure 6.3.1a

Using a template to reduce the size of a graph

The template definition shown in the TEMPLATE DESIGN window in Display 6.3.1b defines three panels. Panel 1 is used to shrink the graph, while Panel 2 is full sized and Panel 3 is extremely small. Panel 1 has its upper right corner 40% of the distance from both the bottom and the left sides. A graph placed in this panel will be restricted to this portion of the graphic page and will, therefore, be reduced to 40% of its original size.

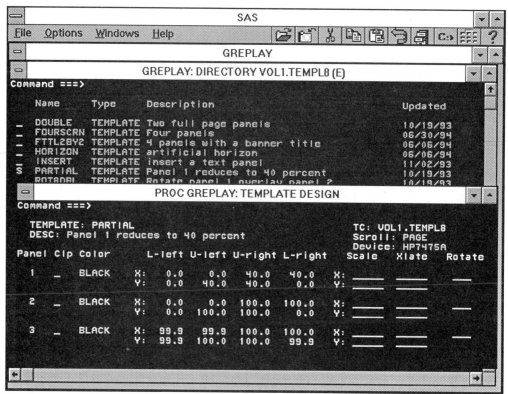

Display 6.3.1b

Using a single template such as Panel 1 in Display 6.3.1b is almost always sufficient to reduce the size of a graph. Occasionally, however, graphs that have been reduced in size using templates are still displayed full size. This is most common when a Graphics Stream File (GSF) such as an HP-GL file is saved and then imported later into another software package such as a word processor.

The software receiving the graph can often be used to easily resize the graph. However, this is not easily done, especially for graphs such as the ones shown in Figure 5.3.2, which do not cover the entire graphics page.

Graphs reduced with templates and later redisplayed often appear full size because the GSF contains no sizing information. If this happens to you one of the following fixes should help you display the graph in reduced size. Section 5.3.2 discusses this problem in relation to GSFs that are transferred to WordPerfect.

Using a border to control size

When importing a GSF file, some plotters and some software packages, such as word processors, attempt to fill the graphics page even when the GSF file was created using a reduced template panel (see Section 5.3.2 for an example).

When this happens, the second panel shown in Display 6.3.1b can be used to force the proper sizing by causing a border to be drawn around the entire graph. The GSLIDE procedure in the following code creates a GRSEG entry (VOL1.CHAPT6.BLANK) that contains only a border. This graph holds graphics space by adding a border to the final graph.

```
proc gslide gout=vol1.chapt6
            name='blank'
            border;
run;
```

The GREPLAY step shown here is written to be used in line mode (NOFS). It identifies the catalog containing the graph (IGOUT=), the catalog containing the template (TC=), the template (TEMPLATE=), and the graphs that are to be placed in each panel (TREPLAY).

```
proc greplay nofs
             igout=vol1.chapt6
             tc=vol1.templ8
             template=partial;
treplay 1:e6_3_1
        2:blank ;
run;
```

In the previous code, the TREPLAY statement associates the panel number with the graphics catalog member, as named in the NAME= option. In this case, the second panel covers the entire graphics page but contains nothing to plot (other than the border).

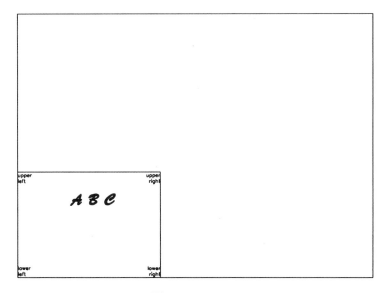

Figure 6.3.1c

Borders can be generated and stored as part of the graph using the BORDER graphics option. When using templates, borders can also be generated with the Color option in the TEMPLATE DESIGN window. When Color is not blank (it is BLACK in Display 6.3.1b), a border of the specified color appears around that panel. This is independent of the BORDER/NOBORDER graphics option.

When the border surrounding the blank space is not desirable, it may be possible to mask it. On some hardware devices, a color that will not be displayed, such as white, can be selected for the border. If the desired color is not available, you may need to add it either to the DEVICE definition or with the COLORS= graphics option. Also, pen plotters can sometimes be directed to a dry pen. When this does not work, it may be possible to use the method described next.

Controlling size without visible borders

A second method of retaining the plot reduction eliminates the border around the entire page. Panel 3 in Display 6.3.1b defines a very small area in the opposite corner from the reduced plot. The following code executes GREPLAY using the third panel:

```
proc greplay nofs
             igout=vol1.chapt6
             tc=vol1.templ8
             template=partial;
treplay 1:e6_3_1
        3:blank ;
run;
```

You may be able to see the barely visible dot indicated by an arrow in the upper right corner of Figure 6.3.1d. The dot is an artifact of the third panel. It is this dot that forces the reduction of the contents of PANEL 1.

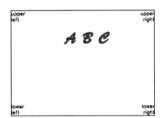

Figure 6.3.1d

SEE ALSO:

Section 5.3.2 - Shows an example of figures that are expanded when loaded into WordPerfect.

Section 6.3.3 - Deals with expanding a graph rather than shrinking it.

6.3.2 Rotating a graph using a template

 When a graph is displayed, the ROTATE option can often be used to change its orientation by 90 degrees. It is also possible to rotate graphs using template panels. As described in Section 6.3.1, template panels are always defined by their four corners, which are associated with coordinates on the graphics page. Typically, panel corners and graph corners correspond, that is, lower left to lower left. This is, however, not required. By changing the associations, the graph can be rotated, inverted, twisted, and otherwise distorted.

It is easy to confuse what is to be shifted. Remember that in the TEMPLATE DESIGN window, L-left (lower left) refers to the lower left corner of the graph, and the coordinate is the location on the page to place that corner. Because associations that are out of order are not seen as mistakes, care must be taken when assigning corners to coordinates. Incorrect assignments can result in plots that are distorted, twisted, or even seen as mirror images (see Section 6.3.5).

The graph is rotated 90 degrees clockwise when the lower left corner of a graph is associated with the upper left corner of the panel (0,100), when the upper left corner of the graph is associated with the upper right panel corner (100,100), and so on around the graph.

Figure 6.3.2a redisplays Figure 6.3.1a unrotated with the coordinates of the corners of the panel superimposed. Notice that the lower left corner of the graph is also the lower left corner of the GSLIDE and both have the panel coordinates of (0,0). The upper right corner of the graph has a panel coordinate of (100,100).

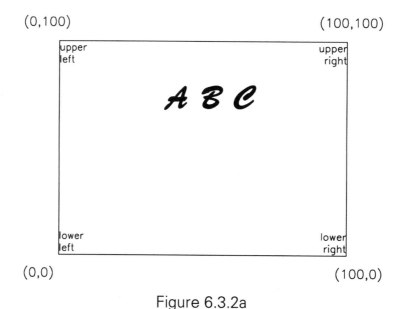

Figure 6.3.2a

In Figure 6.3.2b, Figure 6.3.1 is rotated, again with the panel coordinates shown. The lower left corner of the panel still has the coordinate of (0,0). However, it is now associated with the lower right corner of the GSLIDE graph. The upper right corner of the graph had an unrotated coordinate of (100,100). Now it has the panel coordinate of (100,0). The result is a rotation of 90 degrees.

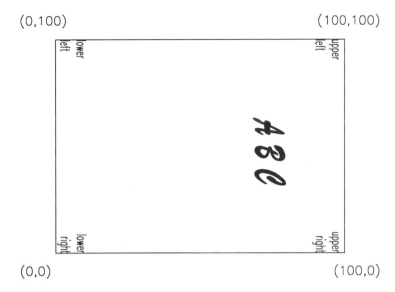

Figure 6.3.2b

These coordinates and panel corners can be matched to the TEMPLATE DESIGN window shown in Display 6.3.2c.

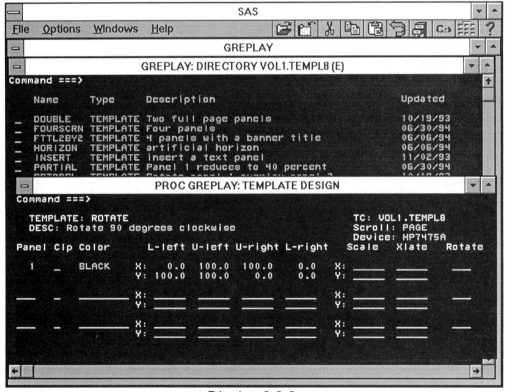

Display 6.3.2c

Notice that the template definition places the lower left corner of the graph at the coordinate of (0,100) and the upper right at (100,0).

The final figure (Figure 6.3.2d) is rotated using the following code and the template panel (VOL1.TEMPL8.ROTATE), which is defined in Display 6.3.2c:

```
proc greplay nofs
              igout=vol1.chapt6
              tc=vol1.templ8
              template=rotate;
treplay 1:e6_3_1;
run;
```

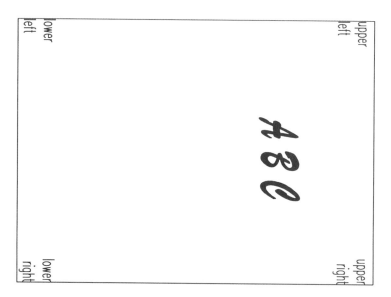

Figure 6.3.2d

MORE INFORMATION:

Carpenter, 1990 - Contains a similar example for rotation using a template.

Gerend, 1988 - Discusses the rotation of multiple plots per page, although some of the notation is misleading.

Kalt, 1986 - Several good examples on plot rotation.

SEE ALSO:

Section 6.3.5 - Expands on the special ordering of the pairing of panel and graph corners.

6.3.3 Zooming in on a portion of the graph

At times, you may need to see details contained in a portion of a graph. It is possible to display this detail by enlarging (zooming) a selected portion of the graph. Zooming in on a portion of a graph and enlarging it using templates is a similar operation to shrinking a graph (Section 6.3.1). Typically, the coordinates of the graphics page used in the template panel definitions range from 0 to 100. This does not have to be the case. Coordinates that exceed these limits actually point to portions of the graphics page that cannot be created. Because GREPLAY only replays the portions of the graph that fall within the bounds of 0 to 100, this portion will be enlarged.

Figure 6.3.3a redisplays a map (Figure 6.2) of the national sales of a travel agency that was generated and stored as a GSEG entry in a catalog (Section 6.2).

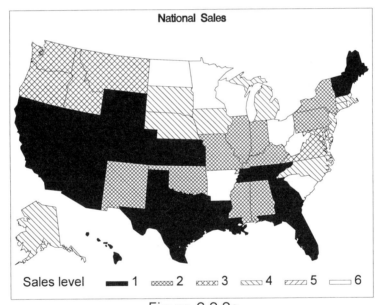

Figure 6.3.3a

Assume that you want to zoom in on the upper-left quadrant of this map (the Pacific Northwest). You can create a template that focuses on this portion of the graph.

The template must be constructed with coordinates that fall outside of the range of 0 to 100. The portion of the graph with coordinates that do fall within this range will be plotted. Figure 6.3.3b shows the coordinates that would be used to zoom in on the upper left corner of the map. The area that will be zoomed is also highlighted with an outline.

Notice that the coordinates of the whole plot are defined so that the portion that is to be plotted is given the coordinates from 0 to 100. This is further illustrated by Figure 6.3.3c, which has superimposed the coordinates from Figure 6.3.3b onto the map from Section 6.2.

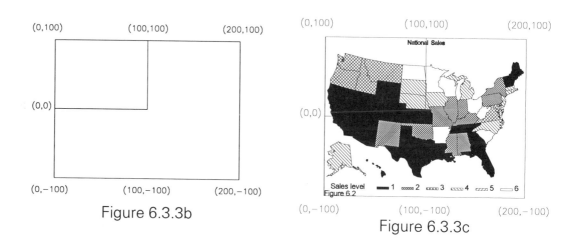

Figure 6.3.3b

Figure 6.3.3c

A template is then constructed, which has the outer corners (of the whole graph) defined with the extended coordinates. The TEMPLATE DESIGN window is shown in Display 6.3.3.d. Because we want to show one-half of the whole graph (in both directions), the corner coordinates of the panel are doubled. The lower left corner has a coordinate of 0,-100. This coordinate was selected so that the lower left corner of the portion of the graph to be plotted will have a coordinate of (0,0).

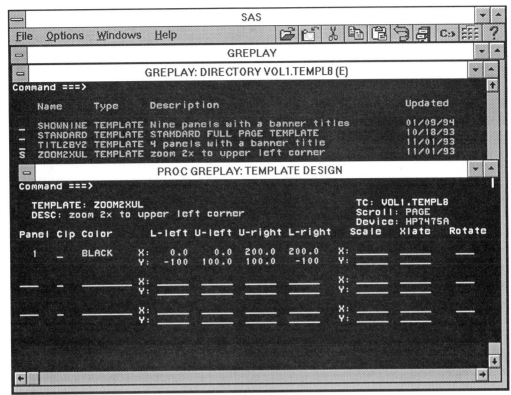

Display 6.3.3d

When this template (ZOOM2XUL) is used to replay the map, the resulting graph (Figure 6.3.3e) zooms in on the upper left corner of the original graph.

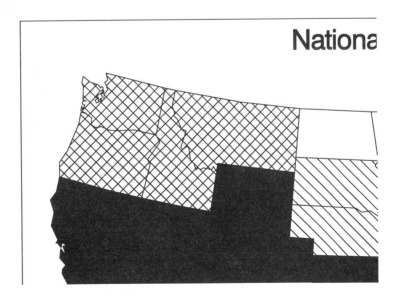

Figure 6.3.3e

At times the zoomed graph is the desired final graph. This is probably not the case for the graph shown in Figure 6.3.3e. By itself, the graph shown is not real useful. The selected portion shows little detail that is not easily seen in the original graph, and the legend information for the map is lost. Rather than display just the zoomed portion, it is possible to save the zoomed portion of the map and then redisplay it along with the legend or some other portion of the original graph.

The detail information for the New England portion of the map is much less clear than for the Pacific Northwest. Both the New England area and the legend areas of the original map can be zoomed separately, the results saved, and then redisplayed on a single graph.

The panel coordinates used to zoom in on New England are shown in Figure 6.3.3f and in the TEMPLATE DESIGN window (Panel 1 in Display 6.3.3h). The inner rectangle indicates the portion that will be zoomed. This portion is selected because it has a lower left corner with coordinates (0,0) and an upper right corner with coordinates (100,100). Because the overall coordinates have a range of 400 in both directions, the selected portion has a width and height that is 25% of the original.

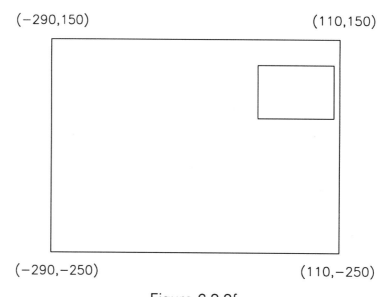

Figure 6.3.3f

The legend is zoomed in a similar fashion. The height of the inner rectangle is 5%, and it has a length of 90%. On the original graph, the legend occupies the space defined with a lower left corner of (10,7) and an upper right corner of (90,12). The legend area is, therefore, 5% high and 80% wide. This means that the vertical range for the zooming template must be 100/.05=2000, and the horizontal range will be 100/.8=125. Because the zoomed portion must have the coordinates (0,0) at the lower left corner, the panel definition has a lower left corner of (-12.5,-140).

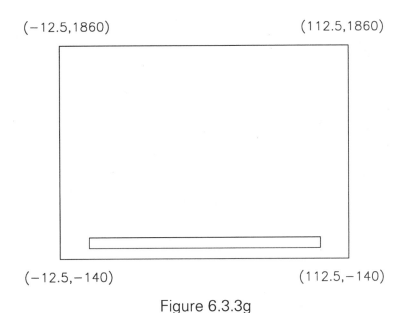

(−12.5,1860)　　　　　　　　　　　　　(112.5,1860)

(−12.5,−140)　　　　　　　　　　　　　(112.5,−140)

Figure 6.3.3g

These two panels and the two panels used to display the zoomed graphs are shown in the TEMPLATE DESIGN window in Display 6.3.3h.

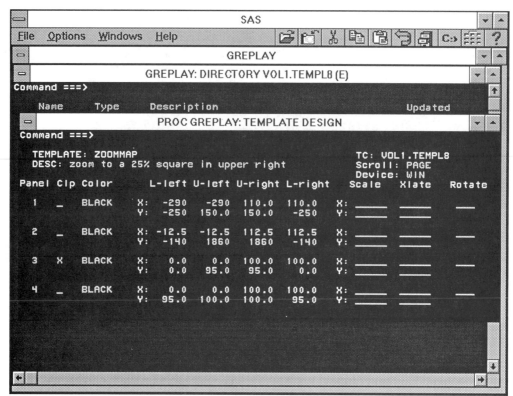

Display 6.3.3h

The following code is used to zoom the two portions of the map using the first two template panels shown in Display 6.3.3h. The MODIFY statement allows you to name the GSEG entry (the default name is TEMPLATE) that is created during the zooming process.

```
goptions nodisplay;

* zoom on new england;
proc greplay nofs
            igout=vol1.chapt6
            gout=vol1.chapt6
            tc=vol1.templ8;
template zoommap;
treplay 1:salesmap;
modify template / name = 'newengl';
run;

* zoom on the legend;
proc greplay nofs
            igout=vol1.chapt6
            gout=vol1.chapt6
            tc=vol1.templ8;
template zoommap;
treplay 2:salesmap;
modify template / name = 'e633lgnd';
run;
```

Once the two zoomed portions of the map have been created and saved, they can be used in a second GREPLAY step.

```
goptions display;
proc greplay nofs
              igout=vol1.chapt6
              tc=vol1.templ8;
template zoommap;
treplay 3:newengl
        4:e6331gnd;
run;
```

The resulting figure (Figure 6.3.3i) is shown next.

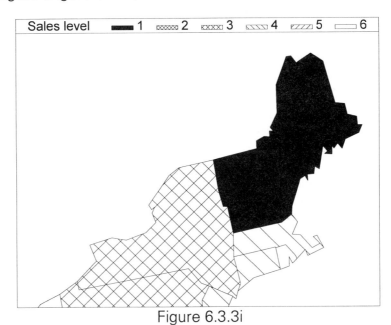

Figure 6.3.3i

MORE INFORMATION:

Carpenter, 1990 - Example zooms in on an area of a map using a template.

Kalt, 1986 - Good example of zooming a graph.

SAS Institute Inc., 1987 - Simple example of using a template to zoom a portion of a graph.

SEE ALSO:

Section 6.3.1 - Deals with shrinking a graph.

6.3.4 Controlling and displaying titles

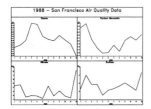

It is not unusual to display several plots on a single page by using templates and GREPLAY. Often, these plots have a common title that appears redundant if it is repeated on each panel. It is possible to create a banner title by using a separate PROC GSLIDE and then to display it in its own template panel.

Following are several ways to create and display a banner title:

- TITLE and FOOTNOTE statements, which utilize options such as ANGLE=, ROTATE=, HEIGHT=, and MOVE=

- LABEL= options in the AXIS statement

- full-sized template panel

- reduced-size template panels.

Use of TITLE, FOOTNOTE, and AXIS statements avoids the use of template panels. However, title placement using the MOVE= options can be tricky.

Using a full-sized title panel

A single, full-sized panel displays a title that has been generated using GSLIDE. Other panels display the plots or graphs of interest. Display 6.3.4a shows the definition of five panels. Notice that the first panel is full sized and that the other four have been reduced so that the top 10% of the graph is only covered by the first panel. The banner title is then displayed in this unused area.

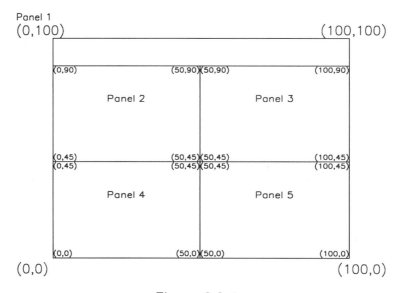

Figure 6.3.4a

The panel coordinates shown in Figure 6.3.4a are used to define the template panels in the TEMPLATE DESIGN window shown in Display 6.3.4b.

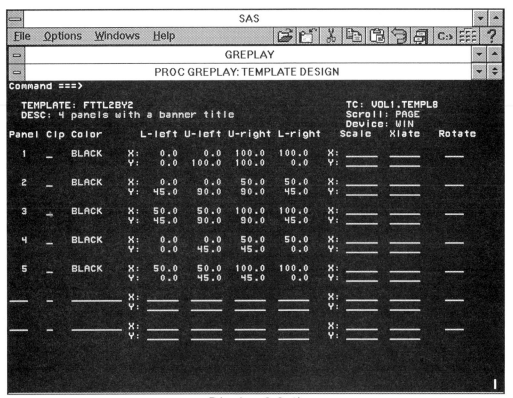

Display 6.3.4b

The following code generates four scatter plots that are saved in the catalog VOL1.CHAPT6. The NODISPLAY option is used so that the graphs are not physically plotted at this time.

```
goptions nodisplay;
proc gplot data=vol1.ca88air
           gout=vol1.chapt6;
where station='SFO';
plot o3*month / name='e634p2';
title1 h=2 f=simplex 'Ozone';
symbol c=black l=1 i=join;
run;

proc gplot data=vol1.ca88air
           gout=vol1.chapt6;
where station='SFO';
plot co*month / name='e634p3';
title1 h=2 f=simplex 'Carbon Monoxide';
run;
```

```
proc gplot data=vol1.ca88air
           gout=vol1.chapt6;
where station='SFO';
plot no3*month / name='e634p4';
title1 h=2 f=simplex 'Nitrate';
run;

proc gplot data=vol1.ca88air
           gout=vol1.chapt6;
where station='SFO';
plot so4*month / name='e634p5';
title1 h=2 f=simplex 'Sulfate';
run;
```

A banner title is then created using GSLIDE and displayed in the full panel using GREPLAY.

```
* Create the title panel;
proc gslide gout=vol1.chapt6
            name='e634full';
title1 h=2 f=duplex '1988 - San Francisco Air Quality Data';
footnote1;
run;

goptions display;
proc greplay nofs
             igout=vol1.chapt6
             tc=vol1.templ8
             template=fttl2by2 ;
treplay 1:e634full
        2:e634p2
        3:e634p3
        4:e634p4
        5:e634p5;
run;
```

This code produces Figure 6.3.4c.

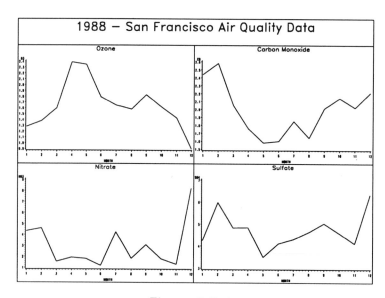

Figure 6.3.4c

MORE INFORMATION:
Carpenter, 1990 - Aspect ratios and their application to template panels is discussed.

Kalt, 1993 - Example places multiple graphs on one page with a common legend.

Redman, 1991 - Detailed example overlays four graphs with a banner title.

6.3.5 Distortion and perspective

Template panels tend to be rectangular, but they do not have to be. Nonrectangular panels can be used to distort images and create the illusion of depth perspective. These panels can often be used to good effect during presentations.

Figure 6.3.5a shows a panel (Panel 1) with its two lower corners at the extremes, while the two upper corners have been moved down and toward the center.

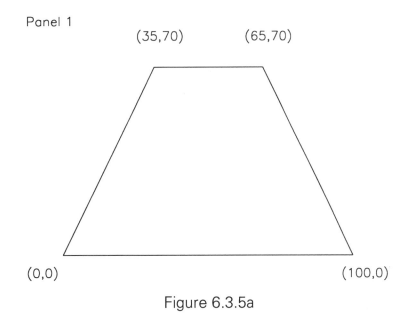

Figure 6.3.5a

These coordinates are used to create a template panel definition for the template HORIZON. The TEMPLATE DESIGN panel is shown in Display 6.3.5b.

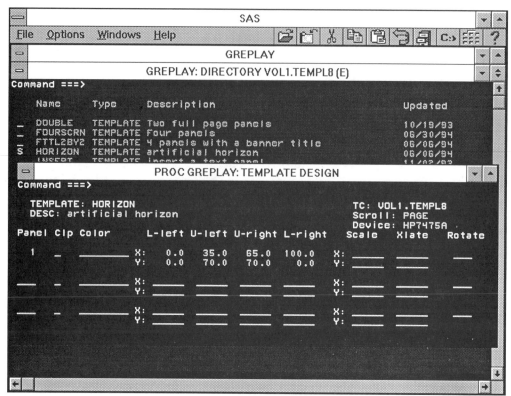

Display 6.3.5b

This panel is used with a simple GSLIDE to display the graph shown in Figure 6.3.5c.

```
goptions nodisplay;
proc gslide gout=vol1.chapt6
            name='e635';
title1 h=4 f=duplex 'Long long ago in a galaxy      ';
title2 h=4 f=duplex 'far far away there was          ';
title3 h=4 f=duplex 'fought a desperate rebellion  ';
title4 h=4 f=duplex 'against a cruel and tyrannical';
title5 h=4 f=duplex 'empire.                         ';
footnote1;
run;

goptions display;
proc greplay nofs
            igout=vol1.chapt6
            tc=vol1.templ8
            template=horizon;
treplay 1:e635;
run;
```

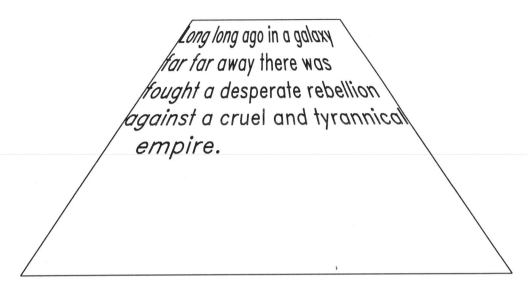

Figure 6.3.5c

Graphs can also be twisted, reversed, and otherwise distorted by manipulating the corners of the template panel.

MORE INFORMATION:
Kalt, 1986 - Examples of perspective. Article includes the template definitions.
Rooth, 1987 - Examples of different ways to use templates.

6.3.6 Using templates to cut, paste, and clip graphs

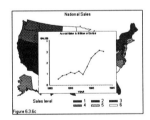

Panel coordinates need not be unique. Nor do they have to define distinct portions of the graphics page. Panels can be defined to overlap and overlay other panels. These overlapping panels can be used as legends, graphics inserts, or for artistic effect. Overlapping panels may or may not mask one another.

Ordinarily, when two or more panels overlap, the graphs from both are displayed. Clipping prevents this by allowing the display of the contents of only one panel at a time. It is as if clipping makes the panel opaque to panels behind it (panels with higher panel numbers). Clipping is requested when the template is defined in the TEMPLATE DESIGN window (or the TDEF statement).

The TEMPLATE DESIGN window shown in Display 6.3.6a defines the template INSERT, which is used in this example. Panel 1 is laid down first, and because clipping is requested (an 'X' is placed in the column labeled 'Clp'), any subsequent panels will be clipped. As is demonstrated here, it does not matter in which order the panels are defined.

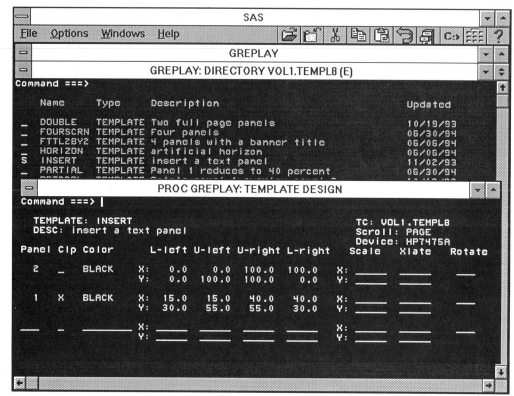

Display 6.3.6a

The following code creates a scatter plot and a text box that overlays the plot using the INSERT template:

```
goptions nodisplay;
proc gslide gout=vol1.chapt6
            name='e636txt';
title1 h=6 f=duplex 'Average Ozone  ';
title2 h=6 f=duplex 'levels exceeded';
title3 h=6 f=duplex '2.6 pphm four  ';
title4 h=6 f=duplex 'months in the  ';
title5 h=6 f=duplex 'area around    ';
title6 h=6 f=duplex 'Livermore.     ';
footnote1;
run;

proc gplot data=vol1.ca88air
           gout=vol1.chapt6;
where station='LIV';
plot o3*month / name='e636'
                vref=2.6;
title1 h=2 f=simplex '1988 Ozone Levels';
title2 h=1.5 f=simplex 'Livermore';
```

```
symbol c=black l=1 i=join v=dot;
run;

goptions display;
proc greplay nofs
             igout=vol1.chapt6
             tc=vol1.templ8
             template=insert;
treplay 1:e636txt
        2:e636;
run;
```

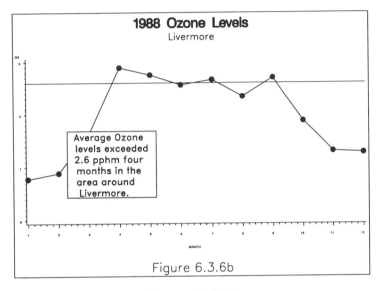

Figure 6.3.6b

The text box in the previous figure is created using PROC GSLIDE. This type of box can also be created using a TITLE statement and the BOX=1 and BLANK=YES options.

Another common use of clipping is to overlay two graphs. A series of graphs with a common background adds interest to a presentation. In Figure 6.3.6c, the map of national sales totals (Figure 6.2) is used as a background for a second graph charting the total annual revenues for the same company.

The template definition for the two panels is very similar to those shown in Display 6.3.6a. The first panel (used for the insert) allows an overlap of 20% around the margins and has the corner coordinates

- upper left (20,80)   upper right (80,80)

- lower left (20,20)   lower right (80,20)

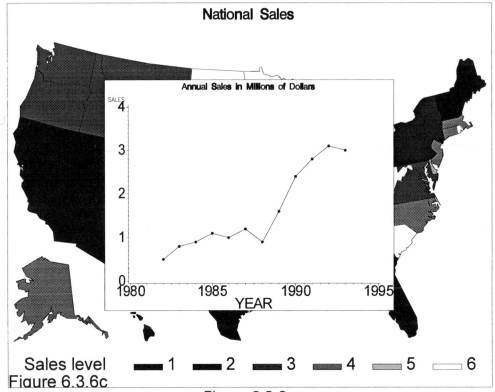

Figure 6.3.6c

MORE INFORMATION:
Carpenter, 1990 - Discusses clipping. However, examples are more
complete in Kalt, 1986.
Kalt, 1986 - Includes examples and template definitions that use clipping.
Rooth, 1987 - Examples restate those in Kalt, 1986.

6.3.7 Creating multiple plots using templates

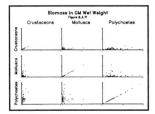

In Section 2.3.3, HPERCENT and VPERCENT are used
with PROC PLOT to split the physical page into nine plots
when using PROC PLOT. A similar plot can be generated
by using templates. The same nine graphs as were
plotted in Figure 2.3.3 are reproduced in this example
using GPLOT.

When producing a number of plots on one page, you should be aware of these factors:

- an equal number of plots both vertically and horizontally helps to preserve the aspect ratio

- as the number of plots increases, the axis labels and scales become smaller and harder to read

- axis scaling should be uniform among the plots so as not to mislead the reader

- auxiliary labels may be needed to supplement missing or reduced axis labels.

In this example, as is typical for this type of plot where the patterns are of primary interest, all of the axis labels and scales are removed. These labels are replaced with GSLIDE titles. In the plot to be generated here, nine scatter plots will be plotted on one page with space left at the top and left side for banner titles (Figure 6.3.7a).

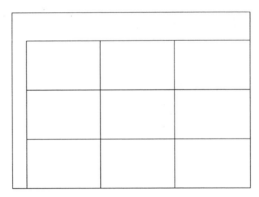

Figure 6.3.7a

The following code generates the nine scatter plots:

```
axis1 order=(0 to 2 by 1)
      label=none;

goptions nodisplay;

proc gplot data=vol1.biomass gout=vol1.chapt6;
plot bmcrus * bmcrus / name='e6371' vaxis= axis1 haxis= axis1;
plot bmcrus * bmmol  / name='e6372' vaxis= axis1 haxis= axis1;
plot bmcrus * bmpoly / name='e6373' vaxis= axis1 haxis= axis1;
plot bmmol  * bmcrus / name='e6374' vaxis= axis1 haxis= axis1;
plot bmmol  * bmmol  / name='e6375' vaxis= axis1 haxis= axis1;
plot bmmol  * bmpoly / name='e6376' vaxis= axis1 haxis= axis1;
plot bmpoly * bmcrus / name='e6377' vaxis= axis1 haxis= axis1;
```

```
plot bmpoly * bmmol  / name='e6378' vaxis= axis1 haxis= axis1;
plot bmpoly * bmpoly / name='e6379' vaxis= axis1 haxis= axis1;
title1 ' ';
footnote ' ';
run;
```

Each of the nine plots utilizes the same axis statement for both axes. This allows comparisons among the plots.

Using the MOVE= option to create the banner titles

The banner title in Figure 6.3.4d was placed on the graph using a full template panel. Using a similar approach, you can also place more complicated banner titles using TITLE statements and the MOVE= option. The trick is to place the titles using units of percent (PCT). The correct percentages are determined by inspection of the template design shown in Display 6.3.7b.

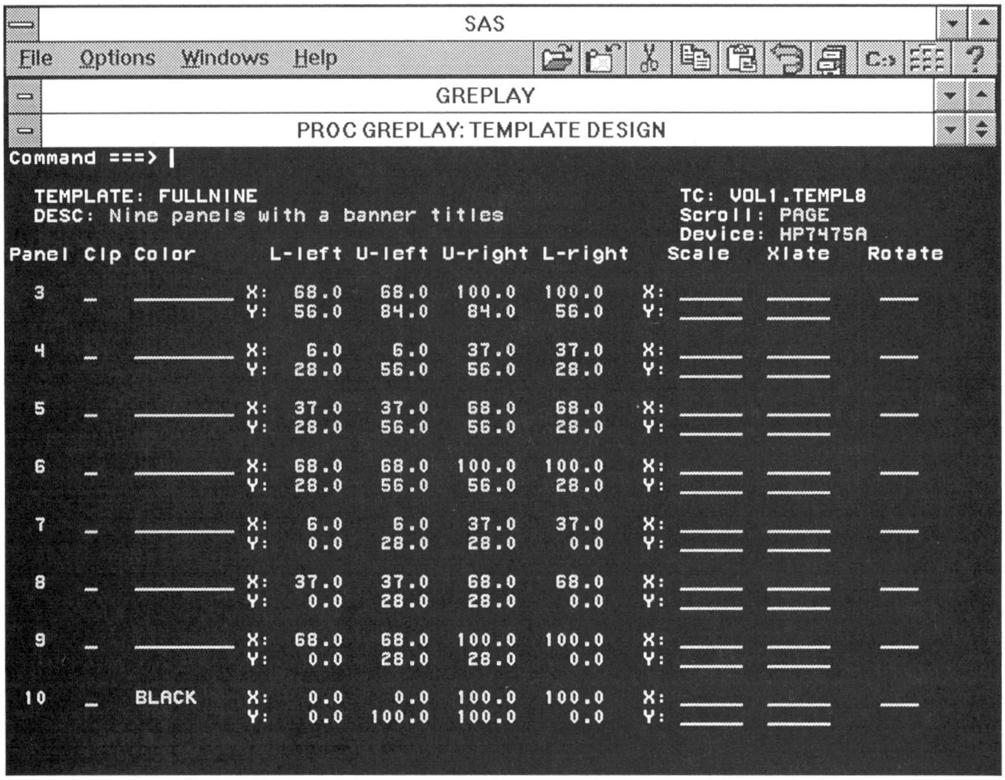

Display 6.3.7b

Inspection of the panel definitions shows that the left title margin has a width of 6% and the top a height of 16%. These panel definitions suggest the positions and heights used in the third and fourth titles in the GSLIDE.

```
* create the titles;
proc gslide gout=vol1.chapt6 name='e637ttl';
title1 'Biomass in GM Wet Weight';
title2 h=1.5 f=simplex 'Figure 6.3.7c';
* Horizontal graph labels;
```

```
title3 h=4pct f=simplex
     move=( 6,84)pct '  Crustaceans'
     move=(37,84)pct '  Molluscs'
     move=(68,84)pct '  Polychaetes';
* Vertical graph labels;
title4 h=4pct a=90 f=simplex
     move=(5,56)pct 'Crustaceans'
     move=(5,28)pct '  Molluscs'
     move=(5,0 )pct 'Polychaetes';
run;
```

The plots and the titles are combined using the following GREPLAY. Together they create Figure 6.3.7c.

```
goptions display;
proc greplay igout=vol1.chapt6 nofs
             tc=vol1.templ8
             template=fullnine;
treplay 1=e6371
        2=e6372
        3=e6373
        4=e6374
        5=e6375
        6=e6376
        7=e6377
        8=e6378
        9=e6379
       10=e637ttl;
run;
```

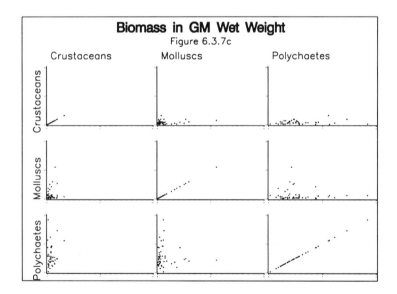

Figure 6.3.7c

SEE ALSO:
Section 2.3.3 - Creates multiple plots using PROC PLOT.
Section 6.3.4 - Examples of titles placed in template panels.

APPENDIX A   Example Databases

The programs included in Appendix A generate the data sets used throughout this book. The programs and program fragments used in the examples are presented as complete programs in Appendix B. All databases are stored and retrieved using the LIBNAME of VOL1.

Because path information and some basic system options vary among operating systems, all of the programs in Appendices A and B assume that the program SETUP.SAS has been executed. The paths and perhaps options statements should be changed before executing on your system.

The example programs and databases can be obtained in electronic form from SAS Online Samples. See the inside back cover for instructions on how to access the online samples. Example programs and databases are also available on diskette from Arthur L. Carpenter at the following address:

> California Occidental Consultants
> 4239 Serena Avenue
> Oceanside, CA 92056-5018

SETUP.SAS

Define *libref*s and paths used by the data creation (Appendix A) and example programs (Appendix B). This SAS code was used for Release 6.08 of the SAS System running under Windows. Path designations, LIBNAME, and FILENAME statements will be different for other operating systems.

```
*************************************************;
* setup.sas;
*
* Setup the libnames etc. for vol1 stuff;
*************************************************;

***********
* define the libname for path to the data sets;
libname vol1 'system specific path information';
***********
* define global options;
options nodate nonumber;
GOPTIONS BORDER NOCHARACTERS NOFILL NOCELL;
***********
* define the path to the HPGL files;
%let pathhpg = system specific path information;
```

BIOMASS.SAS

Biomass (wet weight in grams) estimates were made for several types of soft bottom benthic organisms (critters that live in the mud) over a period of several years along the southern California coast. The BIOMASS data set contains data taken from selected stations and depths during the summer of 1985. The August 5, 1985 'outlier' is a valid datum representing a core that caught a large single organism.

```
*************************************************;
* biomass.sas;
*
* Create the benthos biomass data set.
*************************************************;

data vol1.biomass;
input   @1 STATION $
        @12 DATE DATE7.
        @20 BMPOLY
        @25 BMCRUS
        @31 BMMOL
        @36 BMOTHR
        @41 BMTOTL ;

format date date7.;

label BMCRUS    = 'CRUSTACEAN BIOMASS (GM WET WEIGHT)'
      BMMOL     = 'MOLLUSC BIOMASS (GM WET WEIGHT)   '
      BMOTHR    = 'OTHER BIOMASS (GM WET WEIGHT)     '
      BMPOLY    = 'POLYCHAETE BIOMASS (GM WET WEIGHT)'
      BMTOTL    = 'TOTAL BIOMASS (GM WET WEIGHT)     '
      DATE      = 'DATE                              '
      STATION   = 'STATION ID                        ';

cards;
DL-25       18JUN85 0.4  0.03  0.17 0.02 0.62
DL-60       17JUN85 0.51 0.09  0.14 0.08 0.82
D1100-25    18JUN85 0.28 0.02  0.01 4.61 4.92
D1100-60    17JUN85 0.36 0.05  0.32 0.47 1.2
D1900-25    18JUN85 0.03 0.02  0.11 1.06 1.22
D1900-60    17JUN85 0.54 0.11  0.03 4.18 4.86
D3200-60    17JUN85 0.52 0.14  0.04 0.05 0.75
D3350-25    18JUN85 0.18 0.02  0.11 0    0.31
D6700-25    18JUN85 0.51 0.06  0.03 0.01 0.61
D6700-60    17JUN85 0.32 0.14  0.04 0.22 0.72
D700-25     18JUN85 0.23 0.03  0.02 0.07 0.35
D700-60     17JUN85 1.11 0.32  0.07 0.02 1.52
DL-25       10JUL85 0.92 0.09  0.1  0.03 1.14
DL-60       09JUL85 0.29 0.14  0.03 0.06 0.52
D1100-25    10JUL85 0.14 0.05  0.05 4.79 5.03
D1100-60    09JUL85 0.88 0.07  0.01 0.01 0.97
D1900-25    10JUL85 0.35 0.05  0.05 1.82 2.27
D1900-60    09JUL85 0.87 0.08  0.42 3.35 4.72
D3200-60    09JUL85 0.22 0.1   0.08 0.01 0.41
D3350-25    10JUL85 0.36 0.06  0.01 0.02 0.45
D6700-25    10JUL85 1.84 0.02  0.11 0.05 2.02
```

```
D6700-60    09JUL85 0.47 0.19   0.06 0.06 0.78
D700-25     10JUL85 1.46 0.19   0.12 0.38 2.15
D700-60     09JUL85 0.48 0.18   0.02 0.11 0.79
DL-25       05AUG85 0.92 0.08   0.09 0.02 1.11
DL-60       02AUG85 0.4  0.1    0.59 0.5  1.59
D1100-25    05AUG85 0.18 0.02   0.36 2.33 2.89
D1100-60    02AUG85 0.39 0.12   0.03 0.01 0.55
D1900-25    05AUG85 1.23 0.06   0.04 2.15 3.48
D1900-60    02AUG85 0.56 0.07   0.02 0.11 0.76
D3200-60    02AUG85 0.39 0.11   0.05 0.02 0.57
D3350-25    05AUG85 0.45 44.82  0.02 0.16 45.45
D6700-25    05AUG85 1.13 0.01   0.11 0.04 1.29
D6700-60    02AUG85 0.43 0.15   1.1  0.01 1.69
D700-25     05AUG85 0.31 0.02   0.26 0.03 0.62
D700-60     02AUG85 0.38 0.07   0.12 1.87 2.44
DL-25       26AUG85 0.57 0.01   0.14 0.04 0.76
DL-60       27AUG85 0.46 0.05   0.5  0.18 1.19
D1100-25    26AUG85 0.63 0.02   0.04 0.03 0.72
D1100-60    27AUG85 0.57 0.04   0.09 0.31 1.01
D1900-25    26AUG85 0.26 0.03   0.01 3.89 4.19
D1900-60    27AUG85 0.73 0.07   0.06 0.09 0.95
D3200-60    27AUG85 0.46 0.07   0.02 0.01 0.56
D3350-25    26AUG85 0.57 0.02   0.05 0.05 0.69
D6700-25    26AUG85 0.87 0.01   0.03 0.02 0.93
D6700-60    27AUG85 0.69 0.07   0.03 0.01 0.8
D700-25     26AUG85 0.48 0.19   0.53 0.62 1.82
D700-60     27AUG85 0.25 0.09   0.07 0.01 0.42
run;
```

CA88AIR.SAS

Air quality data was collected from three monitoring sites in California during 1988. The monthly averages for temperature (TEM), humidity (HUM), nitrate (NO3), sulfate (SO4), ozone (O3), and carbon monoxide (CO) concentrations are recorded.

```
**************************************************;
* ca88air.sas
*
* create the SAS data set CA88AIR;
**************************************************;

data vol1.ca88air;
input @1  O3
      @6  CO
      @11 NO3
      @17 SO4
      @22 TEM
      @28 HUM
      @34 DATE
      @40 STATION $3.
      @44 MONTH
  ;
```

```
format date date7.;
cards;
1.58 1.35 10.96 3.18 54.9  59.5  10241 AZU 1
2.77 1.25 12.73 2.96 60.2  58.5  10272 AZU 2
3.59 1.26 15.5  6.11 62.8  58    10301 AZU 3
3.48 1.05 15.01 4.69 63.4  72.75 10332 AZU 4
4.53 0.95 19.69 6.06 67.6  70    10362 AZU 5
3.8  0.93 17.48 7.68 69    74.75 10393 AZU 6
4.84 0.97 19.32 9.41 76.5  79.5  10423 AZU 7
4.33 1.3  18.06 8.84 74.5  78.75 10454 AZU 8
3.95 1.46 17.36 7.95 72.9  75.75 10485 AZU 9
3.18 1.76 22.81 8.93 70.1  76.25 10515 AZU 10
2.18 1.71 14.22 5.59 60    70.75 10546 AZU 11
1.9  0.99 8.7   2.58 54.6  56.5  10576 AZU 12
0.78 1.36 5     2.78 51.9  .     10241 LIV 1
0.89 1.28 8.13  3.7  56.5  .     10272 LIV 2
1.64 0.98 3.58  3.63 59.1  .     10301 LIV 3
2.89 0.94 3.28  3.28 59    .     10332 LIV 4
2.75 0.89 2.6   2.6  59.9  .     10362 LIV 5
2.56 0.84 2.95  2.71 62.7  .     10393 LIV 6
2.66 0.88 3.74  3.72 65.1  .     10423 LIV 7
2.34 0.88 4.63  3.59 65.41 .     10454 LIV 8
2.7  1.06 4.18  3.9  62.1  .     10485 LIV 9
1.88 1.14 6.03  3.99 59.6  .     10515 LIV 10
1.31 1.08 1.94  2.38 54.5  .     10546 LIV 11
1.28 1.45 4.85  2.38 49.8  .     10576 LIV 12
1.28 2.44 4.34  4.25 50.6  77.75 10241 SFO 1
1.38 2.58 4.6   5.98 54.5  70.75 10272 SFO 2
1.6  2.05 1.56  4.83 56.5  68    10301 SFO 3
2.39 1.76 1.93  4.84 58.1  68    10332 SFO 4
2.35 1.58 1.82  3.5  59.5  69.5  10362 SFO 5
1.79 1.6  1.2   4.11 62.5  70    10393 SFO 6
1.65 1.85 4.25  4.31 65.3  72.75 10423 SFO 7
1.58 1.64 1.84  4.63 65    72.75 10454 SFO 8
1.83 2.01 3.08  5.03 63.1  75.25 10485 SFO 9
1.62 2.14 1.81  4.58 61.4  80.25 10515 SFO 10
1.43 2.02 1.33  4.11 56.5  78    10546 SFO 11
0.9  2.21 8.23  6.33 50.4  74.75 10576 SFO 12
run;
```

DOW.SAS

These data are taken from the PC Version 6.04 SAS Sample Library (with the alteration of one value). The data represent the high, low, and closing values of the Dow Jones Stock Market Index during the month of August 1981.

```
****************************************************;
* dow.sas;
*
* create the data set of high, low, and closing
* stock market volume in thousands of shares.
****************************************************;
```

```
* this data is adapted from an example in the SAS Sample
* Library;
**************************************************************
*             S A S   S A M P L E   L I B R A R Y         *
*    NAME: TIMEPLT1                                        *
*    TITLE: STOCK MARKET REPORTING USING PROC TIMEPLOT *
**************************************************************;

data vol1.dow;
input date date7. volume high low close;
label volume='volume in thousands of shares';
format date date7.;
cards;
03AUG81 3219.3 955.48 940.45 946.25
04AUG81 2938.5 951.39 937.40 945.97
05AUG81 4177.8 958.81 942.16 953.58
06AUG81 3975.7 961.47 947.30 892.91
07AUG81 3884.3 954.15 938.45 942.54
10AUG81 2937.7 948.82 935.88 943.68
11AUG81 5262.9 955.48 939.50 949.30
12AUG81 4005.2 955.86 942.26 945.21
13AUG81 3680.8 952.91 938.55 944.35
14AUG81 3714.1 947.77 933.79 936.93
17AUG81 3432.7 939.40 924.37 926.75
18AUG81 4396.7 932.74 916.38 924.37
19AUG81 3517.3 932.08 918.38 926.46
20AUG81 3811.9 935.31 923.52 928.37
21AUG81 2625.9 930.65 917.14 920.57
24AUG81 4736.1 917.43 896.97 900.11
25AUG81 4714.4 904.30 887.46 901.83
26AUG81 3279.6 908.39 893.65 899.26
27AUG81 3676.1 900.49 883.66 889.08
28AUG81 3024.2 898.78 884.80 892.22
;
run;
```

H2OQUAL.SAS

Water quality data was collected during the first six months of 1993 from a
shallow lagoon on the southern California coast. Physical parameters collected
include water depth, temperature, pH, dissolved oxygen, conductivity, and
salinity. Only two stations and one sample time per sample date are included in
this data set.

```
**************************************************;
* h2oqual.sas;
*
* 1993 Water quality data.
**************************************************;
```

```
data vol1.h2oqual
    (keep=datetime station depth temp ph do cond salinity);
input datetime datetime13. @15 station $3.
    depth temp ph do cond salinity;
label datetime = 'date and time of sample collection'
    station  = 'station'
    depth    = 'water depth (ft)'
    temp     = 'temperature (C)'
    ph       = 'pH'
    do       = 'dissolved oxygen'
    cond     = 'conductivity'
    salinity = 'salinity';
format datetime datetime13.;
cards;
06FEB93:09:15 TS3 0 13.6 7.9 8.8 20.3 12.1
06FEB93:09:15 TS3 1 13.5 7.9 8.7 20.4 12.2
06FEB93:09:15 TS3 2 13.5 7.88 8.7 22.1 13.3
06FEB93:09:15 TS3 3 14.1 8.05 9 46.2 29.9
06FEB93:09:15 TS3 4 14.2 8.05 8.9 48.1 31.3
10FEB93:11:51 TS3 0 13.9 7.91 9.5 0.57 0.27
10FEB93:11:51 TS3 1 13.9 7.89 9.5 0.57 0.27
10FEB93:11:51 TS3 2 13.9 7.88 9.4 0.57 0.27
10FEB93:11:51 TS3 3 13.8 7.88 9.5 0.57 0.27
10FEB93:11:51 TS3 4 13.8 7.87 9.4 0.56 0.27


        . . . . . . . . . . . . . . . .
        Not all of the data are included in this appendix
        . . . . . . . . . . . . . . . .


04JUN93:07:20 TS6 0 18.8 8.05 3.6 52.2 34.4
04JUN93:07:20 TS6 1 18.7 8.05 3.6 52.7 34.7
04JUN93:07:20 TS6 2 18.8 8.04 3.5 51.6 33.9
04JUN93:07:20 TS6 3 18.8 8.04 3.4 51.6 33.9
11JUN93:11:42 TS6 0 26.2 8.1 6.3 53 34.9
11JUN93:11:42 TS6 1 26.1 8.1 6.2 53 34.9
11JUN93:11:42 TS6 2 26.1 8.08 6 52.9 34.9
11JUN93:11:42 TS6 3 26.1 8.08 6 53 34.9
16JUN93:15:00 TS6 0 25.9 8.11 8.3 51.6 33.9
16JUN93:15:00 TS6 2 25.8 8.12 8.3 51.3 33.7
16JUN93:15:00 TS6 4 25.6 8.12 8.2 52.1 34.3
run;
```

LAMPARA.SAS

A Lampara net is used in ocean fishing in coastal waters. For this study, it was used to collect data for a number of species over a 12-year period. The data contained here represent the LENGTH and SEX data for one species collected during the summer of 1986.

```
*************************************************;
* lampara.sas;
*
* Create the White Croaker Lampara net length data.
*************************************************;

data vol1.lampara;

input @1 DATE DATE8.
      @10 LENGTH 3.
      @14 SEX $1.
;

format date date7.;

label date   = 'sample date'
      length = 'fish length in mm'
      sex    = 'fish sex (F, M, U)';

cards;
 13MAY86 149 F
 13MAY86 180 M
 13MAY86 174 M
 22MAY86 131 M
 22MAY86 114 M

        .................
        Not all of the data are included in this appendix
        .................

 13AUG86 142 M
 13AUG86 135 M
 13AUG86 142 U
 13AUG86 141 U
;
run;
```

SALESMAP.SAS

Sales data for a national travel agency are compiled by state. The variable CODE is used to indicate business share (CODE=1 indicates the greatest business activity).

```
*************************************************;
* salesmap.sas;
*
* Create a map of sales levels in the US.
*************************************************;
```

```
data vol1.salesmap;
input stcode $2. state 3. code 3. ;

label stcode = 'State code'
      state  = 'state number'
      code   = 'Sales level';

cards;
AL  1    2    ALABAMA
AK  2    4    ALASKA
AZ  4    1    ARIZONA
AR  5    6    ARKANSAS
CA  6    1    CALIFORNIA
CO  8    1    COLORADO
CT  9    4    CONNECTICUT
DE 10    5    DELAWARE
DC 11    3    DISTRICT OF COLUMBIA
FL 12    1    FLORIDA
GA 13    1    GEORGIA
HI 15    1    HAWAII
ID 16    3    IDAHO
IL 17    2    ILLINOIS
IN 18    2    INDIANA
IA 19    4    IOWA
KS 20    1    KANSAS
KY 21    2    KENTUCKY
LA 22    1    LOUISIANA
ME 23    1    MAINE
MD 24    3    MARYLAND
MA 25    4    MASSACHUSETTS
MI 26    4    MICHIGAN
MN 27    6    MINNESOTA
MS 28    2    MISSISSIPPI
MO 29    2    MISSOURI
MT 30    3    MONTANA
NE 31    4    NEBRASKA
NV 32    1    NEVADA
NH 33    1    NEW HAMPSHIRE
NJ 34    4    NEW JERSEY
NM 35    2    NEW MEXICO
NY 36    2    NEW YORK
NC 37    4    NORTH CAROLINA
ND 38    6    NORTH DAKOTA
OH 39    6    OHIO
OK 40    2    OKLAHOMA
OR 41    3    OREGON
PA 42    2    PENNSYLVANIA
RI 44    6    RHODE ISLAND
SC 45    6    SOUTH CAROLINA
SD 46    4    SOUTH DAKOTA
TN 47    1    TENNESSEE
TX 48    1    TEXAS
UT 49    1    UTAH
VT 50    1    VERMONT
VA 51    3    VIRGINIA
WA 53    3    WASHINGTON
WV 54    6    WEST VIRGINIA
WI 55    6    WISCONSIN
WY 56    1    WYOMING
run;
```

APPENDIX B   Example Programs

The programs included in Appendix A generate the data sets used throughout this book. The programs and program fragments used in the examples are presented as complete programs in Appendix B. All databases are stored and retrieved using the LIBNAME of VOL1.

Because path information and some basic system options vary among operating systems, all of the programs in Appendices A and B assume that the program SETUP.SAS has been executed. The paths and perhaps options statements should be changed before executing on your system.

Most of the examples in this book were generated using DEVICE=HP7475A. Unless you use the same device, you need to change this option when you execute the programs in this appendix. Remember, we used Release 6.08 of the SAS System under the Windows environment to generate and test the examples in this book. Therefore, the form of the file-name designation will be somewhat different for your system. Also, if the graphic is to be sent directly to the plotter, the FILENAME statement and the GSNAME= and GSMODE= options are not needed.

The example programs and databases can be obtained in electronic form from the authors and from SAS Online Samples. See the inside back cover for instructions on how to access the online samples.

SETUP.SAS

Define *libref*s and paths used by the data creation (Appendix A) and example programs (Appendix B). This SAS code was used for SAS Release 6.08 running under Windows. Path designations, LIBNAME, and FILENAME statements will be different for other operating systems.

```
***************************************************;
* setup.sas;
*
* Setup the libnames etc. for vol1 stuff;
***************************************************;

***********
* define the libname for path to the data sets;
libname vol1 'system specific path information';
***********
* define global options;
options nodate nonumber;
GOPTIONS BORDER NOCHARACTERS NOFILL NOCELL;
***********
* define the path to the HPGL files;
%let pathhpg = system specific path information;
```

Figure 1.4.1   Demonstrate PROC GTESTIT

```
**************************************************;
* e1_4_1.sas;
*
* Demonstrate the use of PROC GTESTIT;
**************************************************;

FILENAME fileref "&pathhpg\e1_4_1.hpg";
GOPTIONS GSFNAME=fileref DEVICE=hp7475a GSFMODE=replace
noprompt;

proc gtestit pic=1;
run;
```

Figure 1.4.2   Demonstrate HPOS and VPOS

```
**************************************************;
* e1_4_2.sas;
*
* Demonstrate the use of HPOS and VPOS;
**************************************************;

FILENAME fileref "&pathhpg\e1_4_2.hpg";
GOPTIONS GSFNAME=fileref DEVICE=hp7475a GSFMODE=replace
noprompt;

goptions hpos=50 vpos=20;

proc gtestit pic=1;
run;
```

Figure 1.4.3b   Increasing VPOS and HPOS

```
**************************************************;
* e1_4_3b.sas;
*
* Increasing VPOS and HPOS to fit a block chart;
**************************************************;

FILENAME fileref "&pathhpg\e1_4_3b.hpg";
GOPTIONS GSFNAME=fileref DEVICE=hp7475a GSFMODE=replace
noprompt;
goptions vpos=80 hpos=200 htext=2;

proc gchart data=vol1.ca88air;
title1 h=4 'Block Chart of Average Carbon Monoxide';
footnote j=1 h=4 f=simplex 'Figure 1.4.3b';
block month / sumvar=co type=mean
              group=station discrete;
run;
```

Figure 1.4.4   Demonstrate the TARGETDEVICE GOPTION

```
**************************************************;
* e1_4_4.sas;
*
* Demonstrate the use of the TARGETDEVICE goption;
**************************************************;

FILENAME fileref "&pathhpg\e1_4_4.hpg";
GOPTIONS GSFNAME=fileref DEVICE=hp7475a GSFMODE=replace
noprompt
         targetdevice=win;
proc gtestit pic=1;
run;
quit;
```

Figure 2.2   Plotting with PROC UNIVARIATE

```
**************************************************;
* e2_2.sas;
*
* Demonstrate the use of PROC UNIVARIATE;
**************************************************;

proc univariate data=vol1.h2oqual plot;
var temp;
title1 'Water Temperature';
footnote1 j=l 'Figure 2.2';
run;
```

Figure 2.3   A Simple PROC PLOT

```
**************************************************;
* e2_3.sas;
*
* Demonstrate the use of PROC PLOT;
**************************************************;

proc plot data=vol1.ca88air;
plot o3 * month;
title1 '1988 Air Quality Data - Ozone';
footnote 'Figure 2.3';
run;
```

Figure 2.3.1   PROC PLOT Axis Control

```
**************************************************;
* e2_3_1.sas;
*
* Demonstrate the use of PROC PLOT axis control;
**************************************************;

proc plot data=vol1.ca88air;
plot o3 * month / vaxis= 0 to 5 by 1 vexpand vref=4;
title1 '1988 Air Quality Data - Ozone';
footnote1 'Figure 2.3.1';
run;
```

Figure 2.3.2a   PROC PLOT Overlay with the PLOT Statement

```
**************************************************;
* e2_3_2a.sas;
*
* Demonstrate the use of PROC PLOT overlay;
**************************************************;

proc plot data=vol1.ca88air;
plot o3 * month = station;
footnote1 'Figure 2.3.2a';
title1 '1988 Air Quality Data - Ozone';
run;
```

Figure 2.3.2b   PROC PLOT Overlay With the OVERLAY Option

```
**************************************************;
* e2_3_2b.sas;
*
* Demonstrate the use of PROC PLOT overlay;
**************************************************;

proc plot data=vol1.ca88air;
plot o3 * month = 'O' co * month = 'C' / overlay;
where station='SFO';
footnote1 'Figure 2.3.2b';
title1 '1988 Air Quality Data - SFO';
run;
```

Figure 2.3.3   PROC PLOT Multiple Plots Per Page

```
**************************************************;
* e2_3_3.sas;
*
* Place multiple plots per page;
**************************************************;

options linesize=110 pagesize=50;

proc plot data=vol1.biomass hpercent=33 vpercent=33;
plot bmcrus * bmcrus / vaxis= 0 to 2 by 1 haxis= 0 to 2 by 1;
plot bmcrus * bmmol  / vaxis= 0 to 2 by 1 haxis= 0 to 2 by 1;
plot bmcrus * bmpoly / vaxis= 0 to 2 by 1 haxis= 0 to 2 by 1;
plot bmmol  * bmcrus / vaxis= 0 to 2 by 1 haxis= 0 to 2 by 1;
plot bmmol  * bmmol  / vaxis= 0 to 2 by 1 haxis= 0 to 2 by 1;
plot bmmol  * bmpoly / vaxis= 0 to 2 by 1 haxis= 0 to 2 by 1;
plot bmpoly * bmcrus / vaxis= 0 to 2 by 1 haxis= 0 to 2 by 1;
plot bmpoly * bmmol  / vaxis= 0 to 2 by 1 haxis= 0 to 2 by 1;
plot bmpoly * bmpoly / vaxis= 0 to 2 by 1 haxis= 0 to 2 by 1;

footnote1 'Figure 2.3.3';
title1 'Biomass in GM Wet Weight';
run;
```

Figure 2.4a   TIMEPLOT on Sequence Data

```
**************************************************;
* e2_4a.sas;
*
* Use PROC TIMEPLOT to explore the data;
**************************************************;

options ps=50;

proc timeplot data=vol1.dow;
plot low close high/overlay hiloc ref=mean(low);
id date volume;
format volume 6.1 high low close 6.2;
title1 'PROC TIMEPLOT';
footnote1 'Figure 2.4a';
run;
```

Figure 2.4b   TIMEPLOT on Non-sequence Data

```
**************************************************;
* e2_4b.sas;
*
* Use PROC TIMEPLOT to explore the data;
**************************************************;
```

```
options ps=50;

proc timeplot data=vol1.biomass;
plot bmpoly='P' bmcrus='C' /overlay;
where '01aug85'd le date le '31aug85'd;
id date station;
title1 'PROC TIMEPLOT Biomass Data';
footnote1 'Figure 2.4b';
run;
```

Figure 2.5   PROC PLOT Scatter Plot

```
**************************************************;
* e2_5.sas
*
* Create scatter plot prior to the use of PROC REG.
**************************************************;

proc plot data=vol1.h2oqual;
by station;
where depth=0 & station='TS6';
plot ph  * do  ;
title1 'Scatter plot prior to PROC REG';
footnote1 'Figure 2.5';
run;
```

Figure 2.5.1   Plotting with PROC REG

```
**************************************************;
* e2_5_1.sas
*
* Using PROC REG to display relationships.
**************************************************;
proc reg data=vol1.h2oqual;
by station;
where depth=0 & station='TS6';
id datetime;
model ph = do / influence;
plot ph * do;
title1 'Regression of pH and dissolved oxygen';
footnote1 'Figure 2.5.1';
run;
```

Figure 2.5.2   PROC REG - Painting a Point

```
**************************************************;
* e2_5_2.sas
*
* Using PROC REG to display relationships.
* PAINT statement.
**************************************************;

proc reg data=vol1.h2oqual;
by station;
where depth=0 & station='TS6';
id datetime;
model ph = do / influence;
paint datetime = '01apr93:13:40:0'dt;
plot ph * do;
title1 'Regression of pH and dissolved oxygen';
title2 'Paint sample taken 01Apr93 at 13:40';
footnote1 'Figure 2.5.2';
run;
```

Figure 3.2.1   Hardware Fonts

```
****************************************************;
* e3_2_1.sas;
*
* Demonstrate machine fonts and their control;
****************************************************;

FILENAME fileref "&pathhpg\e3_2_1.hpg";
GOPTIONS GSFNAME=fileref DEVICE=hp7475a GSFMODE=replace
noprompt;

proc gslide;
title1 'Figure 3.2.1  title1 defaults: h=2 f=swiss';
title4 h=2 f=none
        'title4 with h=2 & f=none     (hardware font)';
title5 h=2 f=simplex
        'title5 with h=2 & f=simplex  (Software font)';
run;
quit;
```

Figure 3.2.2   Title Options

```
****************************************************;
* e3_2_2.sas;
*
* Demonstrate title options (color, font, and height);
****************************************************;

FILENAME fileref "&pathhpg\e3_2_2.hpg";
GOPTIONS GSFNAME=fileref DEVICE=hp7475a GSFMODE=replace
noprompt;

proc gslide;
title1 'Figure 3.2.2';
title2 h=3 font=swissb 'swissb' color=red f=cartog 'J K L M N';
title3 h=1 f=simplex 'H1' h=2 'H2' h=4 'H4';
run;
```

Figure 3.2.3   Using JUSTIFY to Split a Title

```
****************************************************;
* e3_2_3.sas;
*
* Using the JUSTIFY= option to split a title;
****************************************************;

FILENAME fileref "&pathhpg\e3_2_3.hpg";
GOPTIONS GSFNAME=fileref DEVICE=hp7475a GSFMODE=replace
noprompt;

proc gslide;
title1 h=1.5 justify=left 'Figure 3.2.3'
        justify=l   'second line on left which is a long
segment'
        j=l            'third line on title1'
        j=center    'fourth center top'
        j=c           'fifth in conflict with second'
        j=right      'sixth top right';
title2 'This is the second title';
run;
```

Figure 3.2.4a   Using the ANGLE= and ROTATE= Title Options

```
****************************************************;
* e3_2_4a.sas;
*
* Use of the ANGLE= title option;
****************************************************;

FILENAME filerefa "&pathhpg\e3_2_4a.hpg";
GOPTIONS GSFNAME=filerefa DEVICE=hp7475a GSFMODE=replace
noprompt;

goptions htext=2;
proc gplot data=vol1.ca88air;
plot o3 * month;
title1 '1988 Air Quality Data - Ozone';
title2 angle=90 'OZONE levels at three locations';
title3 angle=90 ' ';
footnote1 angle=-90 rotate=90 'Figure 3.2.4a';
run;
```

Figure 3.2.4b   Using the ANGLE= and ROTATE= AXIS Options

```
****************************************************;
* e3_2_4b.sas;
*
* Use of the ANGLE= title option;
****************************************************;

FILENAME filerefb "&pathhpg\e3_2_4b.hpg";
GOPTIONS GSFNAME=filerefb DEVICE=hp7475a GSFMODE=replace
noprompt;

goptions htext=2;
axis1 label = (f=simplex angle=90 ' '
        j=c angle=90 h=1.1 'Ozone levels at three
locations'
        j=c angle=-90 rotate=90 'Figure 3.2.4b' );

proc gplot data=vol1.ca88air;
plot o3 * month / vaxis=axis1;
title1 '1988 Air Quality Data - Ozone';
footnote1 ;
run;
```

Figure 3.2.5   Superscripts and Subscripts in Titles

```
****************************************************;
* e3_2_5.sas;
*
* Create a subscript and a superscript in a title;
****************************************************;

FILENAME fileref "&pathhpg\e3_2_5.hpg";
GOPTIONS GSFNAME=fileref DEVICE=hp7475a GSFMODE=replace
noprompt;

proc gslide;
title1 'Figure 3.2.5';
title2 f=duplex
        h=6 'Volume is m'
        h=4 move=(+0,+2) '3'
        h=6 move=(+0,-2)  'of H'
        h=4 move=(+0,-2) '2'
        h=6 move=(+0,+2) 'O';
run;
```

Figure 3.2.6   Inserting BY Values in Titles

```
**************************************************;
* e3_2_6.sas;
*
* Inserting BY values into text;
**************************************************;

FILENAME fileref   "&pathhpg\e3_2_6.hpg";
GOPTIONS GSFNAME=fileref  DEVICE=hp7475a GSFMODE=replace
noprompt;
options nobyline;

goptions htext=2;
proc gplot data=vol1.ca88air nocache;
by station;
plot o3 * month;
title1 '1988 Air Quality Data - Ozone';
title2 h=2 f=simplex 'Plots separated by #byvar1';
title3 h=2 f=simplex 'OZONE levels at #byval(station)';
footnote1 j=l h=2 f=simplex 'Figure 3.2.6';
run;
```

Figure 3.3.1a   Logarithmic Scales

```
**************************************************;
* e3_3_1a.sas;
*
* Use the LOGSTYLE=EXPAND option in the AXIS statement.
**************************************************;

FILENAME fileref "&pathhpg\e3_3_1a.hpg";
GOPTIONS GSFNAME=fileref DEVICE=hp7475a GSFMODE=replace
noprompt;
goptions htext=1.5;

data logdata;
do x = -1 to 3 by .1;
  y= 10 ** x;
  output;
end;

axis1 logstyle=expand logbase=10;

proc gplot data=logdata;
plot y * x;
plot y * x / vaxis=axis1;
symbol1 v=none i=join l=1;
title1 'Y = 10' move=(+0,+.5) 'X';
footnote1 j=l h=2 'Figure 3.3.1a';
run;
quit;
```

Figure 3.3.1b   Creating LOG Graph Paper

```
**************************************************;
* e3_3_1b.sas;
*
* Create log graph paper using LOGSTYLE and LOGEXPAND.
**************************************************;

FILENAME fileref "&pathhpg\e3_3_1b.hpg";
GOPTIONS GSFNAME=fileref DEVICE=hp7475a GSFMODE=replace
noprompt;
goptions htext=2;

* define the base as a macro variable;
%let base = 10;
%let min = -1;
%let max = 2;

* create a set of points to plot;
* the variables min and max define the range of the Y axis;
data logdata;
* loop defines major ticks;
do power = &min to &max by 1;
```

```
  y= &base ** power;
  linetype=1;                * major ticks get solid line;
  h=1; output;               * define the left and right;
  h=2; output;               * points for each horizontal
line;
  h=.; output;               * missing value breaks line;
  linetype=2;                * minor ticks get dashed line;
  hold=y;
  do j = 2 to 9;             * loop defines minor ticks;
    y=hold*j;
    h=1; output;
    h=2; output;
    h=.; output;
  end;
end;
run;

* horizontal axis statement;
axis1 minor = (n=4 h=1)
      label = none
      major = (n=6 h=1.5)
      value = none;

* vertical axis statement;
* note n=8 for minor ticks (not 9);
axis2 logstyle=expand logbase=&base
      minor = (n=8 h=1)
      major = (h=1.5)
      value = (f=simplex h=1.5)
      label = none;

proc gplot data=logdata ;
plot y * h = linetype / skipmiss
                        nolegend
                        haxis=axis1
                        vaxis=axis2
                        href=1.0 1.2 1.4 1.6 1.8 2.0;
symbol1 v=none i=join l=1 c=black;
symbol2 v=none i=join l=2 c=black;
title1 "Log Paper (Base &base)";
footnote1 j=l h=1.5 f=simplex 'Figure 3.3.1b';
run;
quit;
```

Figure 3.3.1c   Plotting on LOG Scale Graph Paper

```
**************************************************;
* e3_3_1c.sas;
*
* Plot crustacean biomass using log scales.
**************************************************;

FILENAME fileref "&pathhpg\e3_3_1c.hpg";
GOPTIONS GSFNAME=fileref DEVICE=hp7475a GSFMODE=replace
noprompt;
goptions htext=2;

* define the base as a macro variable;
%let base = 10;
%let min = -2;
%let max = 1;

data bio (keep=date bmcrus linetype)
     minmax (keep=mindate maxdate);
set vol1.biomass (keep=date bmcrus station) end=eof;
retain mindate 999999 maxdate 0 linetype 3;
where station='D3350-25';
output bio;
mindate = min(mindate, date);
maxdate = max(maxdate, date);
if eof then output minmax;
run;

* create a set of points to plot;
* the variables min and max define the range of the Y axis;
data logdata;
set minmax;
* loop defines major ticks;
```

```
do power = &min to &max by 1;
  y= &base ** power;
  linetype=1;              * major ticks get solid line;
  date=mindate; output;        * define the left and right;
  date=maxdate; output;        * points for each horizontal line;
  date=.;         output;      * missing value breaks
line;
  linetype=2;              * minor ticks get dashed line;
  hold=y;
  do j = 2 to 9;          * loop defines minor ticks;
    y=hold*j;
    date=mindate; output;
    date=maxdate; output;
    date=.; output;
  end;
end;
run;

data pltdata;
set logdata (rename=(y=bmcrus)) bio;
run;

* vertical axis statement;
* note n=8 for minor ticks (not 9);
axis1 logstyle=expand logbase=&base
      minor = (n=8 h=1)
      major = (h=1.5)
      value = (f=simplex h=1.5)
      label = none;

axis2 value = (f=simplex h=1.5);

proc gplot data=pltdata ;
plot bmcrus * date = linetype / skipmiss
                    nolegend
                    vaxis=axis1;
                    haxis=axis2
symbol1 v=none i=join l=1 c=black;
symbol2 v=none i=join l=2 c=black;
symbol3 v=dot  i=join l=1 c=black;
title1 "Crustacean Biomass";
footnote1 j=l h=1.5 f=simplex 'Figure 3.1.1c';
run;
quit;
```

Figure 3.3.2   Working with Tick Mark Strings

```
*****************************************************;
* e3_3_2.sas;
*
* Assigning tick mark text using VALUE=;
*****************************************************;

FILENAME fileref "&pathhpg\e3_3_2.hpg";
GOPTIONS GSFNAME=fileref DEVICE=hp7475a GSFMODE=replace
noprompt;

* define the vertical axis ;
axis1 label = (f=duplex h=1 a=90 'Ozone Level')
      order = (0 to 3 by 1)
      minor = (n=1)
      value = (t=3 h=1 'Alert');

* define the horizontal axis ;
axis2 label = (f=duplex h=1 'Monthly Average')
      minor = none
      value = (h=1.5 f=simplex t=1 'Jan'  t=2  'Feb' t=3  'Mar'
                                t=4 f=swissb 'Apr'
                                t=5 f=swissb 'May'
                                t=6  'Jun' t=7  'Jul' t=8  'Aug'
                                t=9  'Sep' t=10 'Oct' t=11 'Nov'
                                t=12 'Dec');

proc gplot data=vol1.ca88air;
where station='SFO';
plot o3 * month / vaxis=axis1
                  haxis=axis2
                  vref=2;
title1 '1988 Air Quality';
title2 h=1.5 f=simplex 'Assigning tick mark text';
footnote1 h=1.5 j=l f=simplex 'Figure 3.3.2';
run;
```

Figure 3.3.3a Unformatted Date Values on an Axis

```
*****************************************************;
* e3_3_3a.sas;
*
* Plotting using dates;
*****************************************************;

FILENAME filerefa "&pathhpg\e3_3_3a.hpg";
GOPTIONS GSFNAME=filerefa DEVICE=hp7475a GSFMODE=replace
noprompt;
goptions htext=1.5;

axis1 label=(h=1.5 a=90 'Volume (X1000)');

proc gplot data=vol1.dow;
plot volume*date=1 / vaxis=axis1;
symbol1 v='V' f=simplex l=1 i=join c=black;
format date 6.;
title1 'Stock Market Analysis of the Dow';
title2 h=2 f=simplex 'Daily Volume';
footnote1 j=l h=1.5 f=simplex 'Figure 3.3.3a';
run;
quit;
```

Figure 3.3.3b Formatted Date Values on an Axis

```
*****************************************************;
* e3_3_3b.sas;
*
* Plotting using dates;
*****************************************************;

FILENAME filerefb "&pathhpg\e3_3_3b.hpg";
GOPTIONS GSFNAME=filerefb DEVICE=hp7475a GSFMODE=replace
noprompt;
goptions htext=1.5;

axis1 label=(h=1.5 a=90 'Volume (X1000)');

proc gplot data=vol1.dow;
plot volume*date=1 / vaxis=axis1;
symbol1 v='V' f=simplex l=1 i=join c=black;
format date date7.;
title1 'Stock Market Analysis of the Dow';
title2 h=2 f=simplex 'Daily Volume';
footnote1 j=l h=1.5 f=simplex 'Figure 3.3.3b';
run;
quit;
```

Figure 3.3.3c Plotting Dates by Week

```
*****************************************************;
* e3_3_3c.sas;
*
* Plotting using dates and the ORDER= option.
*****************************************************;

FILENAME filerefc "&pathhpg\e3_3_3c.hpg";
GOPTIONS GSFNAME=filerefc DEVICE=hp7475a GSFMODE=replace
noprompt;
goptions htext=1.5;

axis1 label=(h=1.5 a=90 f=swiss 'V' f=simplex 'olume
(X1000)');
axis2 order=('03aug81'd to '31aug81'd by week)
      value=(h=1.5);

proc gplot data=vol1.dow;
plot volume*date=1 / vaxis=axis1 haxis=axis2;
symbol1 v='V' f=simplex l=1 i=join c=black;
format date date7.;
title1 'Stock Market Analysis of the Dow';
```

```
title2 h=2 f=simplex 'Daily Volume';
note move=(20,30)pct 'Volumes';

footnote1 j=l h=1.5 f=simplex 'Figure 3.3.3c';
run;
quit;
```

Figure 3.4.1a Legends without the LEGEND Statement

```
****************************************************;
* e3_4_1a.sas;
*
* Legend without a LEGEND Statement.
****************************************************;

FILENAME filerefa "&pathhpg\e3_4_1a.hpg";
GOPTIONS GSFNAME=filerefa DEVICE=hp7475a GSFMODE=replace
noprompt;
goptions htext=2;

axis1 order=('01jun85'd to '01sep85'd by month)
      value=(f=simplex h=1.5);
axis2 label= (h=1.5 a=90 'gm Wet Weight')
      value=(f=simplex h=1.5);

proc gplot data=vol1.biomass;
plot bmtotl * date = station / haxis = axis1 vaxis=axis2;
where station in ('DL-25', 'DL-60', 'D700-25', 'D700-60') ;
symbol1 v=dot    i=join l=1  c=black;
symbol2 v=dot    i=join l=2  c=black;
symbol3 v=circle i=join l=1  c=black;
symbol4 v=circle i=join l=2  c=black;
title1 'Total Biomass at DL and D700';
title3 h=1.5 f=simplex 'Samples taken at 25 and 60 foot
contours';
footnote1 j=l h=1.5 'Figure 3.4.1a';
run;
quit;
```

Figure 3.4.1b Positioning a Legend with Position=

```
****************************************************;
* e3_4_1b.sas;
*
* Positioning a Legend.
****************************************************;

FILENAME filerefb "&pathhpg\e3_4_1b.hpg";
GOPTIONS GSFNAME=filerefb DEVICE=hp7475a GSFMODE=replace
noprompt;

goptions htext=2;
axis1 order=('01jun85'd to '01sep85'd by month)
      value=(f=simplex h=1.5);
axis2 label= (h=1.2 a=90 'gm Wet Weight')
      value=(f=simplex h=1.5);

legend position=(center top)
       across=2
       label=none;

proc gplot data=vol1.biomass;
plot bmtotl * date = station / legend=legend1
                         haxis = axis1 vaxis=axis2;
where station in ('DL-25', 'DL-60', 'D700-25', 'D700-60') ;
symbol1 v=dot    i=join l=1  c=black;
symbol2 v=dot    i=join l=2  c=black;
symbol3 v=circle i=join l=1  c=black;
symbol4 v=circle i=join l=2  c=black;
title1 'Total Biomass at DL and D700';
title3 h=1.5 f=simplex 'Samples taken at 25 and 60 foot
contours';
footnote1 j=l h=1.5 f=simplex 'Figure 3.4.1b';
run;
quit;
```

Figure 3.4.1c Positioning a Legend with the ORIGIN Option

```
****************************************************;
* e3_4_1c.sas;
*
* Positioning a Legend using the ORIGIN option.
****************************************************;

FILENAME filerefc "&pathhpg\e3_4_1c.hpg";
GOPTIONS GSFNAME=filerefc DEVICE=hp7475a GSFMODE=replace
noprompt;
goptions htext=2;

axis1 order=('01jun85'd to '01sep85'd by month)
      value=(f=ximplex h=1.5);
axis2 label= (h=1.5 a=90 'gm Wet Weight')
      value=(f=ximplex h=1.5);

legend origin=(10 pct, 65 pct)
       mode=share
       across=2
       label=none;

proc gplot data=vol1.biomass;
plot bmtotl * date = station / legend=legend1
                         haxis = axis1 vaxis=axis2;
where station in ('DL-25', 'DL-60', 'D700-25', 'D700-60') ;
symbol1 v=dot    i=join l=1  c=black;
symbol2 v=dot    i=join l=2  c=black;
symbol3 v=circle i=join l=1  c=black;
symbol4 v=circle i=join l=2  c=black;
title1 'Total Biomass at DL and D700';
title3 h=1.5 f=simplex 'Samples taken at 25 and 60 foot
contours';
footnote1 j=l h=1.5 f=simplex 'Figure 3.4.1c';
run;
quit;
```

Figure 3.4.2   Using the VALUE= Option

```
****************************************************;
* e3_4_2.sas;
*
* Using the VALUE option to change text.
****************************************************;

FILENAME fileref "&pathhpg\e3_4_2.hpg";
GOPTIONS GSFNAME=fileref DEVICE=hp7475a GSFMODE=replace
noprompt;
goptions htext=2;

axis1 order=('01jun85'd to '01sep85'd by month)
      value=(f=simplex h=1.5);
axis2 label= (h=1.5 a=90 'gm Wet Weight')
      value=(f=simplex h=1.5);

legend origin=(10 pct, 65 pct)
       mode=share
       across=1
       label=none
       value=(f=simplex h=1.2
          t=1 h=1.2 f=swissb 'D700 at 25 feet')
;

proc gplot data=vol1.biomass;
plot bmtotl * date = station / legend=legend1
                         haxis = axis1 vaxis=axis2;
where station in ('DL-25', 'DL-60', 'D700-25', 'D700-60') ;
symbol1 v=dot    i=join l=1  c=black;
symbol2 v=dot    i=join l=2  c=black;
symbol3 v=circle i=join l=1  c=black;
symbol4 v=circle i=join l=2  c=black;
title1 'Total Biomass at DL and D700';
title3 h=1.5 f=simplex 'Samples taken at 25 and 60 foot
contours';
footnote1 j=l h=1.5 f=simplex 'Figure 3.4.2';
run;
quit;
```

Figure 3.4.3   Using the SHAPE= Option

```
**************************************************;
* e3_4_3.sas;
*
* Changing symbol size using the SHAPE option.
**************************************************;

FILENAME fileref "&pathhpg\e3_4_3.hpg";
GOPTIONS GSFNAME=fileref DEVICE=hp7475a GSFMODE=replace
noprompt;

goptions htext=2;
axis1  order=('01jun85'd to '01sep85'd by month)
       value=(f=simplex h=1.5);
axis2  label= (h=1.2 a=90 'gm Wet Weight')
       value=(f=simplex h=1.5);

legend origin=(10 pct, 65 pct)
       mode=share
       across=2
       label=none
       value=(f=simplex h=1.2)
       shape=symbol(8,2)
;

proc gplot data=vol1.biomass;
plot bmtot1 * date = station / legend=legend1
                 haxis = axis1 vaxis=axis2;
where station in ('DL-25', 'DL-60', 'D700-25', 'D700-60') ;
symbol1 v=dot    i=join l=1  c=black;
symbol2 v=dot    i=join l=33 c=black;
symbol3 v=circle i=join l=1  c=black;
symbol4 v=circle i=join l=33 c=black;
title1 'Total Biomass at DL and D700';
title3 h=1.5 f=simplex 'Samples taken at 25 and 60 foot
contours';
footnote1 j=l h=1.5 f=simplex 'Figure 3.4.3';
run;
quit;
```

Figure 4.2   Overlay Two Plots Using GPLOT

```
**************************************************;
* e4_2.sas;
*
* Overlay two plots using GPLOT;
**************************************************;

FILENAME fileref "&pathhpg\e4_2.hpg";
GOPTIONS GSFNAME=fileref DEVICE=hp7475a GSFMODE=replace
noprompt;
goptions htext=2;

* create a cumulative probability distribution histogram
of pH
* values using GPLOT and overlay it with a cumulative
normal
* probability distribution curve with the same mean and
variance.;

* create a summary data set containing the frequencies of pH;
data buckets; set vol1.h2oqual;
keep ph phround;
* round to the nearest tenth (bucket width);
phround = round(ph,.1);
run;

* collect summary statistics on the unrounded value,
* but count the frequency of the rounded value (nrnd);
proc summary data=buckets;
class phround;
var ph phround;
output out=freq n=n nrnd mean=mean std=std;
run;

* determine the expected value for each value of phround;
data pltdata;
set freq;
retain xbar s total .;
keep phround phcuml phnorm;
* the statistics for the distribution have _type_=0;
if _type_ = 0 then do;
```

```
   total = n;
   xbar = mean;
   s = std;
end;
else do;
   prph = nrnd/total;
   phcuml + prph;
   phnorm = probnorm((phround-xbar)/s);
   output;
end;

* plot the cumulative distributions;
proc gplot data=pltdata;
plot phcuml * phround = 1
     phnorm * phround = 2 / overlay
                           vaxis = 0 to 1 by .2
                           haxis = 7.5 to 10 by .5;
label phround = 'pH'
      phcuml  = 'Cumulative Probability';
symbol1 v=none i=stepcj l=1  c=black;
symbol2 v=none i=join   l=2  c=black;
title1 'Cumulative Probability Distribution for pH';
footnote1 j=l h=1.5 f=simplex 'Figure 4.2';
run;
quit;
```

Figure 4.3.1a Error Bars Using INTERPOL Option

```
**************************************************;
* e4_3_1a.sas;
*
* Display error bars using the INTERPOL symbol statement
option.
**************************************************;

FILENAME filerefa "&pathhpg\e4_3_1a.hpg";
GOPTIONS GSFNAME=filerefa DEVICE=hp7475a GSFMODE=replace
noprompt;

goptions htext=2;
proc gplot data=vol1.biomass;
plot bmtot1* date;
symbol1 v=none i=std2mj   c=black l=1;
title1 'Total Biomass';
title2 f=simplex '(using i=std2mj)';
footnote1 j=l h=1.5 f=simplex 'Figure 4.3.1a';
run;
quit;
```

Figure 4.3.1b Error Bars Using Generated Data Points

```
**************************************************;
* e4_3_1b.sas;
*
* Display error bars using data manipulation.
**************************************************;

FILENAME filerefb "&pathhpg\e4_3_1b.hpg";
GOPTIONS GSFNAME=filerefb DEVICE=hp7475a GSFMODE=replace
noprompt;
goptions htext=2;

proc sort data=vol1.biomass
          out=biosort;
by date;
run;

* determine the summary statistics;
proc summary data=biosort;
by date;
var bmtot1;
output out=stats mean=mean stderr=se;
run;
```

```
* create the observations to be plotted;
data all(keep=date biomass);
set stats;
* for each observation create four;
biomass=mean;         output;
biomass=mean+ 2*se;   output;
biomass=mean- 2*se;   output;
biomass=mean;         output;
run;

proc gplot data=all;
plot biomass * date;
symbol1 v=dot i=join  c=black l=1;
title1 'Total Biomass';
footnote1 j=1 h=1.5 f=simplex 'Figure 4.3.1b';
run;
quit;
```

Figure 4.3.2a Generating a Histogram Using GCHART

```
*************************************************;
* e4_3_2a.sas;
*
* Use PROC GCHART on the BIOMASS data;
*************************************************;

FILENAME filerefa "&pathhpg\e4_3_2a.hpg";
GOPTIONS GSFNAME=filerefa DEVICE=hp7475a GSFMODE=replace
noprompt;
goptions htext=2;

proc gchart data=vol1.biomass;
vbar bmtotl;
title1 'Total Biomass Frequency';
title2 h=1.5 f=simplex 'No intervals specified';
footnote1 j=1 h=1.5 f=simplex 'Figure 4.3.2a';
run;
quit;
```

Figure 4.3.2b Generating a Histogram Using GCHART

```
*************************************************;
* e4_3_2b.sas;
*
* Use PROC GCHART selecting BMTOTL < 10;
*************************************************;

FILENAME filerefb "&pathhpg\e4_3_2b.hpg";
GOPTIONS GSFNAME=filerefb DEVICE=hp7475a GSFMODE=replace
noprompt;
goptions htext=2;

* one observation has a large value of BMTOTL;
proc gchart data=vol1.biomass;
vbar bmtotl / midpoints = .5 to 6 by .5;
where bmtotl < 10;
title1 'Total Biomass Frequency';
title2 h=1.5 f=simplex 'Biomass < 10';
footnote1 j=1 h=1.5 f=simplex 'Figure 4.3.2b';
run;
```

Figure 4.3.2c Histogram Generated with Uneven Midpoints

```
*************************************************;
* e4_3_2c.sas;
*
* Use PROC GCHART using midpoints;
*************************************************;

FILENAME filerefc "&pathhpg\e4_3_2c.hpg";
GOPTIONS GSFNAME=filerefc DEVICE=hp7475a GSFMODE=replace
noprompt;
goptions htext=2;

axis1 value=(h=1.5 f=simplex);

axis2 value=(h=1.5 f=simplex)
      label=(h=1.5 f=simplex);

* one observation has a large value of BMTOTL;
proc gchart data=vol1.biomass;
vbar bmtotl / midpoints = .5 to 6 by .5, 30
              raxis=axis1
              maxis=axis2;
title1 'Total Biomass Frequency';
title2 h=1.5 f=simplex 'Using uneven midpoints';
footnote1 j=1 h=1.5 f=simplex 'Figure 4.3.2c';
run;
quit;
```

Figure 4.3.2d Using GPLOT to Generate a Histogram

```
*************************************************;
* e4_3_2d.sas;
*
* Use PROC PLOT to generate a histogram;
*************************************************;

libname gdevice0 "&pathhpg";

FILENAME filerefd "&pathhpg\e4_3_2d.cgm";
GOPTIONS GSFNAME=filerefd DEVICE=cgmwpca GSFMODE=replace
noprompt;
goptions htext=2;

* Create a grouping format;
proc format;
value grp
   .5 = '<0.75'
  1.0 = '1.0'
  1.5 = '1.5'
  2.0 = '2.0'
  2.5 = '2.5'
  3.0 = '3.0'
  3.5 = '3.5'
  4.0 = '4.0'
  4.5 = '4.5'
  5.0 = '5.0'
  5.5 = '5.5'
  6.0 = '6.0'
  7.0 = '>6.25'
  other = ' ';
run;

* Group the observations into buckets;
data group (keep=group bmtotl);
set vol1.biomass (keep=bmtotl);
group = round(bmtotl,.5);
* Combine 0-.25 with .25-.75;
if group=0 then group=.5;
* combine all groups > than 6.25 into one bucket;
group = min(7, group);
run;

proc sort data=group;
by group;
run;
```

```
* determine the observation count for each bucket;
proc summary data=group;
by group;
var group;
output out=count n=freq;
run;

* Create the data set used to plot
* PLTVAR is used to separate SYMBOLS and PATTERNS;
data plot(keep=freq group pltvar);
set count;
* Each point becomes four.
* Each bar is centered on the midpoint and has a width of .5;
tgroup = group;
tfreq = freq;
*Create a broken horizontal axis;
if _n_=1 then do;
   pltvar=1;
     freq=0.02;
             group=0;    output;
             group=6.4; output;
     pltvar=2;
             group=6.6; output;
             group=7.4; output;
end;
* separate the count in the largest group;
if tgroup le 6 then pltvar=3; else pltvar=4;
group = tgroup - .25; freq =      0 ; output;   *lower
left corner;
                      freq =   tfreq; output;   *upper
left corner;
group = tgroup + .25;           output;   *upper
right corner;
                      freq =   0 ; output;   *lower
right corner;
run;

* Axis and pattern control;
* Horizontal axis ;
axis1 order= 0 to 7.5 by .5
      style=0
      major=none
      minor=none
      label=(h=2 f=simplex)
      value=(h=1.5 f=simplex a=55)
      offset=(0cm);
* Vertical axis ;
axis2 offset=(0 cm)
      order=0 to 16 by 2
      value=(h=1.5 f=simplex)
      minor=none;

* define fill patterns (1 & 2 used for horiz. axis);
pattern1 v=me c=black;
pattern2 v=me c=black;
pattern3 v=me c=black;
pattern4 v=m1x45 c=black;

symbol1 i=join c=black l=1;
symbol2 i=join c=black l=1;
symbol3 i=join c=black l=1;
symbol4 i=join c=black l=2;

proc gplot data=plot;
plot freq*group=pltvar / areas=4
                        haxis=axis1
                        vaxis=axis2
                        nolegend;
format group grp5.;
label freq  = 'Frequency'
      group = 'grams wet weight';
title1 h=2.5 f=swiss 'Total Biomass Frequency';
title2 h=2 f=simplex 'Histogram with broken horizontal
axis';
footnote1 j=l h=2 f=simplex 'Figure 4.3.2d';
run;
quit;
```

Figure 4.3.3a GPLOT Example Plot

```
*************************************************;
* e4_3_3a.sas;
*
* Create multiple axes on one plot.
*************************************************;

FILENAME filerefa "&pathhpg\e4_3_3a.hpg";
GOPTIONS GSFNAME=filerefa DEVICE=hp7475a GSFMODE=replace
noprompt;
```

```
goptions htext=2;
proc gplot data=vol1.ca88air;
plot co*month=station;
symbol1 v='A' l=1  i=join c=black;
symbol2 v='L' l=2  i=join c=black;
symbol3 v='S' l=14 i=join c=black;
title1 '1988 Carbon Monoxide Readings';
footnote1 j=l h=1.5 f=simplex 'Figure 4.3.3a';
run;
```

Figure 4.3.3b Multiple Axes on One Plot

```
*************************************************;
* e4_3_3b.sas;
*
* Create multiple axes on one plot.
*************************************************;

FILENAME filerefb "&pathhpg\e4_3_3b.hpg";
GOPTIONS GSFNAME=filerefb DEVICE=hp7475a GSFMODE=replace
noprompt;
goptions htext=2;

data air1 (keep=yvar month pltvar);
set vol1.ca88air(keep=month co station);
by station;
retain pltvar offset;

* hold the current value of month;
tmon = month;

* Create dummy axes for each station;
* Allow three vertical units for each axis with one unit
between
* each plot.;
if _n_=1 then do;
   pltvar=1;
   * axis for SFO;
   yvar=0; month=12; output;
           month=0;  output;
   yvar=3;           output;
   yvar=.;           output;
   * axis for LIV;
   yvar=4; month=12; output;
           month=0;  output;
   yvar=7;           output;
   yvar=.;           output;
   * axis for AZU;
   yvar=8; month=12; output;
           month=0;  output;
   yvar=11;          output;
   yvar=.;           output;
   month=tmon;
end;

if first.station then do;
   * The data for each station is offset vertically to fit
   * with the dummy axes.;
   if station = 'AZU' then do;
      offset=8;
      pltvar=2;
   end;
   else if station = 'LIV' then do;
      offset=4;
      pltvar=3;
   end;
   else do;
      offset = 0;
      pltvar=4;
   end;
end;

yvar = co + offset;
output;
run;

* Control the vertical axis;
axis1 order = 0 to 11 by 1
      label = (h=1.5 f=simplex 'ppm')
      minor=none
      style=0;
* Control the horizontal axis;
axis2 minor=none
      style=0;
```

```
* Define the symbols for each subplot;
* SYMBOL1 controls the axes;
symbol1 v=none c=black l=1 i=join;
symbol2 v='A' c=black l=1 i=join f=simplex;
symbol3 v='L' c=black l=1 i=join f=simplex;
symbol4 v='S' c=black l=1 i=join f=simplex;

* Define a format for the vertical axis;
proc format;
value vert 0,4,8  = '0'
           3,7,11 = '3'
             other = ' ';
run;

* Plot the data;
proc gplot data=air1;
plot yvar*month=pltvar / nolegend
                         skipmiss
                         vaxis=axis1
                         haxis=axis2;
format yvar vert.;
title1 '1988 Carbon Monoxide Readings';
footnote1 j=l h=1.5 f=simplex 'Figure 4.3.3b';
run;
quit;
```

Figure 4.3.3c Separating Three Variables

```
**************************************************;
* e4_3_3c.sas;
*
* Create multiple axes on one plot.
**************************************************;

goptions reset=all border htext=2;

FILENAME filerefc "&pathhpg\e4_3_3c.hpg";
GOPTIONS GSFNAME=filerefc DEVICE=hp7475a GSFMODE=replace
noprompt;

* control the labels and values for both axes;
axis1 value=(h=1.5 f=simplex)
      label=(h=1.5 f=simplex);
* Plot the data;
proc gplot data=vol1.biomass;
where station = 'D700-60';
plot bmothr*date ='O'
     bmcrus*date ='C'
     bmpoly*date ='P' / overlay
                        vaxis=axis1 haxis=axis1;
symbol1 v='O' c=black f=swiss;
symbol2 v='C' c=black f=swiss;
symbol3 v='P' c=black f=swiss;
title1 'Biomass at D700-60';
title2 h=1.5 f=swiss 'C' f=simplex 'rustacean  '
              f=swiss 'P' f=simplex 'olychaete  '
              f=swiss 'O' f=simplex 'ther';
footnote1 j=l h=2 f=simplex 'Figure 4.3.3c';
run;
```

Figure 4.3.3d Separating Values of a Variable

```
**************************************************;
* e4_3_3d.sas;
*
* Create multiple axes on one plot.
**************************************************;

FILENAME filerefd "&pathhpg\e4_3_3d.hpg";
GOPTIONS GSFNAME=filerefd DEVICE=hp7475a GSFMODE=replace
noprompt;
goptions htext=2;

data bio1 (keep=yvar date  pltvar);
set vol1.biomass (keep=date station bmcrus bmpoly bmothr);
where station='D700-60';
retain pltvar;
```

```
* hold the current value of date ;
tdte = date ;

* Create dummy axes for each station;
* Allow three vertical units for each axis with one unit
between
* each plot.;
if _n_=1 then do;
   pltvar=1;
   * axis for bmothr;
   yvar=0;     date='01sep85'd; output;
               date='15jun85'd; output;
   yvar=0.50;                   output;
   yvar=.;                      output;
   * axis for bmpoly;
    yvar=0.75; date='01sep85'd; output;
               date='15jun85'd; output;
   yvar=1.25;                   output;
   yvar=.;                      output;
   * axis for bmcrus;
   yvar=1.50; date='01sep85'd; output;
              date='15jun85'd; output;
   yvar=2.00;                   output;
   yvar=.;                      output;
   date=tdte;
end;

* The data for each taxa is offset vertically to fit
* with the dummy axes.;
* BMOTHR there is no offset;
   pltvar=2;
   yvar = bmothr;
   output;
* BMPOLY is placed in the middle axis ;
* the offset is .75;
   pltvar=3;
   yvar = bmpoly + .75;
   output;
* BMCRUS is placed in the upper axis;
* the offset is 1.50;
   pltvar=4;
   yvar = bmcrus + 1.50;
   output;
run;

* Control the vertical axis;
axis1 order = 0 to 2 by .25
      label = (h=1.5 f=simplex a=90 'gm wet weight')
      value=(h=1.5 f=simplex)
      minor=none
      major=none
      style=0;
* Control the horizontal axis;
axis2 minor=none
      order= '15jun85'd, '01jul85'd, '15jul85'd,
             '01aug85'd, '15aug85'd, '01sep85'd
      label=(h=1.5 f=simplex)
      value=(h=1.5 f=simplex)
      style=0;

* Define the symbols for each subplot;
* SYMBOL1 controls the axes;
symbol1 v=none c=black l=1 i=join f=;
symbol2 v='O' c=black l=1 i=join f=swiss;
symbol3 v='P' c=black l=1 i=join f=swiss;
symbol4 v='C' c=black l=1 i=join f=swiss;

* Define a format for the vertical axis;
proc format;
value vert 0.0, 0.75, 1.5 = '0'
           0.5, 1.25, 2.0 = '.5'
           other  = ' ';
run;

* Plot the data;
proc gplot data=bio1;
plot yvar*date =pltvar / nolegend
                         skipmiss
                         vaxis=axis1
                         haxis=axis2;
format yvar vert.;
title1 'Biomass at D700-60';
title2 h=1.5 f=swiss 'C' f=simplex 'rustacean  '
              f=swiss 'P' f=simplex 'olychaete  '
              f=swiss 'O' f=simplex 'ther';
footnote1 j=l h=2 f=simplex 'Figure 4.3.3d';
run;
quit;
```

Figure 4.3.3e GPLOT with the PLOT2 Statement

```sas
****************************************************;
* E4_3_3e.sas
*
* Specialized plot for concentration values.
*
****************************************************;
* define global options;
options nomtrace nosymbolgen nomprint;
goptions reset=all nopolygonclip nopclip nopolygonfill;
GOPTIONS BORDER NOCHARACTERS NOFILL NOCELL;
****************************************************;
FILENAME filerefe "&pathhpg\E4_3_3e.hpg";
GOPTIONS GSFNAME=filerefe DEVICE=hp7475a GSFMODE=replace
noprompt;

****************************************************;
* generate the test data set;
data toplot;
input patient $3. @5 strdate $8. conc100 conc30 conc10
percd8 cd8_cd38;
cards;
50x 12/8/92  5.8  6.2 1.1 44 388
50x 2/15/93 19   10.7 2.9 43 387
50x 3/25/93  9.5  5.5 2   47 302
50x 4/15/93  7.9  2.1 2.9 48 467
;


%macro concplt(pervar, var, varstrg);
****************************************************;
* incoming data assumptions
*    - data set named TOPLOT
*    - variable are: patient code ($) - patient id
*                    strdate ($) - label for horiz. axis
*                    conc100, conc30, conc10 - scaled conc
values
*                    &pervar - percent variable
*                    &var - variable value
*    - conc values are scaled to pervar
*    - data are sorted by patient id
*    - data are ordered within patient id
*    - all patients have the same number of data points
*;

* split the data, creating plot reference points;
data conc (keep=patient point ptorder
                ptype conc conc2 symnum symnum2);
set toplot;
by patient;
* the data point must be plotted in a specific order;
ptorder+1;
* point is used as the horizontal variable;
if first.patient then point=0;
point+1;
* create a macro var containing each date string;
ii = left(put(point,2.));
call symput('date'||ii,strdate);
* total number of points;
if last.patient then do;
   totpts = left(put(point,2.));
   call symput('totpts',totpts);
   axpts = left(put(point+1,2.));
   call symput('axpts',axpts);
end;

* output the line data (plotted by PLOT2);
* the variables symnum and symnum2 point to SYMBOL
statements;
* ptype separates points to be plotted on PLOT or PLOT2;
conc = .; symnum=3; ptype='2';
symnum2=4; conc2 = &pervar*10; ptorder+1; output conc;
symnum2=5; conc2 = &var;       ptorder+1; output conc;

* create pseudo points for the histograms;
* histograms plotted using PLOT statement;
conc2 = .; symnum2=5; ptype='1';
holdpt = point;
* three vertical bars: conc100, conc30, and conc10;
* create the four corners of each of the three bars for
each POINT;
```

```sas
* conc100;
symnum = 1;
point=holdpt-.375; conc=0;        ptorder+1; output conc;
                   conc=conc100;  ptorder+1; output conc;
point=holdpt-.125;                ptorder+1; output conc;
                   conc=0;        ptorder+1; output conc;
* conc30;
symnum = 2;
point=holdpt-.125; conc=0;        ptorder+1; output conc;
                   conc=conc30;   ptorder+1; output conc;
point=holdpt+.125;                ptorder+1; output conc;
                   conc=0;        ptorder+1; output conc;
* conc10;
symnum = 3;
point=holdpt+.125; conc=0;        ptorder+1; output conc;
                   conc=conc10;   ptorder+1; output conc;
point=holdpt+.375;                ptorder+1; output conc;
                   conc=0;        ptorder+1; output conc;
point=holdpt;
run;

* data are sorted so that SYMBOLs are used at the correct
time.;
proc sort data=conc;
by patient symnum symnum2 ptype ptorder;
run;

* gplot axis and legend statements;
axis1 major = none
      offset = (0,0)
      label = none
      minor = (n=1 h=1)
      value = (h=1 f=simplex angle=55  ' '
         %do i = 1 %to &totpts;
            "&&date&i"
         %end; ' ')
      order = (0 to &axpts by 1);

axis2 major = (h=1)
      offset = (0)
      label = (h=2.5 'CELL %')
      order = (0 to 100 by 10)
      minor = none;

axis3 major = (h=1)
      offset = (0)
      label = (h=1.5 'CELL COUNT')
      order = (0 to 1000 by 100)
      minor = none;

legend1 across=3
        position=(bottom center outside)
        label=none
        shape=bar(5,.8)
        value=('CONC. 100:1' 'CONC. 30:1' 'CONC. 10:1');

legend2 across=2
        position=(bottom center outside)
        label=none
        shape=symbol(5,.5)
        value=("% &varstrg" "&varstrg");

goption hby=0;
proc gplot data=conc;
by patient;
plot conc * point = symnum / areas=3
                            skipmiss
                            legend=legend1
                            vaxis=axis2
                            haxis=axis1;

plot2 conc2*point = symnum2/ vaxis=axis3
                            legend=legend2
                            skipmiss;

symbol1 v=none c=black i=join l=1;
symbol2 v=none c=black i=join l=1;
symbol3 v=none c=black i=join l=1;
symbol4 v='U' c=black i=join l=1 f=marker  h=.5;
symbol5 v='U' c=black i=join l=1 f=markere h=.5;

pattern1 v=solid c=black;
pattern2 v=m2x45 c=black;
pattern3 v=empty c=black;
```

```
label conc2 = 'CELL COUNT'
      conc  = 'COUNT %';
title1  f=duplex h=1.5 'Patient code #byval(patient)';
title2  f=simplex h=1.5 "&varstrg";
footnote h=1.5 j=l f=simplex 'Figure 4.3.3e';
run;
%mend concplt;
**************************************************;
%concplt(percd8, cd8_cd38, CD8+ CD38+)
```

Figure 4.3.4a Butterfly Plots

```
**************************************************;
* e4_3_4a.sas;
*
* Create butterfly plots.
**************************************************;

FILENAME filerefa "&pathhpg\e4_3_4a.hpg";
GOPTIONS GSFNAME=filerefa DEVICE=hp7475a GSFMODE=replace
noprompt;
goptions htext=2;

data air1 (keep=yvar month pltvar);
set vol1.ca88air(keep=month co station);
by station;
retain pltvar offset;

* hold the current value of month;
tmon = month;

* Create dummy axes for each station;
* Allow six vertical units for each axis with one unit
between
* each plot.;
if _n_=1 then do;
   pltvar=0;
   * axis for SFO;
   yvar=0; month=0;   output;
   yvar=6;            output;
   yvar=3;            output;
            month=12; output;
   yvar=.;            output;
   * axis for LIV;
   yvar=7; month=0;   output;
   yvar=13;           output;
   yvar=10;           output;
            month=12; output;
   yvar=.;            output;
   * axis for AZU;
   yvar=14;month=0;   output;
   yvar=20;           output;
   yvar=17;           output;
            month=12; output;
   yvar=.;            output;
   month=tmon;
end;

if first.station then do;
   plt+1;
   * The data for each station is offset vertically to fit
   * with the dummy axes.;
   if station = 'AZU' then offset=17;
   else if station = 'LIV' then offset=10;
   else offset = 3;
end;

* Each butterfly plot is made up of three sets of lines
* with a common SYMBOL statement;
* Upper line;
pltvar = plt*3-2; yvar = offset + co; output;
* Lower line;
pltvar = plt*3-1; yvar = offset - co; output;
* Hilo line;
pltvar = plt*3  ; yvar = offset      ; output;
                  yvar = offset - co; output;
                  yvar = offset + co; output;
                  yvar = offset      ; output;

run;

* Control the vertical axis;
axis1 order = 0 to 20 by 1
      label = (h=1.5 f=simplex 'ppm')
      value = (h=1.2 f=simplex)
      minor=none
      style=0;
```

```
* Control the horizontal axis;
axis2 minor=none;
      label=(h=1.5 f=simplex)
      value=(h=1.5 f=simplex);

* Define the symbols for each subplot;
* SYMBOL1 controls the axes;
symbol1 v=none c=black l=1 i=join r=10;

* Define a format for the vertical axis;
proc format;
value vert 0,7,14  = '3'
           6,13,20 = '3'
           3,10,17 = '0'
           4       = 'SFO'
           11      = 'LIV'
           18      = 'AZU'
           other   = ' ';
run;

* Plot the data;
proc gplot data=air1;
plot yvar*month=pltvar / nolegend
                         skipmiss
                         vaxis=axis1
                         haxis=axis2;
format yvar vert.;
title1 '1988 Carbon Monoxide Readings';
footnote1 j=l h=1.5 f=simplex 'Figure 4.3.4a';
run;
quit;
```

Figure 4.3.4b Butterfly Plots

```
**************************************************;
* e4_3_4b.sas;
*
* Create butterfly plots.
**************************************************;

FILENAME filerefb "&pathhpg\e4_3_4b.hpg";
GOPTIONS GSFNAME=filerefb DEVICE=hp7475a GSFMODE=replace
noprompt;

data bio1;
set vol1.biomass (keep= date bmcrus bmmol bmpoly bmothr);
* Adjust date for successive sample dates;
if date='17jun85'd then date='18jun85'd;
else if date='09jul85'd then date='10jul85'd;
else if date='02aug85'd then date='05aug85'd;
else if date='26aug85'd then date='27aug85'd;
run;

proc sort data=bio1;
by date;
run;

proc means data=bio1 noprint;
by date;
var bmcrus bmmol bmpoly bmothr;
output out=bio2 mean=mncrus mnmoll mnpoly mnothr;
run;

data bio3 (keep=yvar date pltvar);
set bio2 (keep=date mnpoly mnmoll mncrus mnothr);
retain pltvar;

* Create dummy axes for each taxa;

* Allow one vertical units for each axis with .25 units
* between each plot.;
if _n_=1 then do;

   * hold the current value of date ;
   tdte = date ;

   pltvar=1;
   * axis for MNPOLY;
   yvar=0;      date='15jun85'd;  output;
   yvar=1;                        output;
   yvar=.5;                       output;
                date='01sep85'd;  output;
```

```
yvar=.;                              output;
  * axis for MNMOLL;
  yvar=1.25; date='15jun85'd;    output;
  yvar=2.25;                     output;
  yvar=1.75;                     output;
           date='01sep85'd;      output;
  yvar=.;                        output;
  * axis for MNOTHR;
  yvar=2.50; date='15jun85'd;    output;
  yvar=3.50;                     output;
  yvar=3.00;                     output;
           date='01sep85'd;      output;
  yvar=.;                        output;
  date = tdte;
end;

* Each butterfly plot is made up of three sets of lines
* each with a common SYMBOL statement;
* the horizontal value for each point is date;

* BMPOLY (centered vertically on .5);
* Upper line;
pltvar = 2; yvar =  .5  + mnpoly/2; output;
* Lower line;
pltvar = 3; yvar =  .5  - mnpoly/2; output;
* Hilo line;
pltvar = 4; yvar =  .5  + mnpoly/2; output;
            yvar =  .5  - mnpoly/2; output;
            yvar =  .;              output;

* BMMOLL (centered vertically on 1.75);
* Upper line;
pltvar = 5; yvar = 1.75 + mnmoll/2; output;
* Lower line;
pltvar = 6; yvar = 1.75 - mnmoll/2; output;
* Hilo line;
pltvar = 7; yvar = 1.75 + mnmoll/2; output;
            yvar = 1.75 - mnmoll/2; output;
            yvar =  .;              output;

* BMOTHR (centered vertically on 3.00);
* Upper line;
pltvar = 8; yvar = 3.00 + mnothr/2; output;
* Lower line;
pltvar = 9; yvar = 3.00 - mnothr/2; output;
* Hilo line;
pltvar =10; yvar = 3.00 + mnothr/2; output;
            yvar = 3.00 - mnothr/2; output;
            yvar =  .;              output;
run;

* Control the vertical axis;
axis1 order = 0 to 3.5 by .25
      label = (h=1.2 a=90 'gm Wet Weight')
      value = (h=1.3)
      minor=none
      style=0;
* Control the horizontal axis;
axis2 minor=none
      order= '15jun85'd, '01jul85'd, '15jul85'd,
             '01aug85'd, '15aug85'd, '01sep85'd
      value = (h=1.3)
      style=0;

* Define the symbols for each subplot;
* SYMBOL1 controls the axes;
symbol1 v=none c=black l=1 i=join r=10;

* Define a format for the vertical axis;
proc format;
value vert 0,1,1.25, 2.25, 2.5, 3.5 = '.5'
           .5, 1.75, 3 = '0'
           .75      = 'BMPOLY'
           2        = 'BMMOLL'
           3.25     = 'BMOTHR'
           other    = ' ';
run;

* Plot the data;
proc gplot data=bio3;
plot yvar*date =pltvar / nolegend
                         skipmiss
                         vaxis=axis1
                         haxis=axis2;
```

```
format yvar vert.;
title1 'Biomass Averaged Across Stations';
footnote1 j=l h=2 f=simplex 'Figure 4.3.4b';
run;
quit;
*/ *;
```

Figure 4.3.5 Box-Whisker Plots

```
***************************************************;
* e4_3_5.sas;
*
* Create box-whisker plots.
***************************************************;

FILENAME fileref "&pathhpg\e4_3_5.hpg";
GOPTIONS GSFNAME=fileref DEVICE=hp7475a GSFMODE=replace
noprompt;

proc sort data=vol1.ca88air (keep=co station)
          out=caair;
by station co;
run;

* determine the median, and quartile statistics for each
station;
proc univariate data=caair noprint;
by station;
var co;
output out=stats median=median
                 q1=q1 q3=q3 qrange=qrange;
run;


* Determine the whisker endpoints;
* Whisker endpoints are the most extreme data values that
are
* within 1.5*qrange of the quartiles.;
data stats2;
merge stats caair;
by station;
retain lowpt highpt;
drop co;
if first.station then do;
  lowpt=.; highpt=.;
end;

* does this point determine the whisker end point?;
if q1-1.5*qrange <= co <= q3+1.5*qrange then do;
  * look for the smallest value that is between
  * q1-1.5*qrange and q1;
  if lowpt=. then lowpt = co;
  * look for the largest value that is between
  * q3+1.5*qrange and q3;
  if highpt=. then highpt = co;
  else highpt=max(highpt,co);
end;

if last.station then output;
run;


* combine the stats with the data and retain extreme
points;
data both;
merge stats2 caair;
by station;
if first.station then do;
  * Build the box and whiskers from the summary stats;
  stacnt + 1;

  * Whiskers are dotted lines;
  pltvar=1;
  * start at the top whisker;
  xvar=stacnt   ; yvar=highpt       ; output;
                  yvar=q3           ; output;
  xvar=.        ;                     output;
  xvar=stacnt   ; yvar=lowpt        ; output;
                  yvar=q1           ; output;
  xvar=.        ;                     output;

  * The box is a solid line;
  pltvar=2;
  xvar=stacnt+.3; yvar=q3           ; output;
                  yvar=median       ; output;
```

```
       xvar=stacnt-.3;                        output;
       xvar=stacnt+.3;                        output;
                      yvar=q1        ;  output;
       xvar=stacnt-.3;                        output;
                      yvar=q3        ;  output;
       xvar=stacnt+.3;                        output;
       xvar=.         ;                output;

   end;

   * plot outliers;
   xvar=stacnt;
   yvar=co;

   * Determine where this point falls;
   * Extreme outliers;
   if co < q1-3*qrange or co > q3+3*qrange then do;
       pltvar=4;
       output;
   end;
   else if co < q1-1.5*qrange or co > q3+1.5*qrange then do;
       pltvar=3;
       output;
   end;
   run;


   * Control the vertical axis;
   axis1 label=(h=1.5 f=simplex a=90 'p.p.m.')
         value=(h=1.5 f=simplex);

   * Control the horizontal axis;
   axis2 label=(h=1.5 f=simplex 'STATIONS')
         order=(0 to 4 by 1)
         major=none
         minor=none
         value= (h=1.5 f=simplex
                  t=1 ' ' t=2 'AZU' t=3 'LIV' t=4 'SFO' t=5 ' ');

   * Define the symbols;
   symbol1 v=none c=black l=2 i=join;
   symbol2 v=none c=black l=1 i=join;
   symbol3 v=circle c=black;
   symbol4 v=diamond c=black;


   * Plot the data;
   proc gplot data=both;
   plot yvar*xvar=pltvar / nolegend
                           skipmiss
                           vaxis=axis1
                           haxis=axis2;
   title1 h=2 '1988 Carbon Monoxide Readings';
   footnote1 j=l h=2 f=simplex 'Figure 4.3.5';
   run;
   quit;
```

Figure 4.3.6 Cluster Analysis Plots

```
******************************************************;
* e4_3_6.sas;
*
* Connect points in a cluster.
******************************************************;

FILENAME fileref "&pathhpg\e4_3_6.hpg";
GOPTIONS GSFNAME=fileref DEVICE=hp7475a GSFMODE=replace
noprompt;

proc fastclus data=vol1.h2oqual
     mean=meanclus
     out=outclus
     maxclusters=4
     noprint
     ;
var depth temp ph do cond salinity;
run;

* sort the cluster mean data;
proc sort data=meanclus;
by cluster;
run;
```

```
* sort the raw data with the cluster assignments;
proc sort data=outclus;
by cluster;
run;

%macro pltclus(xvar, yvar);
* create a macro to plot any two data variables;

* Combine the cluster means with the rawdata;
* Select two plotting variables;
data both (keep=cluster &xvar &yvar);
set meanclus (keep= cluster &xvar &yvar)
     outclus  (keep= cluster &xvar &yvar);
by cluster;
retain xmean ymean;
* the first value for each cluster contains the summary
info;
if first.cluster then do;
    xmean= &xvar;
    ymean= &yvar;
    output;
end;
else if &xvar>. and &yvar>. then do;
    * for each point output two observations that form the
line
    * segment from the centroid to the data point;
    output;
    &xvar = xmean;
    &yvar = ymean;
    output;
end;

* graph the clusters using GPLOT;
proc gplot data=both;
plot &yvar * &xvar = cluster;

symbol1 line=1 i=join c=black v=square;
symbol2 line=1 i=join c=black v=circle;
symbol3 line=1 i=join c=black v=triangle;
symbol4 line=1 i=join c=black v=star;
symbol5 line=1 i=join c=black v=diamond;
title1 'Water Quality Cluster Analysis';
footnote h=2 f=simplex j=l 'Figure 4.3.6';
%mend pltclus;


*****************************;

*%pltclus(temp, salinity)  run;
*%pltclus(ph  , salinity)  run;
 %pltclus(do  , salinity)  run;
```

Figure 4.4.1a GCHART of the Lampara Length Data

```
*************************************************;
* e4_4_1a.sas;
*
* GCHART of the Lampara length data.
*************************************************;

FILENAME filerefa "&pathhpg\e4_4_1a.hpg";
GOPTIONS GSFNAME=filerefa DEVICE=hp7475a GSFMODE=replace
noprompt;

proc gchart data=vol1.lampara;
vbar length;
title1 'Lampara Length Data';
footnote1 h=2 f=simplex j=l 'Figure 4.4.1a';
run;
quit;
```

Figure 4.4.1bc Unevenly Spaced Vertical Axes

```
*****************************************************;
* e4_4_1bc.sas;
*
* Probability plots.
* Produces unevenly spaced axis scales using formats.
*****************************************************;

FILENAME filerefb "&pathhpg\e4_4_1b.hpg";
FILENAME filerefc "&pathhpg\e4_4_1c.hpg";
GOPTIONS GSFNAME=filerefb DEVICE=hp7475a GSFMODE=replace
noprompt;

* Generate normal probabilities (y) and two data sets
* that can be used to generate formats.;
data norm (keep= x x2 y y2)
     f1 (keep=fmtname start label)
     f2 (keep=fmtname start label fuzz);
length start label $12;
retain fuzz .05;
do x = -4 to 4 by .1;
  x2 = x;
  y = probnorm(x);
  y2 = y;
  output norm;

  * Prepare to generate a format (PRNORM.) to convert
  * normal values to probabilities;
  fmtname = 'prnorm';
  start = put(x,4.1);
  label = put(y,8.3);
  output f1;

  * Prepare to generate a format (PROBIT.) to convert
  * probabilities to normal values;
  fmtname = 'probit';
  start = put(y,9.7);
  label = put(x,4.1);
  output f2;
end;
label x = 'Normal Scores';
run;

* create the two formats from the control data sets;
proc format cntlin=f1;
proc format cntlin=f2;
run;

axis1 label=none
      value=(h=1.5 f=simplex);

axis2 label=(h=1.5 f=simplex)
      value=(h=1.5 f=simplex);

proc gplot data=norm;
plot y*x / vaxis=axis1 haxis=axis2;
plot2 y2*x / vaxis=axis1;
format y2 probit.;
symbol1 v=none l=1 i=join c=black r=2;
title1 'Cumulative Normal Distribution';
title2 h=1.5 f=simplex 'Based on Probabilities';
title3 h=1.5 f=simplex a=90 'Probability';
title4 h=1.5 f=simplex a=-90 'Normal Scores';
footnote1 h=2 f=simplex j=l 'Figure 4.4.1b';
run;

GOPTIONS GSFNAME=filerefc;
proc gplot data=norm;
plot x*x / vaxis=axis1 haxis=axis2;
plot2 x2*x / vaxis=axis1;
format x2 prnorm.;
symbol1 v=none l=1 i=join c=black r=2;
title1 'Cumulative Normal Distribution';
title2 h=1.5 f=simplex 'Vertical Scale Based on Normal Scores';
title3 h=1.5 f=simplex a=90 'Normal Scores';
title4 h=1.5 f=simplex a=-90 'Probability';
footnote1 h=2 f=simplex j=l 'Figure 4.4.1c';
run;
quit;
```

Figure 4.4.1de Probability and Quantile Plots

```
*****************************************************;
* e4_4_1de.sas;
*
* Produce a Probability plot for the Lampara data.
*****************************************************;

FILENAME filerefd "&pathhpg\e4_4_1d.hpg";
FILENAME filerefe "&pathhpg\e4_4_1e.hpg";
GOPTIONS GSFNAME=filerefd DEVICE=hp7475a GSFMODE=replace
noprompt;

* Generate normal quantiles (x), probabilities (y), and two
* data sets that can be used to generate formats.;
data norm (keep=x y)
     f1 (keep=fmtname start label)
     f2 (keep=fmtname start label fuzz);
length start label $12;
retain fuzz .05;
do x = -4 to 4 by .1;
  y = probnorm(x);
  output norm;

  * Prepare to generate a format (PRNORM.) to convert
  * normal quantiles to probabilities;
  fmtname = 'prnorm';
  start = put(x,4.1);
  label = put(y,8.3);
  output f1;

  * Prepare to generate a format (PROBIT.) to convert
  * probabilities to normal quantiles;
  fmtname = 'probit';
  start = put(y,9.7);
  label = put(x,4.1);
  output f2;
end;
label x = 'Normal Quantiles';
run;

* create the two formats from the control data sets;
proc format cntlin=f1;
proc format cntlin=f2;
run;

* convert the length information to standard normal;
proc standard data=vol1.lampara
              out=standard
              mean=0 std=1;
var length;
run;

* Determine the length frequencies for the lampara data;
proc freq data=standard noprint;
table length / out=percent;
run;

* Calculate the cumulative length probabilities;
data cumulpr (keep= length cumulpr cumnorm x y);
set percent (in=inper) norm ;
if not inper then do;
   length = x;
   cumulpr = .;
end;
else do;
   cumulpr + (percent/100);
   cumnorm = probit(cumulpr);
end;
label length  = 'Standardized Lengths (normal quantiles)'
      cumulpr = 'cumulative probabilities'
      cumnorm = 'normal quantiles';
run;

* Axis and symbol definitions;
* Axis1 used to plot probabilities;
axis1 order= 0 to 1 by .1
      value=(h=1.5 f=simplex)
      label=none;
* Axis2 used to plot normal quantiles;
axis2 order= -4 to 4 by 1
      value=(h=1.5 f=simplex)
      label=none;

axis3 label=(h=1.5 f=simplex)
      value=(h=1.5 f=simplex);
* symbol1 is used with the data;
symbol1 v=dot c=black;
```

```
* symbol2 is used to control the normal line;
symbol2 i=join v=none l=1 c=black;

* Plot the probabilities with the second axis
* formatted to normal quantiles;
proc gplot data=cumulpr;
plot cumulpr*length=1 / vaxis=axis1 haxis=axis3;
plot2 y*length=2 / vaxis=axis1;
format y probit.;
title1 'Cumulative Normal Distribution';
title2 h=1.5 f=simplex 'Vertical Scale Based on Probabilities';
title3 h=1.5 f=simplex a=90 'Cumulative Probability';
title4 h=1.5 f=simplex a=-90 'Normal Quantiles';
footnote1 h=2 f=simplex j=l 'Figure 4.4.1d';
run;

* Plot the normal scores with the second axis
* formatted to probabilities;
GOPTIONS GSFNAME=filerefe;
proc gplot data=cumulpr;
plot cumnorm*length=1 / vaxis=axis2 haxis=axis3;
plot2 x*length=2 / vaxis=axis2;
format x prnorm.;
title1 'Cumulative Normal Distribution';
title2 h=1.5 f=simplex 'Vertical Scale Based on Normal Quantiles';
title3 h=1.5 f=simplex a=90 'Normal Quantiles';
title4 h=1.5 f=simplex a=-90 'Probability';
footnote1 h=2 f=simplex j=l 'Figure 4.4.1e';
run;
quit;
```

Figure 4.4.2a Nonequal Axis Scaling

```
**************************************************;
* e4_4_2a.sas;
*
* Demonstrate non-equal scaling of the axes.
**************************************************;

FILENAME filerefa "&pathhpg\e4_4_2a.hpg";
GOPTIONS GSFNAME=filerefa DEVICE=hp7475a GSFMODE=replace
noprompt;

data design (keep= x y pltvar);
* Create a square centered on (5,5) with a side of length 5;
pltvar=1;
x= 0; y= 0; output;
x= 0; y=10; output;
x=10; y=10; output;
x=10; y= 0; output;
x= 0; y= 0; output;

* Create a circle centered on (5,5) with a radius of length 5;
pltvar=2;
pi = arcos(-1);
do alpha = 0 to 2*pi by 2*pi/100;
  x=5*cos(alpha)+5;
  y=5*sin(alpha)+5;
  output;
end;
run;

proc gplot data=design;
plot y*x=pltvar / nolegend;
symbol1 v=none i=j l=1 c=black r=2;
title1 'Creating Axes with Equal Scales';
title2 h=1 f=simplex 'Circle within a Square';
footnote1 h=2 f=simplex j=l 'Figure 4.4.2a';
run;
```

Figure 4.4.2b Using HSIZE to Adjust the Scale

```
**************************************************;
* e4_4_2b.sas;
*
* Demonstrate equal scaling using HSIZE.
**************************************************;

FILENAME filerefb "&pathhpg\e4_4_2b.hpg";
GOPTIONS GSFNAME=filerefb DEVICE=hp7475a GSFMODE=replace
```

```
noprompt;

data design (keep= x y pltvar);
* Create a square centered on (5,5) with a side of length
5;
pltvar=1;
x= 0; y= 0; output;
x= 0; y=10; output;
x=10; y=10; output;
x=10; y= 0; output;
x= 0; y= 0; output;

* Create a circle centered on (5,5) with a radius of length
5;
pltvar=2;
pi = arcos(-1);
do alpha = 0 to 2*pi by 2*pi/100;
  x=5*cos(alpha)+5;
  y=5*sin(alpha)+5;
  output;
end;
run;

goptions hsize=5;
proc gplot data=design;
plot y*x=pltvar / nolegend;
symbol1 v=none i=j l=1 c=black r=2;
title1 'Creating Axes with Equal Scales';
title2 h=1 f=simplex 'Adjusting the HSIZE GOPTION';
footnote1 h=2 f=simplex j=2 'Figure 4.4.2b';
run;
```

Figure 4.4.2c Using Titles to Adjust the Scale

```
**************************************************;
* e4_4_2c.sas;
*
* Adjust the horizontal axis scale by adding blank titles.
**************************************************;

FILENAME filerefc "&pathhpg\e4_4_2c.hpg";
GOPTIONS GSFNAME=filerefc DEVICE=hp7475a GSFMODE=replace
noprompt;

data design (keep= x y pltvar);
* Create a square centered on (5,5) with a side of length
5;
pltvar=1;
x= 0; y= 0; output;
x= 0; y=10; output;
x=10; y=10; output;
x=10; y= 0; output;
x= 0; y= 0; output;

* Create a circle centered on (5,5) with a radius of length
5;
pltvar=2;
pi = arcos(-1);
do alpha = 0 to 2*pi by 2*pi/100;
  x=5*cos(alpha)+5;
  y=5*sin(alpha)+5;
  output;
end;
run;

axis1 label=(h=1.5 f=simplex a=90 'Y axis')
      value=(h=1.5 f=simplex);
axis2 label=(h=1.5 f=simplex 'X axis')
      value=(h=1.5 f=simplex);

proc gplot data=design;
plot y*x=pltvar / nolegend
            vaxis=axis1 haxis=axis2;
symbol1 v=none i=j l=1 c=black r=2;
title1 'Creating Axes with Equal Scales';
title2 h=1.5 f=simplex 'Padding the Margins';
title3 h=10.9 f=simplex a=-90 ' ';
title4 h=10.9 f=simplex a= 90 ' ';
footnote1 h=2 f=simplex j=l 'Figure 4.4.2c';
run;
quit;
```

Figure 4.4.2d Using the Range to Adjust the Scale

```
**************************************************;
* e4_4_2d.sas;
*
* Equal scaling by adjusting the range of the longer axis;
**************************************************;

FILENAME filerefd "&pathhpg\e4_4_2d.hpg";
GOPTIONS GSFNAME=filerefd DEVICE=hp7475a GSFMODE=replace
noprompt;

data design (keep= x y pltvar);
* Create a square centered on (5,5) with a side of length 5;
pltvar=1;
x= 0; y= 0; output;
x= 0; y=10; output;
x=10; y=10; output;
x=10; y= 0; output;
x= 0; y= 0; output;

* Create a circle centered on (5,5) with a radius of length 5;
pltvar=2;
pi = arcos(-1);
do alpha = 0 to 2*pi by 2*pi/100;
   x=5*cos(alpha)+5;
   y=5*sin(alpha)+5;
   output;
end;
run;

* Select the range of the longer axis such that:
* range = (range_short)*(length_long)/(length_short);
axis1 order= -5 to 15 by 5
      value=(h=1.5 f=simplex)
      label=(h=1.5 f=simplex)
      minor=(n=4);
axis2 value=(h=1.5 f=simplex)
      label=(h=1.5 f=simplex) a=90 'Y Axis');
proc gplot data=design;
plot y*x=pltvar / nolegend haxis=axis1 vaxis=axis2;
symbol1 v=none i=j l=1 c=black r=2;
title1 'Creating Axes with Equal Scales';
title2 h=1.5 f=simplex 'Adjusting the Axis Range';
footnote1 h=2 f=simplex j=l 'Example 4.4.2d';
run;
```

Figure 4.5.1 Create a GFONT Histogram

```
**************************************************;
* e4_5_1.sas;
*
* Create a GFONT containing a histogram of values.
**************************************************;

FILENAME fileref "&pathhpg\e4_5_1.hpg";
GOPTIONS GSFNAME=fileref DEVICE=hp7475a GSFMODE=replace
noprompt;

* Determine the cell frequencies for each dateXsex;
proc freq data=vol1.lampara;
by date;
table sex / noprint out=percent;
run;

* Add a null value to dates without all three sex groups;
data groups (keep=date sex);set percent (keep=date);
by date;
if first.date then do sex = 'F', 'M', 'U';
   output;
end;
run;

* Fill empty cells with a zero percent and
* count the total catch (data to be plotted);
data percent2 (keep=date sex percent)
     totcatch (keep=date totcatch pltvar);
merge percent (in=inper) groups;
by date sex;
* Add zero values for empty cells;
if not inper then do;
   percent=0;
   count=0;
end;
   output percent2;
* Determine the total catch for each date;
if first.date then do;
   totcatch=0;
   pltvar+1;
end;
totcatch + count;
if last.date then output totcatch;
label totcatch = 'Total Catch';
run;

data fontdata (keep=char seg x y lp ptype);
set percent2 (keep=date sex percent);
by date;
length char $1;
retain char ' ' ptype 'V';
if first.date then do;
   pltvar + 1;
   char = put(pltvar,1.);
   * define the outline;
   seg=1; lp='L';
   x=  0; y=  0; output;
          y=100; output;
   x=100;        output;
          y=  0; output;
          y= 50; output;
   x=  0;        output;
end;

* Draw the histogram bars;
* Bar height is determined by the data,
* the width coordinates (x) are F=0-33, M=33=66, and
* U=66-100;
seg=2; lp='P'; y=percent;
if sex = 'F' then do;
   x= 0; y=0;          output;
         y=percent; output;
   x=33;               output;
end;
else if sex = 'M' then do;
   x=33; y=percent; output;
   x=66;               output;
end;
else if sex = 'U' then do;
   x=66; y=percent; output;
   x=100;              output;
          y=0;         output;
   x=0;                output;
end;
run;

* Define the gfont library;
libname gfont0 "&pathhpg";

* Create the GFONT (HISTO);
proc gfont data=fontdata
          name=histo
          filled
          nodisplay;
run;

* Define the axis statements;
axis1 order=0 to 20 by 5
      value=(h=1.5 f=simplex)
      label=(h=1.5 f=simplex)

axis2 order='01may86'd to '0lsep86'd by month
      value=(h=1.5 f=simplex)
      label=(h=1.5 f=simplex);

* Display the total catch using the user-defined font;
proc gplot data=totcatch;
plot totcatch*date=pltvar /
    nolegend
    vaxis= axis1
    haxis= axis2;
title1 'Total Catch';
title2 h=1.5 f=simplex
    'Bars show percentage for each sex (F, M, U)';
footnote1 h=2 j=l f=simplex 'Figure 4.5.1';
symbol1 f=histo c=black h=3 v=1;
symbol2 f=histo c=black h=3 v=2;
symbol3 f=histo c=black h=3 v=3;
symbol4 f=histo c=black h=3 v=4;
symbol5 f=histo c=black h=3 v=5;
symbol6 f=histo c=black h=3 v=6;
symbol7 f=histo c=black h=3 v=7;
symbol8 f=histo c=black h=3 v=8;
run;
quit;
```

Figure 4.5.2   Creating Sunflower Plots

```
************************************************;
* e4_5_2.sas;
*
* Create and display a sunflower GFONT.
************************************************;

FILENAME fileref "&pathhpg\e4_5_2.hpg";
GOPTIONS GSFNAME=fileref DEVICE=hp7475a GSFMODE=replace
noprompt;

* create the data used to create the font;
data fontdata(keep=char seg x y lp ptype);
length char $1;
retain char ' ';
twopi = 2*arcos(-1);
quarter = twopi/4;
do pltvar = 1 to 20 by 1;
  char = substr('ABCDEFGHIJKLMNOPQRSTUV',pltvar,1);
  * define the center point as a circle with radius 10;
  seg=0;  lp='p';
  ptype='w';  x =   0; y=100; output;
  ptype='v';  x =  50; y= 60; output;
  ptype='c';  x =  50; y= 50; output;
  ptype='v';  x =  40; y= 50; output;
  ptype='c';  x =  50; y= 50; output;
  ptype='v';  x =  50; y= 40; output;
  ptype='c';  x =  50; y= 50; output;
  ptype='v';  x =  60; y= 50; output;
  ptype='c';  x =  50; y= 50; output;
  ptype='v';  x =  50; y= 60; output;

  * for pltvars > 1 include petals;
  lp='l';
  if pltvar>1 then do seg = 1 to pltvar;
    * Divide the circle into pltvar parts, draw a line for
    * each part.  Shift the angle by one quarter turn to
    * make the first vertical;
    angle = twopi/pltvar*(seg-1) + quarter;
    x= 50; y = 50;  output;
    x= 50*cos(angle)+50; y=50*sin(angle)+50; output;
    * for the very last point draw back to the center;
    if seg=pltvar then do;
      x= 50; y = 50;  output;
    end;
  end;
end;

* Define the gfont library;
libname gfont0 "&pathhpg";

* Create the GFONT (HISTO);
proc gfont data=fontdata
           name=sunflwr
           filled
           nodisplay;
run;

* Plot the daily stock market high with the sunflower
* petals representing the trading volume (500,000 shares);
*
* Adjust the volume to a number between 1 and 20;
data dow;
set vol1.dow;
pltvar = ceil(volume/500);
output;

* Each of the twenty symbol statements must be requested
* even if all are not used on the plot.  PLTVAR=n points to
* the Nth activated symbol statement, not just SYMBOLn.;
* Create 20 points that will not be plotted, but will activate
* each of the 20 symbol statements;
if _n_=1 then do pltvar=1 to 20;
  high=.;
  output;
end;
run;

* Define the axis statements;
axis1 value=(h=1.5 f=simplex)
      label=(h=1.5 f=simplex);

axis2 order= '03aug81'd to '31aug81'd by week
      value=(h=1.5 f=simplex)
      label=(h=1.5 f=simplex);

* Display the closing high;
proc gplot data=dow;
plot high*date=pltvar /
     vaxis=axis1 haxis=axis2
     nolegend;
```

```
title1 'Daily Trading Highs';
title2 h=1.5 f=simplex 'Petals represent trading volume in
500,000 shares';
footnote1 h=2 j=l f=simplex 'Figure 4.5.2';
symbol1  f=sunflwr c=black h=2 v=A;
symbol2  f=sunflwr c=black h=2 v=B;
symbol3  f=sunflwr c=black h=2 v=C;
symbol4  f=sunflwr c=black h=2 v=D;
symbol5  f=sunflwr c=black h=2 v=E;
symbol6  f=sunflwr c=black h=2 v=F;
symbol7  f=sunflwr c=black h=2 v=G;
symbol8  f=sunflwr c=black h=2 v=H;
symbol9  f=sunflwr c=black h=2 v=I;
symbol10 f=sunflwr c=black h=2 v=J;
symbol11 f=sunflwr c=black h=2 v=K;
symbol12 f=sunflwr c=black h=2 v=L;
symbol13 f=sunflwr c=black h=2 v=M;
symbol14 f=sunflwr c=black h=2 v=N;
symbol15 f=sunflwr c=black h=2 v=O;
symbol16 f=sunflwr c=black h=2 v=P;
symbol17 f=sunflwr c=black h=2 v=Q;
symbol18 f=sunflwr c=black h=2 v=R;
symbol19 f=sunflwr c=black h=2 v=S;
symbol20 f=sunflwr c=black h=2 v=T;
run;
quit;
```

Figure 5.3.1 Selected GOPTIONS

```
* using the FILENAME statement to identify the GSFNAME
file;
filename fileref 'myplots\xyplt.hpg';

goptions noborder
        gsfname=fileref
        device=hp7475a
        gsfmode=replace noprompt;
```

Figure 5.3.2   BORDER versus NOBORDER

```
************************************************;
* e5_3_2.sas;
*
* Demonstrate differences of the BORDER and NOBORDER
options;
************************************************;

FILENAME filerefa "&pathhpg\e5_3_2a.hpg";
FILENAME filerefb "&pathhpg\e5_3_2b.hpg";
GOPTIONS GSFNAME=filerefa DEVICE=hp7475a GSFMODE=replace
noprompt;

goptions border;
proc gslide;
title j=l h=2 f=simplex 'Figure 5.3.2a';
title2 h=2 j=c f=duplex 'Using the';
title3 h=2 j=c f=duplex 'BORDER GOPTION';
run;

goptions noborder gsfname=filerefb;
proc gslide;
title j=l h=2 f=simplex 'Figure 5.3.2b';
title2 h=2 j=c f=duplex 'Using the';
title3 h=2 j=c f=duplex 'NOBORDER GOPTION';
run;
```

Figure 5.6.4 Demonstrate the Use of Gray Scales

```
***************************************************;
* e5_6_4.sas;
*
* Demonstrate gray-scales;
***************************************************;

libname gdevice0 "&pathhpg";

goptions reset=all border;
FILENAME fileref "&pathhpg\e5_6_4.cgm";
GOPTIONS GSFNAME=fileref DEVICE=cgmwp6ga GSFMODE=replace
noprompt;

proc gslide;
title1 h=2 f=swiss j=c 'Demonstrate the use of Gray-Scales';
note h=10 c=gray00 j=c f=marker 'Q' c=gray22 'Q' c=gray33 'Q'
                         c=gray44 'Q' c=gray55 'Q' c=gray66 'Q';
note j=c h=1.8 f=simplex
c=gray00 'gray00        gray22        gray33'
      '         gray44        gray55        gray66';
note h=10 c=gray77 j=c f=marker 'Q' c=gray88 'Q' c=gray99 'Q'
                         c=grayaa 'Q' c=graybb 'Q' c=graycc 'Q';
note h=1.8 f=simplex
c=gray00 'gray77        gray88        gray99'
      '         grayaa        graybb        graycc';
note h=10 c=graydd j=c f=marker 'Q' c=grayee 'Q' c=grayff 'Q';
note j=c f=simplex
c=gray00 'graydd        grayee        grayff';
footnote j=1 h=2 f=simplex 'Figure 5.6.4';
run;
quit;
```

Figure 5.7.1 Stacked Bar Chart

```
***************************************************;
* e5_7_1.sas;
*
* Use GCHART to demonstrate a stacked bar chart;
***************************************************;

FILENAME fileref "&pathhpg\e5_7_1.hpg";
GOPTIONS GSFNAME=fileref DEVICE=hp7475a GSFMODE=replace
noprompt;

proc gchart data=vol1.lampara;
title 'Stacked Histogram';
footnote j=1 h=2 f=simplex 'Figure 5.7.1';
vbar length / subgroup=sex
          midpoints = 100 110 120 130 140 150 160 170 180 190
200;
pattern1 value=l1 c=black;
pattern2 value=x1 c=blue;
pattern3 value=r1 c=green;
run;
```

Figure 5.7.2 GPLOT and the AREAS= Option

```
***************************************************;
* e5_7_2.sas;
*
* Use Gplot to demonstrate a plot of layers;
***************************************************;

FILENAME fileref "&pathhpg\e5_7_2.hpg";
GOPTIONS GSFNAME=fileref DEVICE=hp7475a GSFMODE=replace
noprompt;

data inverse;
do x = .10 to 2 by .05;
    y1 = 1/x;
    y2 = 1/x + 1;
    output;
end;

proc gplot data=inverse;
```

```
footnote j=1 h=2 f=simplex 'Figure 5.7.2';
title 'Layers Plot of an Inverse Function';
title2 h=2 j=c f=simplex
        'Vertical Width Of The Upper Layer Is Constant';
plot y1*x y2*x / overlay haxis = 0 to 2 by .5
                        areas=2;

symbol1 i=join v=none l=1;
symbol2 i=join v=none l=2;

pattern1 value=m3n90 color=black;
pattern2 value=m3n0 color=red;
run;
quit;
```

Figure 5.7.3 Block Charts

```
***************************************************;
* e5_7_3.sas;
*
* Use GCHART to build block charts;
***************************************************;

FILENAME fileref "&pathhpg\e5_7_3.hpg";
GOPTIONS GSFNAME=fileref DEVICE=hp7475a GSFMODE=replace
noprompt;

proc gchart data=vol1.lampara;
title1 'Block Chart';
footnote j=1 h=2 f=simplex 'Figure 5.7.3';
block length / group=sex
          midpoints = 110 140 170 200;
run;
```

Figure 5.7.4 Optical Illusion

```
***************************************************;
* e5_7_4.sas;
*
* Use Vertical bars to demonstrate an illusion;
***************************************************;

FILENAME fileref "&pathhpg\e5_7_4.hpg";
GOPTIONS GSFNAME=fileref DEVICE=hp7475a GSFMODE=replace
noprompt;

proc gchart data=vol1.lampara;
title 'Patterns Seem to Create Leaning Towers';
footnote j=1 h=2 f=simplex 'Figure 5.7.4';
vbar length / patternid=midpoint
              midpoints = 120 140 160 180 ;
pattern1 value=l1 color=black;
pattern2 value=r1 color=black;
pattern3 value=l1 color=black;
pattern4 value=r1 color=black;
run;
```

Figure 5.7.5 Comparison of Group Size

```
***************************************************;
* e5_7_5.sas;
*
* Comparison of four data display styles.
* Which size group, 120 or 160 is larger?
***************************************************;

FILENAME fileref "&pathhpg\e5_7_5.hpg";
GOPTIONS GSFNAME=fileref DEVICE=hp7475a GSFMODE=replace
noprompt;

goption nodisplay htext=2 ftext=simplex;
proc gchart data=vol1.lampara gout=chpt5;
title1 'Frequency Comparison of';
title2 h=2 j=c f=duplex '120mm and 160mm Size Groups';
```

```
footnote j=1 h=2 f=simplex 'Figure 5.7.5';
vbar length / midpoints = 120 140 160 180 name='vbar';
hbar length / midpoints = 120 140 160 180 name='hbar';
pie  length / midpoints = 120 140 160 180 name='pie1';
pie  length / midpoints = 120 140 160 180 explode=160 name='
pie2';
run;

goptions display;
proc greplay igout=chpt5 nofs;
tc vol1.templ8;

template fourscrn;
treplay 1='vbar'
        2='hbar'
        3='pie1'
        4='pie2';
run;
quit;
```

Figure 5.7.6a Nonaligned Axes

```
**************************************************;
* e5_7_6a.sas;
*
* Plot with two non-aligned axes;
**************************************************;

FILENAME filerefa "&pathhpg\e5_7_6a.hpg";
GOPTIONS GSFNAME=filerefa DEVICE=hp7475a GSFMODE=replace
noprompt;

proc gplot data=vol1.ca88air;
plot o3 * month = 'O';
plot2 co * month = 'C';
where station='SFO';
title1 '1988 Air Quality Data - SFO';
title2 h=2 f=simplex 'Two Non-aligned Axes';
footnote1 j=1 h=2 'Figure 5.7.6a';
run;
quit;
```

Figure 5.7.6b Nonaligned Axes

```
**************************************************;
* e5_7_6b.sas;
*
* Plot with two non-aligned axes;
**************************************************;

FILENAME filerefb "&pathhpg\e5_7_6b.hpg";
GOPTIONS GSFNAME=filerefb DEVICE=hp7475a GSFMODE=replace
noprompt;

axis1 order=880 to 1040 by 20
      value=(h=1.5 f=simplex)
      label=(h=1.5 a=90 f=simplex 'Daily High');
axis2 order='27jul81'd to '31aug81'd by 7
      value=(h=1.5 f=simplex)
      label=(h=1.5 f=simplex 'DATE');
axis3 order=0 to 6000 by 2000
       value=(h=1.5 f=simplex)
      label=(h=1.5 a=-90 f=simplex 'VOLUME in 1000 Shares');

proc gplot data=vol1.dow;
plot high * date / vaxis=axis1
                   haxis=axis2;
plot2 volume*date/ vaxis=axis3;
title1 'Dow HIGH and VOLUME';
footnote1 j=1 h=2 'Figure 5.7.6b';
symbol1 i=join v='H' f=simplex l=1 c=black;
symbol2 i=join v='V' f=simplex l=2 c=black;
run;
quit;
```

Figure 5.7.7 SCATTER Statement in G3D

```
**************************************************;
* e5_7_7.sas;
*
* SCATTER statement in PROC G3D;
**************************************************;

FILENAME fileref "&pathhpg\e5_7_7.hpg";
GOPTIONS GSFNAME=fileref DEVICE=hp7475a GSFMODE=replace
noprompt;

data air; set vol1.ca88air;
if station='AZU' then do;
    shapevar='club';
    colorvar='black';
end;
else if station='LIV' then do;
    shapevar='spade';
    colorvar='blue';
end;
else if station='SFO' then do;
    shapevar='heart';
    colorvar='green';
end;
* temperatures range from 40 to 80;
* create a scaled variable based on temperature (ranges
from 0
to 3);
min=40; max=80;
sizevar = (tem-min)/(max-min)*3;
run;

proc g3d data=air;
scatter o3 * co = no3 / size=sizevar
                        shape=shapevar
                        color=colorvar
                        grid;
title1 h=2 f=swiss '1988 Air Quality Data';
title2 h=2 f=simplex 'Temperature Relationship to CO, O'
          h=1 move=(+0,-.5) '3'
          h=2 move=(+0,+.5) ', and NO'
          h=1 move=(+0,-.5) '3';
title3 h=1.2 f=simplex 'Symbol size relates to
Temperature';
title4 h=1.2 f=simplex 'Symbol color relates to Season';
title5 h=1.2 f=simplex 'AZU (club)   LIV (spade)   SFO
(heart)';
footnote j=1 h=2 f=simplex 'Figure 5.7.7';
run;
```

Figure 6.2 National Sales Map

```
**************************************************;
* e6_2.sas;
*
* Create and store a map of the US.
**************************************************;

FILENAME fileref "&pathhpg\e6_2.hpg";
GOPTIONS GSFNAME=fileref DEVICE=hp7475a GSFMODE=replace
noprompt;

proc gmap map=maps.us
          data=vol1.salesmap
          gout=vol1.chapt6;
id state;
choro code / coutline=black
             name='salesmap'
             discrete;
pattern1 v=msolid c=black;
pattern2 v=m5x45  c=black;
pattern3 v=m1x45  c=black;
pattern4 v=m1n135 c=black;
pattern5 v=m1n45  c=black;
pattern6 v=empty  c=black;

title1 'National Sales';
footnote1 j=1 h=2 f=simplex 'Figure 6.2';
run;
```

Display 6.2.1 Open the GREPLAY Window

```
****************************************************;
* e6_2_1.sas;
*
* Demonstrate the use of PROC GREPLAY.
****************************************************;

proc greplay igout= vol1.chapt6;
run;
```

Figure 6.3 Displaying the TEMPLATE DIRECTORY Window

```
****************************************************;
* e6_3.sas;
*
* Use PROC GREPLAY to display the TEMPLATE DIRECTORY window.
****************************************************;

proc greplay igout= vol1.chapt6
             tc= sashelp.templt;
run;
```

Figure 6.3.1a GSLIDE Example Plot

```
****************************************************;
* e6_3_1a.sas;
*
* Store a GSLIDE example plot.
****************************************************;

FILENAME filerefa "&pathhpg\e6_3_1a.hpg";
GOPTIONS GSFNAME=filerefa DEVICE=hp7475a GSFMODE=replace
noprompt;

proc gslide gout=vol1.chapt6 name='e6_3_1';
title1 f=simplex h=2 j=l 'upper' j=r 'upper';
title2 f=simplex h=2 j=l 'left' j=r 'right';
note f=brush h=6 j=c ' A B C';
footnote1 f=simplex h=2 j=l 'lower' j=r 'lower';
footnote2 f=simplex h=2 j=l 'left' j=r 'right';
run;
```

Figure 6.3.1c Using a Border to Control Size

```
****************************************************;
* e6_3_1c.sas;
*
* replay 6.3.1a using a reduced size template.
****************************************************;

FILENAME filerefc "&pathhpg\e6_3_1c.hpg";
GOPTIONS GSFNAME=filerefc DEVICE=hp7475a GSFMODE=replace
noprompt;

proc gslide gout=vol1.chapt6
            name='blank'
            border;
run;

proc greplay nofs
             igout=vol1.chapt6
             tc=vol1.templ8
             template=partial;
treplay 1:e6_3_1
        2:blank ;
run;
```

Figure 6.3.1d Contolling Size without a Border

```
****************************************************;
* e6_3_1d.sas;
*
* replay 6.3.1a using a reduced size template.
****************************************************;

FILENAME filerefd "&pathhpg\e6_3_1d.hpg";
GOPTIONS GSFNAME=filerefd DEVICE=hp7475a GSFMODE=replace
noprompt;

proc gslide gout=vol1.chapt6
            name='blank'
            border;
run;

proc greplay nofs
             igout=vol1.chapt6
             tc=vol1.templ8
             template=partial;
treplay 1:e6_3_1
        3:blank ;
run;
```

Figure 6.3.2a Display Panel Coordinates

```
****************************************************;
* e6_3_2a.sas;
*
* replay 6.3.1 overlayed with the panel coordinates.
****************************************************;

FILENAME filerefa "&pathhpg\e6_3_2a.hpg";
GOPTIONS GSFNAME=filerefa DEVICE=hp7475a GSFMODE=replace
noprompt;
goptions noborder;

* create a GSLIDE with the panel coordinates;
proc gslide gout=vol1.chapt6
            name='coords';
title1 f=simplex h=2 j=l '(0,100)' j=r '(100,100)';
footnote1 f=simplex h=2 j=l '(0,0)' j=r '(100,0)';
run;

proc greplay nofs
             igout=vol1.chapt6
             tc=vol1.templ8
             template=e632;
treplay 1:coords
        2:e6_3_1;
run;
quit;
```

Figure 6.3.2b Rotate Displaying Panel Coordinates

```
****************************************************;
* e6_3_2b.sas;
*
* replay 6.3.1 overlayed with the panel coordinates.
****************************************************;

FILENAME filerefb "&pathhpg\e6_3_2b.hpg";
GOPTIONS GSFNAME=filerefb DEVICE=hp7475a GSFMODE=replace
noprompt;
goptions noborder;
```

```
proc greplay nofs
            igout=vol1.chapt6
            tc=vol1.templ8
            template=e632;
treplay 1:coords
         3:e6_3_1;
run;
quit;
```

```
proc greplay nofs
            igout=vol1.chapt6
            tc=vol1.templ8
            template=e632;
treplay 1:e6_3_3b
         2:e633line;
run;
quit;
```

Figure 6.3.2d Rotate Using Template Coordinates

```
****************************************;
* e6_3_2d.sas;
*
* replay 6.3.1 using a rotated template.
****************************************;

FILENAME filerefd "&pathhpg\e6_3_2d.hpg";
GOPTIONS GSFNAME=filerefd DEVICE=hp7475a GSFMODE=replace
noprompt;

proc greplay nofs
            igout=vol1.chapt6
            tc=vol1.templ8
            template=rotate;
treplay 1:e6_3_1;
run;
```

Figure 6.3.3a Sales Map to be Zoomed

```
See code for Figure 6.2
```

Figure 6.3.3b Zoom Panel Coordinates

```
****************************************;
* e6_3_3b.sas;
*
* Create a slide of the coordinates used to zoom X 2
* to the upper left corner;
****************************************;

FILENAME filerefb "&pathhpg\e6_3_3b.hpg";
GOPTIONS GSFNAME=filerefb DEVICE=hp7475a GSFMODE=replace
noprompt;
goptions noborder;

goptions nodisplay;
* create a GSLIDE with the panel coordinates;
proc gslide gout=vol1.chapt6
            name='e6_3_3b';
title1 f=simplex h=2 j=l '(0,100)'
                   j=c '(100,100)'
                   j=r '(200,100)';
title2 f=simplex h=2 m=(0,50)pct '(0,0)';
footnote1 f=simplex h=2 j=l '(0,-100)'
                     j=c '(100,-100)'
                     j=r '(200,-100)';
run;
proc gslide gout=vol1.chapt6
            name='e6331line';
title1 draw=(0,50,50,50,50,100)pct;
footnote1 ' ';
run;
```

Figure 6.3.3c Graphic Overlayed with Zoom Coordinates

```
****************************************;
* e6_3_3c.sas;
*
* replay 6.2 overlayed with the panel coordinates shown in
6.3.3b.
****************************************;

FILENAME filerefc "&pathhpg\e6_3_3c.hpg";
GOPTIONS GSFNAME=filerefc DEVICE=hp7475a GSFMODE=replace
noprompt;

goptions display;
proc greplay nofs
            igout=vol1.chapt6
            tc=vol1.templ8
            template=e633;
treplay 1:e6_3_3B
         2:e633line
         3:salesmap;
run;
quit;
```

Figure 6.3.3e Zooming Using Panel Coordinates

```
****************************************;
* e6_3_3e.sas;
*
* replay 6.2 using a template to zoom in on the upper left
corner.
****************************************;

FILENAME filerefd "&pathhpg\e6_3_3e.hpg";
GOPTIONS GSFNAME=filerefd DEVICE=hp7475a GSFMODE=replace
noprompt;

proc greplay nofs
            igout=vol1.chapt6
            tc=vol1.templ8
            template=zoom2xul;
treplay 1:salesmap;
run;
```

Figure 6.3.3f Zooming on a Map

```
****************************************;
* e6_3_3f.sas;
*
* Create a slide of the coordinates used to zoom
* new england;
****************************************;

FILENAME filereff "&pathhpg\e6_3_3f.hpg";
GOPTIONS GSFNAME=filereff DEVICE=hp7475a GSFMODE=replace
noprompt;
goptions noborder;
goptions display;
```

```
goptions nodisplay;
* create a GSLIDE with the panel coordinates;
proc gslide gout=vol1.chapt6
             name='e6_3_3f';
title1 f=simplex h=2 j=l '(-290,150)'
                   j=r '(110,150)';
footnote1 f=simplex h=2 j=l '(-290,-250)'
                         j=r '(110,-250)';
run;
proc gslide gout=vol1.chapt6
             name='e633flin';
title1 draw=(72,63,72,88,98,88,98,63,72,63)pct;
footnote1 ' ';
run;

goptions display;
proc greplay nofs
             igout=vol1.chapt6
             tc=vol1.templ8
             template=e632;
treplay 1:e6_3_3f
        2:e633flin;
run;
quit;
```

Figure 6.3.3g Zooming on a Legend

```
****************************************************;
* e6_3_3g.sas;
*
* zoom on 6.2 using coordinates shown in 6.3.3f
****************************************************;

FILENAME filerefg "&pathhpg\e6_3_3g.hpg";
GOPTIONS GSFNAME=filerefg DEVICE=hp7475a GSFMODE=replace
noprompt;

goptions nodisplay;

* zoom on new england;
proc greplay nofs
             igout=vol1.chapt6
             gout=vol1.chapt6
             tc=vol1.templ8;
template zoommap;
treplay 1:salesmap;
modify template / name = 'newengl';
run;

* zoom on the legend;
proc greplay nofs
             igout=vol1.chapt6
             gout=vol1.chapt6
             tc=vol1.templ8;
template zoommap;
treplay 2:salesmap;
modify template / name = 'e633lgnd';
run;

goptions display;
proc greplay nofs
             igout=vol1.chapt6
             tc=vol1.templ8;
template zoommap;
treplay 3:newengl
        4:e633lgnd;
run;
quit;
```

Figure 6.3.3i   Placing Zoomed Graphs

```
****************************************************;
* e6_3_3i.sas;
*
* zoom on 6.2 using coordinates shown in 6.3.3f&g
****************************************************;
```

```
FILENAME filerefi "&pathhpg\e6_3_3i.hpg";
GOPTIONS GSFNAME=filerefi DEVICE=hp7475a GSFMODE=replace
noprompt;

goptions nodisplay;

* zoom on new england;
proc greplay nofs
             igout=vol1.chapt6
             gout=vol1.chapt6
             tc=vol1.templ8;
template zoommap;
treplay 1:salesmap;
modify template / name = 'newengl';
run;

* zoom on the legend;
proc greplay nofs
             igout=vol1.chapt6
             gout=vol1.chapt6
             tc=vol1.templ8;
template zoommap;
treplay 2:salesmap;
modify template / name = 'e633lgnd';
run;

goptions display;
proc greplay nofs
             igout=vol1.chapt6
             tc=vol1.templ8;
template zoommap;
treplay 3:newengl
        4:e633lgnd;
run;
quit;
```

Figure 6.3.4c Display a Banner Style Title

```
****************************************************;
* e6_3_4c.sas;
*
* Display four panels and a title banner
* using a full sized overlayed title panel.
****************************************************;

FILENAME filerefc "&pathhpg\e6_3_4c.hpg";
GOPTIONS GSFNAME=filerefc DEVICE=hp7475a GSFMODE=replace
noprompt;

goptions nodisplay;
proc gplot data=vol1.ca88air
           gout=vol1.chapt6;
where station='SFO';
plot o3*month / name='e634p2';
title1 h=2 f=simplex 'Ozone';
symbol c=black l=1 i=join;
run;

proc gplot data=vol1.ca88air
           gout=vol1.chapt6;
where station='SFO';
plot co*month / name='e634p3';
title1 h=2 f=simplex 'Carbon Monoxide';
run;

proc gplot data=vol1.ca88air
           gout=vol1.chapt6;
where station='SFO';
plot no3*month / name='e634p4';
title1 h=2 f=simplex 'Nitrate';
run;

proc gplot data=vol1.ca88air
           gout=vol1.chapt6;
where station='SFO';
plot so4*month / name='e634p5';
title1 h=2 f=simplex 'Sulfate';
run;
```

```
* Create the title panel;
proc gslide gout=vol1.chapt6
             name='e634full';
title1 h=2 f=duplex '1988 - San Francisco Air Quality Data';
footnote1;
run;

goptions display;
proc greplay nofs
             igout=vol1.chapt6
             tc=vol1.templ8
             template=fttl2by2 ;
treplay 1:e634full
        2:e634p2
        3:e634p3
        4:e634p4
        5:e634p5;
run;
```

Figure 6.3.5c Display Titles Using Perspective

```
***********************************************;
* e6_3_5c.sas;
*
* Display titles using perspective.
***********************************************;

FILENAME filerefc "&pathhpg\e6_3_5c.hpg";
GOPTIONS GSFNAME=filerefc DEVICE=hp7475a GSFMODE=replace
noprompt;

goptions nodisplay;
proc gslide gout=vol1.chapt6
             name='e635';
title1 h=4 f=duplex 'Long long ago in a galaxy      ';
title2 h=4 f=duplex 'far far away there was          ';
title3 h=4 f=duplex 'fought a desperate rebellion  ';
title4 h=4 f=duplex 'against a cruel and tyrannical';
title5 h=4 f=duplex 'empire.                        ';
footnote1;
run;

goptions display;
proc greplay nofs
             igout=vol1.chapt6
             tc=vol1.templ8
             template=horizon;
treplay 1:e635;
run;
```

Figure 6.3.6b Template Overlays

```
***********************************************;
* e6_3_6.sas;
*
* Display text on a graphic using a template.
***********************************************;

FILENAME fileref "&pathhpg\e6_3_6.hpg";
GOPTIONS GSFNAME=fileref DEVICE=hp7475a GSFMODE=replace
noprompt;

goptions nodisplay;
proc gslide gout=vol1.chapt6
             name='e636txt';
title1 h=6 f=duplex 'Average Ozone   ';
title2 h=6 f=duplex 'levels exceeded';
title3 h=6 f=duplex '2.6 pphm four   ';
title4 h=6 f=duplex 'months in the   ';
title5 h=6 f=duplex 'area around     ';
title6 h=6 f=duplex 'Livermore.      ';
footnote1;
run;
```

```
proc gplot data=vol1.ca88air
             gout=vol1.chapt6;
where station='LIV';
plot o3*month / name='e636'
                vref=2.6;
title1 h=2 '1988 Ozone Levels';
title2 h=1.5 f=simplex 'Livermore';
symbol c=black l=1 i=join v=dot;
footnote f=simplex h=2 'Figure 6.3.6b';
run;

goptions display;
proc greplay nofs
             igout=vol1.chapt6
             tc=vol1.templ8
             template=insert;
treplay 1:e636txt
        2:e636;
run;
```

Figure 6.3.6c Template Overlay of a Map

```
***********************************************;
* e6_3_6c.sas;
*
* Overlay a graph on top of a map using a template.
***********************************************;

libname gdevice0 "&pathhpg";

goptions reset=all border;
FILENAME filerefc "&pathhpg\e6_3_6c.cgm";
GOPTIONS GSFNAME=filerefc DEVICE=cgmwpga GSFMODE=replace
noprompt;
goptions nodisplay;

data sales;
year=1982; sales=0.5; output;
year=1983; sales=0.8; output;
year=1984; sales=0.9; output;
year=1985; sales=1.1; output;
year=1986; sales=1.0; output;
year=1987; sales=1.2; output;
year=1988; sales=0.9; output;
year=1989; sales=1.6; output;
year=1990; sales=2.4; output;
year=1991; sales=2.8; output;
year=1992; sales=3.1; output;
year=1993; sales=3.0; output;
run;

goptions htext=2;
proc gplot data=sales gout=vol1.chapt6;
plot sales*year / name='annsales'
                haxis = 1980 to 1995 by 5;
symbol1 c=black v=dot i=join l=1;
title1 'Annual Sales in Millions of Dollars';
run;

proc gmap map=maps.us
          data=vol1.salesmap
          gout=vol1.chapt6;
id state;
choro code / coutline=black
             name='e636sale'
             discrete;
pattern1 v=msolid c=gray00;
pattern2 v=msolid c=gray33;
pattern3 v=msolid c=gray66;
pattern4 v=msolid c=gray99;
pattern5 v=msolid c=graycc;
pattern6 v=msolid c=grayff;

title1 'National Sales';
footnote f=simplex h=2 j=l 'Figure 6.3.6c';
run;
```

```
goptions display;
proc greplay nofs
            igout=vol1.chapt6
            tc=vol1.templ8
               template=insert2;
treplay 1:annsales
        2:e636sale;
run;
quit;
```

```
goptions display;
proc greplay igout=vol1.chapt6 nofs
            tc=vol1.templ8
               template=fullnine;
treplay 1=e6371
        2=e6372
        3=e6373
        4=e6374
        5=e6375
        6=e6376
        7=e6377
        8=e6378
        9=e6379
       10=e637ttl;
run;
quit;
```

Figure 6.3.7a Template Preview

```
**************************************************;
* e6_3_7a.sas;
*
* Preview the template;
**************************************************;

FILENAME filerefa "&pathhpg\e6_3_7a.hpg";
goptions reset=all border
        DEVICE=hp7475a noprompt
        GSFNAME=filerefa GSFMODE=replace;

goptions display;
proc greplay igout=vol1.chapt6 nofs
            tc=vol1.templ8;
preview fullnine;
run;
quit;
```

Figure 6.3.7c Banner Titles on Multiple Plots

```
**************************************************;
* e6_3_7c.sas;
*
* Place multiple plots per page;
**************************************************;

FILENAME filerefc "&pathhpg\e6_3_7c.hpg";
goptions reset=all
        DEVICE=hp7475a noprompt
        GSFNAME=filerefc GSFMODE=replace;

axis1 order=(0 to 2 by 1)
      label=none;

goptions nodisplay;

proc gplot data=vol1.biomass gout=vol1.chapt6;
plot bmcrus * bmcrus / name='e6371' vaxis= axis1 haxis= axis1;
plot bmcrus * bmmol  / name='e6372' vaxis= axis1 haxis= axis1;
plot bmcrus * bmpoly / name='e6373' vaxis= axis1 haxis= axis1;
plot bmmol  * bmcrus / name='e6374' vaxis= axis1 haxis= axis1;
plot bmmol  * bmmol  / name='e6375' vaxis= axis1 haxis= axis1;
plot bmmol  * bmpoly / name='e6376' vaxis= axis1 haxis= axis1;
plot bmpoly * bmcrus / name='e6377' vaxis= axis1 haxis= axis1;
plot bmpoly * bmmol  / name='e6378' vaxis= axis1 haxis= axis1;
plot bmpoly * bmpoly / name='e6379' vaxis= axis1 haxis= axis1;
title1 ' ';
footnote ' ';
run;

* create the titles;
proc gslide gout=vol1.chapt6 name='e637ttl';
title1 'Biomass in GM Wet Weight';
title2 h=1.5 f=simplex 'Figure 6.3.7c';
* Horizontal graph labels;
title3 h=4pct f=simplex
      move=( 6,84)pct ' Crustaceans'
      move=(37,84)pct ' Molluscs'
      move=(68,84)pct ' Polychaetes';
* Vertical graph labels;
title4 h=4pct a=90 f=simplex
      move=(5,56)pct 'Crustaceans'
       move=(5,28)pct ' Molluscs'
       move=(5,0 )pct 'Polychaetes';
run;
```

REFERENCES

SAS Institute Documentation

SAS Institute Inc. (1993), *SAS/ETS User's Guide, Version 6, Second Edition.* Cary, NC: SAS Institute Inc.

SAS Institute Inc. (1990), *SAS/GRAPH Software: Reference, Version 6, First Edition.* Cary, NC: SAS Institute Inc.

SAS Institute Inc. (1991), *SAS/GRAPH Software: Usage, Version 6, First Edition.* Cary, NC: SAS Institute Inc.

SAS Institute Inc. (1994), *SAS Guide to Report Writing: Examples, Version 6, First Edition.* Cary, NC: SAS Institute Inc.

SAS Institute Inc. (1991), *SAS Language and Procedures: Usage 2, Version 6, First Edition.* Cary, NC: SAS Institute Inc.

SAS Institute Inc. (1990), *SAS Language: Reference, Version 6, First Edition.* Cary, NC: SAS Institute Inc.

SAS Institute Inc. (1988), *SAS Procedures Guide, Release 6.03 Edition.* Cary, NC: SAS Institute Inc.

SAS Institute Inc. (1990), *SAS Procedures Guide, Version 6, Third Edition.* Cary, NC: SAS Institute Inc.

SAS Institute Inc. (1990), *SAS/STAT User's Guide, Version 6, Fourth Edition.* Cary, NC: SAS Institute Inc.

SAS Institute Inc. (1991), SAS Technical Report P-215, *SAS/GRAPH Software: Changes and Enhancements, Release 6.07,* Cary, NC: SAS Institute Inc.

SAS Institute Inc. (1991), SAS Technical Report P-222, *Changes and Enhancements to Base SAS Software, Release 6.07, First Edition.* Cary, NC: SAS Institute Inc.

SAS Technical Support Document TS252B, (1993), *Exporting SAS/GRAPH Output to Microsoft Word for Windows,* V2.04.
Cary, NC: SAS Institute Inc.

SAS Technical Support Document TS252G, (1993). *Exporting SAS/GRAPH Output to WordPerfect for DOS.* V2.02, 5/23/93,
Cary, NC: SAS Institute Inc.

SAS Technical Support Document TS252P, (1994), *Exporting SAS/GRAPH Output to WordPerfect for Windows 6.0A Maintenance,* 5/31/94. Cary,
NC: SAS Institute Inc.

Articles, Papers, and Books

Anonymous. (1987), "Unusual SAS/GRAPH Applications," *SAS Communications,* Vol. XII, No. 4. Cary, NC: SAS Institute Inc. pp. 36-38.

Benoit, Patricia. (1985), "Statistical Graphs Made Possible by the SAS/GRAPH ANNOTATE Facility Under VMS," *Proceedings of the Tenth Annual SUGI Conference.* Cary, NC: SAS Institute Inc. pp. 228-234.

Bessler, LeRoy. (1994a), "Chart Smart: Design Graphs, Maps, and Tables for Effective Communication," in *Proceedings of the Nineteenth Annual SUGI Conference.* Cary, NC: SAS Institute Inc. pp. 697-706.

Bessler, LeRoy. (1994b), "Most Effective Use of PROC GMAP: Solutions for Professional-grade Statistical Mapping," in *Proceedings of the Nineteenth Annual SUGI Conference.* Cary, NC: SAS Institute Inc. pp. 881-886.

Buckner, Glen and Terry Allen. (1988), "Using SAS/GRAPH Software to Create Graphics for Data Analysis," in *Proceedings of the Thirteenth Annual SUGI Conference.* Cary, NC: SAS Institute Inc. pp. 1087-1092.

Carpenter, Arthur L. (1989), "The GPLOT Procedure: Quick Tricks for the New User," in *Proceedings of the Fourteenth Annual SUGI Conference.* Cary, NC: SAS Institute Inc. pp. 591-596.

Carpenter, Arthur L. (1990), "Using the Template Facility in the GREPLAY Procedure: Zoom, Cut, and Paste Using the Panel Coordinates," in *Proceedings of the Fifteenth Annual SUGI Conference.* Cary, NC: SAS Institute Inc. pp. 651-655.

Carpenter, Arthur L. (1991), "Marie Annotate: How Not to Lose Your Head When Enhancing SAS/GRAPH Output," in *Proceedings of the Sixteenth Annual SUGI Conference.* Cary, NC: SAS Institute Inc. pp. 743-747.

Carpenter, Arthur L. (1992), "Little Orphan Annotate: How to Dress Up SAS/GRAPH Output," *Proceedings of the Seventeenth Annual SUGI Conference.* Cary, NC: SAS Institute Inc. pp. 549-554.

Carpenter, Arthur L. (1994a), "The Annotate Facility: A Quick Start to an Easy Overview," in *Proceedings of the Nineteenth Annual SUGI Conference.* Cary, NC: SAS Institute Inc. pp. 1423-1428.

Carpenter, Arthur L. (1994b), "Visualization of Scientific Data: Specialty Graphs Without Using Annotate," in *Proceedings of the Nineteenth Annual SUGI Conference.* Cary, NC: SAS Institute Inc. pp. 731-739.

Cassidy, Deb. (1994), "Move=(+0,+5): Making SAS/GRAPH Work For You," in *Proceedings of the Nineteenth Annual SUGI Conference.* Cary, NC: SAS Institute Inc. pp. 803-808.

Cleveland, W. and R. McGill. (1984a), "Graphical Perception: Theory, Experimentation, and Application to the Development of Graphical Methods," *Journal of the American Statistical Association,* Vol. 79. No. 387. pp. 531-554.

Cleveland, W. and R. McGill. (1984b), "The Many Faces of a Scatterplot," *Journal of the American Statistical Association,* Vol. 79. No. 388. pp. 807-822.

Corning, Betsy. (1994a), "Designing and Producing Effective Graphs with SAS/GRAPH Software-Using Graphic Elements Effectively," in *Observations,* Vol. 3, No. 2. Cary, NC: SAS Institute Inc. pp.73-86.

Corning, Betsy. (1994b), "Designing and Producing Effective Graphs with SAS/GRAPH Software-Making Graphs Informative," in *Observations,* Vol. 3, No. 3. Cary, NC: SAS Institute Inc. pp. 3-17.

Corning, Betsy. (1994c), "Designing and Producing Effective Graphs with SAS/GRAPH Software-Presenting Data Effectively," in *Observations,* Vol. 3, No. 4. Cary, NC: SAS Institute Inc. pp. 4-20.

Easter, Gretel, (1993), "Input/Output," in *Observations,* Vol. 3, No. 1. Cary, NC: SAS Institute Inc. p. 57.

Freund, R. and R. Littell. (1986), *SAS System for Regression, Second Edition.* Cary, NC: SAS Institute Inc.

Friendly, M. (1990), "The SAS System for Statistical Graphics," in *Proceedings of the Fifteenth Annual SUGI Conference.* Cary, NC: SAS Institute Inc. pp. 1425-1430.

Friendly, M. (1991), *SAS System for Statistical Graphics.* First Edition. Cary, NC: SAS Institute Inc.

Gerend, P. and R. Raftery. (1988), "Using the SAS/GRAPH Template Facility to Rotate Multiple Plots Per Page in Batch Computing," in *Proceedings of the Thirteenth Annual SUGI Conference.* Cary, NC: SAS Institute Inc. pp. 370-372.

Griffin, Lori. (1994), "Importing SAS Graphic Files into WordPerfect (Comparing several device drivers to determine which produces the best result.)," in *Proceedings of the Nineteenth Annual SUGI Conference.* Cary, NC: SAS Institute Inc. pp. 726-730.

Kalt, M. (1986), "Creative Uses of PROC GREPLAY," in *Proceedings of the Eleventh Annual SUGI Conference.* Cary, NC: SAS Institute Inc. pp. 985-991.

Kalt, M. (1993), "Input/Output," in *Observations*, Vol. 2, No. 4. Cary, NC: SAS Institute Inc. pp. 63-64.

Kalt, M. and J. Redman. (1993a), "Customizing Axes Using SAS Date and Time Values," in *Observations*, Vol. 2, No. 3. Cary, NC: SAS Institute Inc. pp. 22-29.

Kalt, M. and J. Redman. (1993b). "Picture This," in *Observations*, Vol. 2, No. 4. Cary, NC: SAS Institute Inc. pp. 67-69.

Larus, John M. (1987), "Graphical Displays of Nonhierarchical Cluster Analysis Solutions," in *Proceedings of the Twelfth Annual SUGI Conference.* Cary, NC: SAS Institute Inc. pp. 1089-1095.

Latour, Dominique and Martin Johnson. (1992), "Input/Output," in *Observations*, Vol. 1, No. 2. Cary, NC: SAS Institute Inc. pp. 55-57.

Olmstead, Ann. (1985), "Box Plots Using SAS/GRAPH Software," in *Proceedings of the Tenth Annual SUGI Conference.* Cary, NC: SAS Institute Inc. pp. 888-894.

⚹ McGill, R., J.W. Tukey, and W. Larsen. (1978), "Variations of Box Plots," in *The American Statistician*, Vol. 32, No. 1. pp. 12-16.

Mendelson, Irene. (1994), "Use Origin and Length to Pinpoint and Match up Multiple Graphs," in *Proceedings of the Nineteenth Annual SUGI Conference*. Cary, NC: SAS Institute Inc. pp. 155-156.

⚹ Sall, J. (1990), "Leverage Plots for General Linear Hypotheses," *in The American Statistician*, Vol. 44, No. 4. pp. 308-315.

Redman, Jude. (1991), "Input/Output," in *Observations*, Vol. 1, No. 1. Cary, NC: SAS Institute Inc. pp. 59-61.

Redman, Jude. (1993), "Input/Output," in Observations, Vol. 2, No. 3. Cary, NC: SAS Institute Inc. pp. 58-60.

Rooth, N. (1987), "PROC GREPLAY -- Developing a Presentation That Your Users Will Appreciate," in *Proceedings of the Twelfth Annual SUGI Conference*. Cary, NC: SAS Institute Inc. pp. 168-174.

Tufte, Edward. (1983), *The Visual Display of Quantitative Information*. Cheshire, CN: Graphics Press.

⚹ Wainer, Howard. (1984), "How to Display Data Badly," in *The American Statistician*, Vol. 38, No. 2. pp. 137-147.

Westerlund, Earl. (1994), "Using BY Variable Text Substitution to Add Data Values to SAS/GRAPH Titles and Footnotes," in *Proceedings of the Nineteenth Annual SUGI Conference*. Cary, NC: SAS Institute, Inc. pp. 153-154.

Wind, J. (1993), "Tools and Techniques to Integrate and Map Geographic Data Using SAS/GRAPH Software," in *Proceedings of the Eighteenth Annual SUGI Conference*. Cary, NC: SAS Institute Inc. pp. 721-729.

cal Index

Axis Control

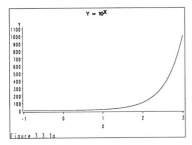

Page 50, Figure 3.3.1a

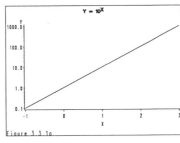

Page 50, Figure 3.3.1a

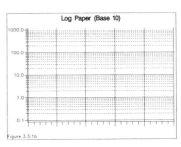

Page 52, Figure 3.3.1b

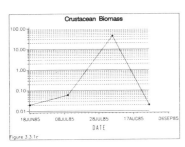

Page 54, Figure 3.3.1c

Page 56, Figure 3.3.2

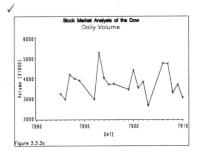

Page 58, Figure 3.3.3a

Axis Control (continued)

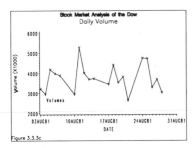

Page 59, Figure 3.3.3c

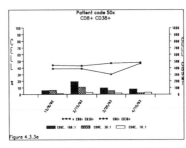

Page 88, Figure 4.3.3e

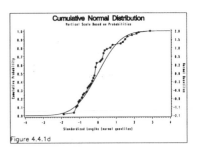

Page 106, Figure 4.4.1d

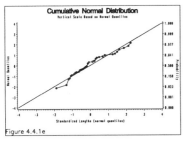

Page 107, Figure 4.4.1e

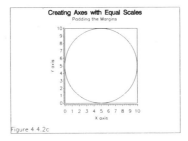

Page 112, Figure 4.4.2c

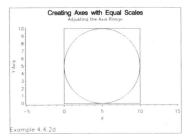

Page 113, Figure 4.4.2d

Gmap Examples

Page 151, Figure 6.2

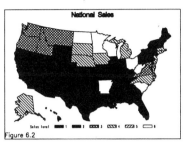

Page 167, Figure 6.3.3a

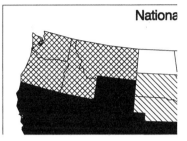

Page 169, Figure 6.3.3e

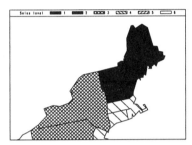

Page 173, Figure 6.3.3i

Goptions

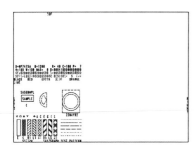

Page 5, Figure 1.4.1a

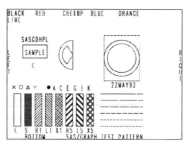

Page 8, Figure 1.4.2

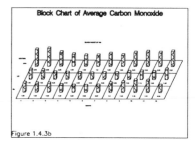

Page 9, Figure 1.4.3b

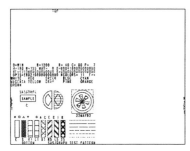

Page 11, Figure 1.4.4

Histograms

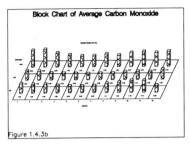

Page 9, Figure 1.4.3b

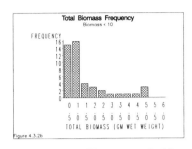

Page 74, Figure 4.3.2b

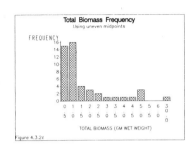

Page 75, Figure 4.3.2c

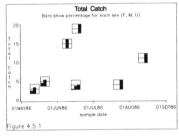

Page 78, Figure 4.3.2d

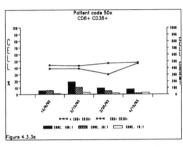

Page 88, Figure 4.3.3e

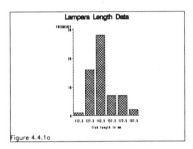

Page 101, Figure 4.4.1a

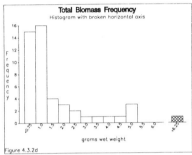

Page 118, Figure 4.5.1

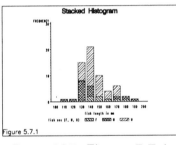

Page 137, Figure 5.7.1

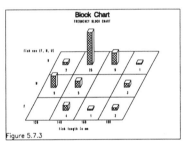

Page 140, Figure 5.7.3

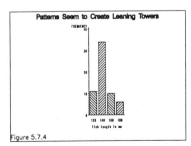

Page 141, Figure 5.7.4

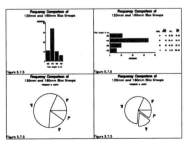

Page 143, Figure 5.7.5

Legend Control

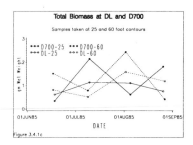

Page 64, Figure 3.4.1c

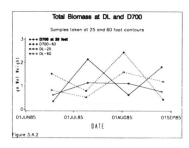

Page 65, Figure 3.4.2

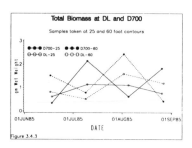

Page 66, Figure 3.4.3

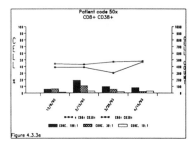

Page 88, Figure 4.3.3e

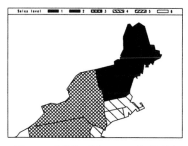

Page 173, Figure 6.3.3i

Miscellaneous

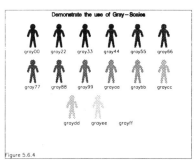

Page 135, Figure 5.6.4

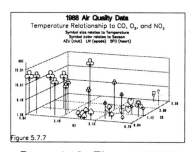

Page 148, Figure 5.7.7

Multiple Plots

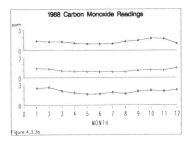

Page 82, Figure 4.3.3b

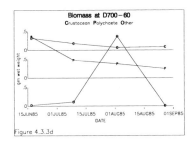

Page 85, Figure 4.3.3d

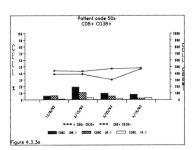

Page 88, Figure 4.3.3e

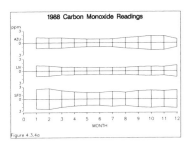

Page 91, Figure 4.3.4a

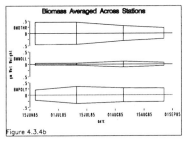

Page 93, Figure 4.3.4b

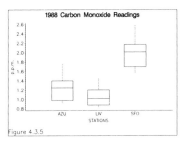

Page 96, Figure 4.3.5

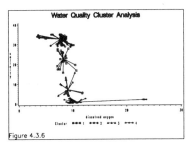

Page 99, Figure 4.3.6

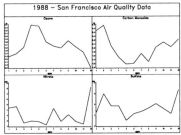

Page 176, Figure 6.3.4c

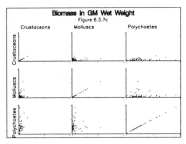

Page 185, Figure 6.3.7c

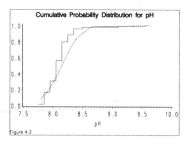

Page 69, Figure 4.2

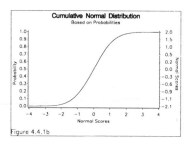

Page 103, Figure 4.4.1b

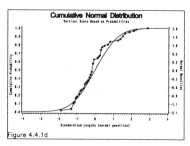

Page 106, Figure 4.4.1d

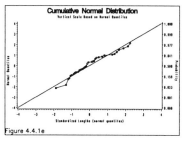

Page 107, Figure 4.4.1e

Scatter Plots

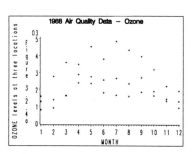

Page 43, Figure 3.2.4a

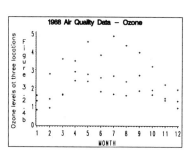

Page 44, Figure 3.2.4b

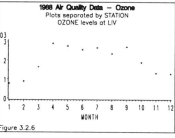

Page 48, Figure 3.2.6

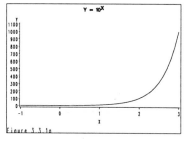

Page 50, Figure 3.3.1a

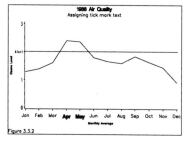

Page 56, Figure 3.3.2

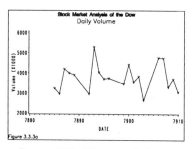

Page 58, Figure 3.3.3a

Scatter Plots (continued)

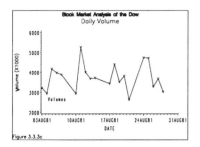

Page 59, Figure 3.3.3c

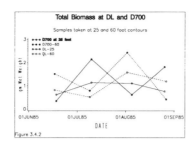

Page 65, Figure 3.4.2

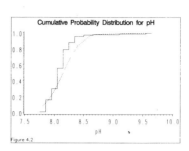

Page 69, Figure 4.2

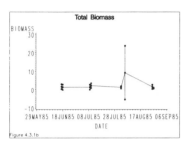

Page 73, Figure 4.3.1b

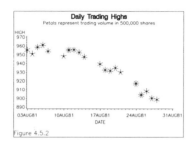

Page 122, Figure 4.5.2

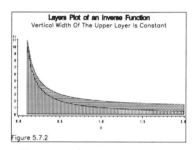

Page 139, Figure 5.7.2

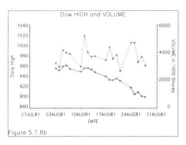

Page 146, Figure 5.7.6b

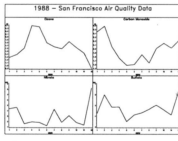

Page 176, Figure 6.3.4c

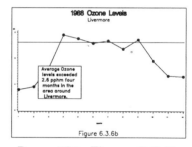

Page 181, Figure 6.3.6b

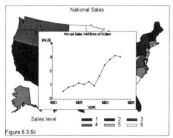

Page 182, Figure 6.3.6c

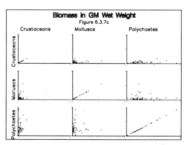

Page 185, Figure 6.3.7c

Specialty Plots

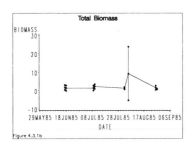

Page 73, Figure 4.3.1b

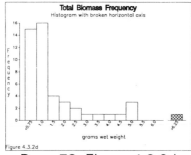

Page 78, Figure 4.3.2d

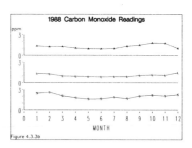

Page 82, Figure 4.3.3b

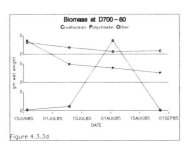

Page 85, Figure 4.3.3d

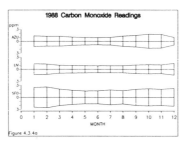

Page 91, Figure 4.3.4a

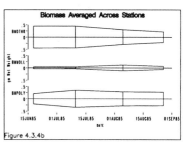

Page 93, Figure 4.3.4b

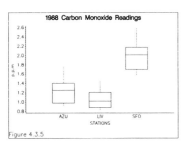

Page 96, Figure 4.3.5

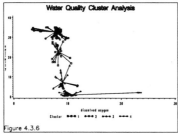

Page 99, Figure 4.3.6

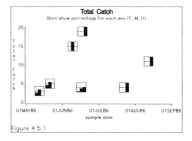

Page 118, Figure 4.5.1

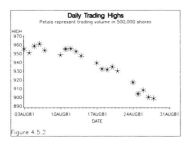

Page 122, Figure 4.5.2

Symbol and Pattern Control

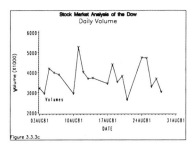

Page 59, Figure 3.3.3c

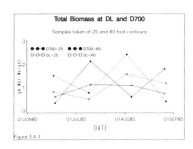

Page 66, Figure 3.4.3

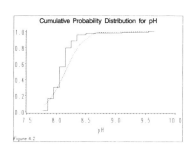

Page 69, Figure 4.2

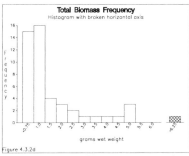

Page 78, Figure 4.3.2d

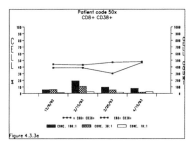

Page 88, Figure 4.3.3e

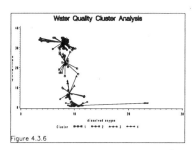

Page 99, Figure 4.3.6

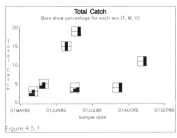

Page 118, Figure 4.5.1

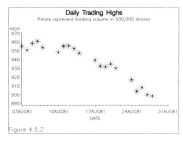

Page 122, Figure 4.5.2

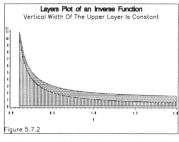

Page 139, Figure 5.7.2

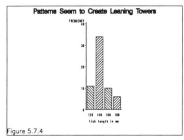

Page 141, Figure 5.7.4

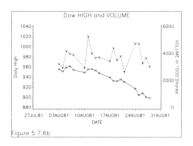

Page 146, Figure 5.7.6b

Templates

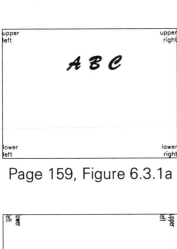

Page 159, Figure 6.3.1a

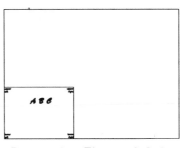

Page 161, Figure 6.3.1c

Page 163, Figure 6.3.1d

Page 166, Figure 6.3.2d

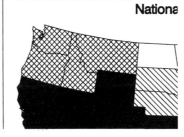

Page 169, Figure 6.3.3e

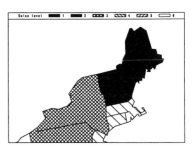

Page 173, Figure 6.3.3i

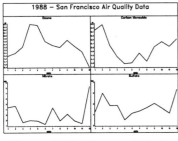

Page 176, Figure 6.3.4c

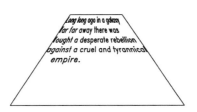

Page 179, Figure 6.3.5c

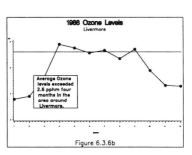

Page 181, Figure 6.3.6b

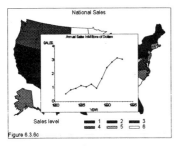

Page 182, Figure 6.3.6c

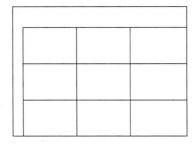

Page 183, Figure 6.3.7a

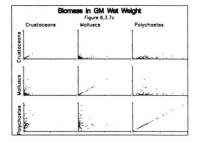

Page 185, Figure 6.3.7c

Text Characteristics

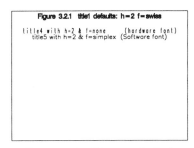

Page 40, Figure 3.2.1

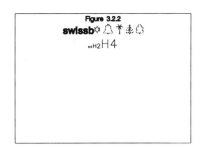

Page 41, Figure 3.2.2

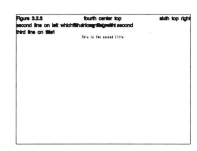

Page 42, Figure 3.2.3

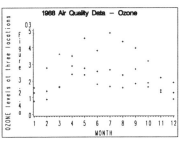

Page 43, Figure 3.2.4a

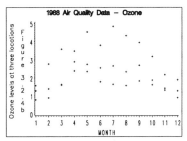

Page 44, Figure 3.2.4b

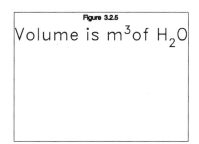

Page 46, Figure 3.2.5

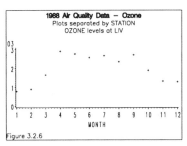

Page 48, Figure 3.2.6

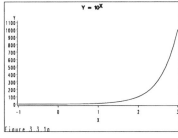

Page 50, Figure 3.3.1a

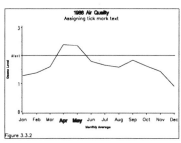

Page 56, Figure 3.3.2

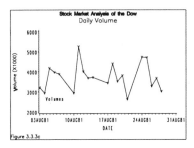

Page 59, Figure 3.3.3c

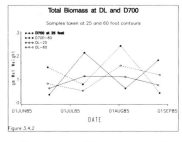

Page 65, Figure 3.4.2

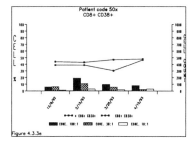

Page 88, Figure 4.3.3e

Text Characteristics (continued)

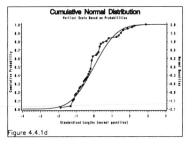

Page 106, Figure 4.4.1d

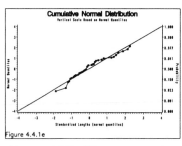

Page 107, Figure 4.4.1e

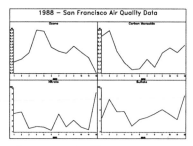

Page 176, Figure 6.3.4c

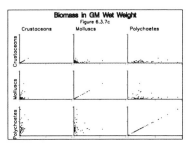

Page 185, Figure 6.3.7c

Index